A Listening/ Speaking Skills Book

mosaic two

A Listening/ Speaking Skills Book

With Learning Strategies and Language Functions

Third Edition

mosaic two

Jami Ferrer-Hanreddy
Trainer/Consultant
Milwaukee, Wisconsin

Elizabeth Whalley
San Francisco State University

The McGraw-Hill Companies, Inc.

New York   St. Louis   San Francisco   Auckland   Bogotá   Caracas   Lisbon
London   Madrid   Mexico City   Milan   Montreal   New Delhi   San Juan
Singapore   Sydney   Tokyo   Toronto

This is an EBI book.

McGraw-Hill
*A Division of The **McGraw·Hill** Companies*

Mosaic Two
A Listening/Speaking Skills Book
Third Edition

5 6 7 8 9 0   DOC   DOC   0

ISBN 0-07-020636-8
ISBN 0-07-114514-1

This book was set in Times Roman by Clarinda.

The editors were Tim Stookesberry, Bill Preston, and John Chapman, the designers were
Lorna Lo, Suzanne Montazer, Francis Owens, and Elizabeth Williamson; the production
supervisor was Phyllis Snyder; the project editor was Stacey Sawyer; the cover was
designed by Francis Owens; the cover illustrator was Laura Tarrish; the photo researcher
was Cindy Robinson, Seaside Publishing; illustrations were done by David Bohn, Axelle
Fortier, Rick Hackney, Lori Heckelman, and Sally Richardson.

R. R. Donnelley & Sons Company, Crawfordsville, IN, was printer and binder.
Phoenix Color Corporation was cover separator and printer.

Library of Congress Catalog Card Number: 98-82406.

INTERNATIONAL EDITION

When ordering this title, use ISBN 0-007-114514-1

Cover credit: SCRABBLE, the gameboard design, rules, and other indicia are U.S. trademarks
of and © 1996 Hasbro, Inc. All rights reserved. Used with permission. Outside the United States
and Canada: Scrabble® board game tiles used by permission of J. W. Spears & Sons PLC.

Photo credits:

Page 1 © Erika Stone/Photo Researchers, Inc.; *2* © Robert Isaacs/Photo Researchers, Inc.; *5* (*left*) ©
Bettmann Archive; *5* (*right*) © UPI/Bettmann Archive; *9* © Richard Pasley/Stock, Boston; *10* ©
Underwood & Underwood/Bettmann Archive; *11* © Bettmann Archive; *13* © UPI/Bettmann
Archive; *14* © Michael Hayman/Stock, Boston; *16* © UPI/Bettmann Archive; *21* (*top left*) © AP
Wide World Photos; *21* (*top right*) © AP Wirephoto; *21* (*bottom left*) © UPI/Bettmann Archive;

(credits continued on page 270)

Contents

CHAPTER one

Language and Learning

CHAPTER two

Danger and Daring

CHAPTER **three**

Man and Woman

CHAPTER **four**

Mysteries Past and Present

CHAPTER **five**

Transitions

CHAPTER **six**

The Mind   **75**

CHAPTER **seven**

Working   **93**

CHAPTER eight

Breakthroughs 111

CHAPTER nine

Art and Entertainment 127

Preface
to the Third Edition

The Mosaic Two Program

The Mosaic Two Program consists of four texts and a variety of supplemental materials for high-intermediate to low-advanced students seeking to improve their English language skills. Each of the four texts in this program is carefully organized by chapter theme, vocabulary, grammar structures, and where possible, learning strategies and language functions. As a result, information introduced in a chapter of any one of the Mosaic Two texts corresponds to and reinforces material taught in the same chapter of the other three books, creating a truly integrated, four-skills approach.

The Mosaic Two program is highly flexible. The texts in this series may be used together or separately, depending on students' needs and course goals. The books in this program include:

- **A Content-Based Grammar.** Designed to teach grammar through content, this text introduces, practices, and applies grammatical structures through the development of high-interest chapter topics. This thematic approach motivates students because they are improving their mastery of grammatical structures and vocabulary while expanding their own knowledge.
- **A Content-Based Writing Book.** This text takes students step-by-step through the writing process—from formulating ideas through the revision stage. Writing assignments progress from paragraphs to essays, and students write about interesting, contemporary subjects from the sciences, social sciences, and humanities that are relevant to their current or future academic coursework.

- **A Listening/Speaking Skills Book.** This text teaches learning strategies and language functions, while maintaining a strong focus on both listening and speaking. Each chapter includes a realistic listening passage on an interesting topic related to the chapter theme. Short conversations also provide comprehension practice, while a variety of speaking activities reinforce the use of language in context.
- **A Reading Skills Book.** The selections in this text help students develop their reading skills in a meaningful rather than a mechanical way—enabling them to successfully tackle other academic texts. The three readings per chapter come from a variety of authentic sources, such as textbooks, magazines, newspapers, interviews, and so on, and are accompanied by pre- and post-reading exercises, including skimming, scanning, making inferences, paraphrasing, and group problem solving.

Supplemental Materials

In addition to the four core texts outlined above, various supplemental materials are available to assist users of the third edition, including:

Instructor's Manual

Extensively revised for the new edition, this manual provides instructions and guidelines for using the four core texts separately or in various combinations to suit particular program needs. For each of the core texts, there is a separate section with answer keys, teaching tips, additional activities, and other suggestions. The testing materials have been greatly expanded in this edition.

Audio Program for *Mosaic Two: A Listening/Speaking Skills Book*

 Completely re-recorded for the new edition, the audio program is designed to be used in conjunction with those exercises that are indicated with a cassette icon in the student text. Complete tapescripts are now included in the back of the student text.

Audio Program to Accompany *Mosaic Two: A Reading Skills Book*

 This new optional audio program contains selected readings from the student text.

These taped selections of poems, articles, stories, and speeches enable students to listen at their leisure to the natural oral discourse of native readers for intonation and modeling. Readings that are included in this program are indicated with a cassette icon in the student text.

Video/Video Guide

New to this edition, the video program for Mosaic Two contains authentic television segments that are coordinated with the twelve chapter themes in the four texts. A variety of pre- and post-viewing exercises and activities for this video are available in a separate Video Guide.

Mosaic Two: A Listening/ Speaking Skills Book, Third Edition

Rationale and Chapter Organization

Mosaic Two: A Listening/Speaking Skills Book, Third Edition, is unique among listening/ speaking materials currently available. Most other materials focus on either listening or speaking and teach either learning strategies or language functions. This text teaches learning strategies *and* language functions, while maintaining a strong focus on *both* listening and speaking.

The text consists of twelve chapters. One learning strategy and one language function are presented in each chapter. Every chapter includes a realistic listening passage on a high-interest topic related to the chapter theme and is accompanied by interactive listening exercises. Short conversations also provide highly realistic listening comprehension practice. A variety of speaking activities then reinforce the use of learning strategies and language functions in context. The three main parts of each chapter can be summarized as follows:

- **Getting Started.** A section called **Sharing Your Experience** presents discussion questions designed to tap students' prior knowledge of aspects of the chapter theme. These questions are followed by a **Vocabulary** section consisting of one or more exercises that provide comprehension practice for key words that will appear in the listening passage.

- **Skill A.** This part is always a presentation of a learning strategy essential for academic success. Explanations are both thorough and easy to follow. "This presentation is followed by **Listen In** exercises based on a high-interest listening passage and **Speak Out** activities designed to provide practice of the strategy in realistic contexts.
- **Skill B.** This part is always a presentation of a language function. Here, thorough and clear explanations are complemented by an abundance of useful idiomatic expressions. This presentation is followed by a **Conversations** section and **Listen In** exercises designed to promote comprehension of the language function, as well as **Speak Out** activities to provide practice of the language function and idioms in realistic contexts.

New to the Third Edition

1. **Streamlined Design.** The two-color design and revised art program make this edition more appealing to today's students. It is also more user friendly because many directions have been shortened and clarified, exercises and activities have been numbered, and key information has been highlighted in shaded boxes and charts.

2. **New Chapter Theme on Breakthroughs.** The new edition features an entirely new theme for Chapter Eight: Breakthroughs. In addition, themes for several other chapters have been broadened to include new content.

3. **Did You Know?** This entirely new boxed feature opens the chapter with interest-catching information designed to arouse curiosity about the chapter theme, stimulate thought and conversation, and enhance motivation for learning.

4. **Focus on Testing.** Also appearing in each chapter, this new boxed feature simulates a standardized listening test, such as the listening portion of the TOEFL. It gives students the opportunity to practice listening for information in a controlled situation, where they are not able to interact with the speaker(s) or allowed to rewind the tape and listen again.

5. **Listening Passages.** Along with the usual variety of academic lectures, listening passages are presented in a variety of other formats, including radio programs, informal discussions, and a formal "downlink" discussion. In addition, all listening passages have been rewritten to include interactive dialogue involving several speakers. This interactivity makes the passage more natural; at the same time, it helps break up some longer passages into more manageable "chunks" of listening material.

6. **Conversations.** Conversations in this section, which were used in the previous edition only to illustrate language functions, are now presented with accompanying listening exercises designed to teach the use of language functions in realistic contexts.

7. **Skills Chart.** A chart summarizing the listening exercises and speaking activities follows the preface.

8. **Tapescripts:** All tapescripts are now in back of the student text.

9. **Answer Keys.** Answer keys for all exercises are in the Instructor's Manual.

General Teaching Suggestions

1. Read through an entire chapter and listen to the taped material for that chapter before teaching any portion of it.

2. The interactive comprehension and production activities are carefully designed for maximum appeal to students. Since no two classes are alike, however, activities can

be readily adapted and personalized, allowing for a great deal of flexibility. For example, activities can be modified to reflect such variables as local information, current events, names of students, and students' personal interests and experiences.

3. To facilitate the various role-plays and other interactive activities, you will probably need to disinhibit yourself and the students to some degree. To this end, you can use the personal information you know about the students: What amuses them? What saddens them? What excites them? Using a few bits of personal information in a relaxed and safe environment can greatly increase both individual participation and class rapport.

4. To facilitate maximum student participation during speaking activities, allow students to interact without interruption as much as possible unless there are misunderstandings or miscommunications. Keep notes and give feedback after students have completed an activity. In this way, you can avoid having students look to you for judgment after each sentence they utter.

5. During small group activities, heterogeneous groups—where all proficiency levels are represented—are generally recommended. However, there are occasions when it is advisable to put all of the more proficient students in one group so that they cannot dominate the less proficient students. Whether *you* place students in groups or they form their own groups, be sure to change the groupings periodically. Doing this will help promote strong class rapport as well as expose students to a greater variety of voices and speaking styles for listening practice.

6. The exercises are designed to teach skills, not to test proficiency. However, students will generally need to be reminded that it is all right to make errors. They are not expected to be competent at each task already, but rather, through the process of learning from errors, to *become* competent.

7. This text provides more practice exercises and activities in each chapter than most teachers would be able to use in a week of class time. Therefore, if you wish to complete a chapter a week, you may have to choose among the activities provided.

Specific Teaching Suggestions

Did You Know? To use this feature as a listening exercise, read each item as a question: (Did you know . . . ?) and have students answer "yes" or "no." Or have students work in pairs, taking turns asking each other the questions (in this case, the student listening should close his or her book).

To use this feature as a speaking activity, discuss each item in pairs, small groups, or as a class. Students can add their own "Did you know . . . ?" items to the ones given in the text. As an extension activity providing reading and research practice, students can look up additional items appropriate to the chapter theme.

Sharing Your Experience. This section allows students to relate their own knowledge, background, and experience to the chapter theme. Most questions are open ended; there are no right or wrong answers, and students should be encouraged to share whatever they can. A suggested time frame for discussing these questions is about fifteen minutes. If students are reluctant to participate, try having them write out their answers for homework the night before.

Vocabulary. The vocabulary exercises can be done in class or as homework. Doing them cooperatively in pairs or groups is an excellent way for students to learn the words while gaining extra speaking practice.

Skill A—Learning Strategy. Explanatory material is provided for each skill. Students can read this material at home or in class before or after you discuss the skill with them. Or you can read the material aloud to them while you put key points on the board.

Skill A—Listen In. Students listen to the passage on the cassette and do the accompanying exercises. You may need to do several items as examples and perhaps stop the tape more frequently than is suggested in the text for some groups of students.

Skill A—Speak Out. The focus here is on speaking, but the activities also involve active listening. Both whole class and small group activities are provided; these vary in length from about ten minutes to a whole class period.

Skill B—Language Function and Conversations. A language function is presented and then illustrated in a listening exercise using short conversations. This section helps students master idioms, stress and intonation patterns, and body language associated with the language function. The listening exercise is designed to teach, not test. For students who have difficulty, you may have them:
a. read along as they listen.
b. listen and repeat short selections of the conversation.
c. listen and pantomime facial expressions and gestures they think the speakers would use.
d. fill in cloze passages you have created from the conversations.

Skill B—Listen In. This section gives students the opportunity to listen for uses (or misuses) of the language function in the passage or the conversations. You may need to stop the tape frequently for some students, but you should work toward building their comprehension of increasingly longer chunks of language.

Skill B—Speak Out. These activities provide natural language contexts in which to practice the language function. They are designed to maximize student interaction and verbal output. Accordingly, you will want to provide feedback that facilitates rather than inhibits this interaction as students play the various games, participate in role-plays, or team up for debates (see item 4 under General Teaching Suggestions). The time

frame for these activities can vary from ten minutes to a whole class period.

Focus on Testing. In this feature, which simulates a standardized listening test, students listen for specific information. They listen to a passage once only, then answer questions that follow. After they finish this mini-test, you should let them listen to the items again, then go over the answers and any questions they might have.

Dedication

To the memory of Cindy Strauss, Gertrude and Stanley Whalley, and Fred Goldstein.

And for Joe and Gracie, who have never read a word, yet consummately provide the context for the work in wordless ways.

Acknowledgments

First, we wish to acknowledge the expertise, imagination, and inspiration of those whose contributions to the first and second editions helped lay the foundation for the third: Steven Carlson, Marilyn Bernstein, Steven Marx, William G. Carter, and Steven Hollander. We are indebted to Eirik Børve, who included us in the ground-breaking first edition project, and ever grateful to Mary McVey Gill for her monumental efforts in pulling such a project together, her most excellent editorial work, and her friendship.

We wish to express our deepest appreciation to Thalia Dorwick and Tim Stookesberry for their acumen and persistence in choosing to pursue a third edition and for treating us in style; to Bill Preston for his most excellent and unflagging editorial support; to John Chapman for his superb editorial assistance at a crucial point in the process; and to Lila M. Gardner for her ability to provide both a calming effect and desperately needed editorial wizardry when the going got tough.

Judy Tanka deserves the prize for most exceptional editor. She read every word, always had positive suggestions for problem areas, and even caught typos from the second edition!

We are also grateful to others who have provided creative suggestions and other support: Susan Ammons; Steve Aron; Connie Bendel; Mary, Louise, Elizabeth and Roger Dunn; Sue Garfield; Osha Hanfling; Manouso Manos; David Marimont; DeeDee Quinn; Rufus Rusty Russell III; Ann Stromberg; Pat Sutton; and, of course, the folks down at the Plant.

We heartily acknowledge the assistance of the staff at the Palo Alto Public Library and the support of San Francisco State University.

Finally, our thanks to the following reviewers whose comments, both favorable and critical, were of great value in the development of the third edition of the Interactions/Mosaic series:

Jean Al-Sibai, University of North Carolina; Janet Alexander, Waterbury College; Roberta Alexander, San Diego City College; Julie Alpert, Santa Barbara City College; Anita Cook, Tidewater Community College; Anne Deal Beavers, Heald Business College; Larry Berking, Monroe Community College; Deborah Busch, Delaware County Community College; Patricia A. Card, Chaminade University of Honolulu; José A. Carmona, Hudson County Community College; Kathleen Carroll, Fontbonne College; Consuela Chase, Loyola University; Lee Chen, California State University; Karen Cheng, University of Malaya; Gaye Childress, University of North Texas; Maria Conforti, University of Colorado; Earsie A. de Feliz, Arkansas State University; Elizabeth Devlin-Foltz, Montgomery County Adult Education; Colleen Dick, San Francisco Institute of English; Marta Dmytrenko-Ahrabian, Wayne State University; Margo Duffy, Northeast Wisconsin Technical; Magali Duignan, Augusta College; Janet Dyar, Meridian Community College; Anne Ediger, San Diego City College; D. Frangie, Wayne State University; Robert Geryk, Wayne State University; Jeanne Gibson, American Language Academy; Kathleen Walsh Greene, Rhode Island College; Myra Harada, San Diego Mesa College; Kristin Hathhorn, Eastern Washington University; Mary Herbert, University of California, Davis; Joyce Homick, Houston Community College; Catherine Hutcheson, Texas Christian University; Suzie Johnston, Tyler Junior College; Donna Kauffman, Radford University; Emmie Lim, Cypress College; Patricia Mascarenas, Monte Vista Comunity School; Mark Mattison, Donnelly College; Diane Peak, Choate Rosemary Hall; James Pedersen, Irvine Valley College; Linda Quillan, Arkansas State University; Marnie Ramker, University of Illinois; Joan Roberts, The Doane Stuart School; Doralee Robertson, Jacksonville University; Ellen Rosen, Fullerton College; Jean Sawyer, American Language Academy; Frances Schulze, College of San Mateo; Sherrie R. Sellers, Brigham Young University; Tess M. Shafer, Edmonds Community College; Heinz F. Tengler, Lado International College; Sara Tipton, Wayne State University; Karen R. Vallejo, Brigham Young University; Susan Williams, University of Central Florida; Mary Shepard Wong, El Camino College; Cindy Yoder, Eastern Mennonite College; Cheryl L. Youtsey, Loyola University; Miriam Zahler, Wayne State University; Maria Zien, English Center, Miami; Yongmin Zhu, Los Medanos College; Norma Zorilla, Fresno Pacific College.

Summary of Listening/Speaking Exercises and Activities for Learning Strategies and Language Functions

Chapter	Learning Strategies	Listening Exercises	Speaking Activities
one	• listening for the main point	• listen for parts of lecture and main points	• share language autobiographies • discuss how speakers make points
two	• noting specific details	• select note-taking method • take notes	• make a presentation from an outline
three	• abbreviating: when and how	• take notes and abbreviate whenever possible	• discuss meanings of common and unusual abbreviations
four	• using illustrations in note taking	• use illustrations for note taking	• describe uncharted solar systems • use illustrations in notes • compare findings
five	• understanding and making analogies	• note analogies	• create analogies
six	• listening for comparisons and contrasts	• note words that signal comparison or contrast • fill in a chart	• compare/contrast various dream scenarios • analyze dreams • compare findings
seven	• listening for causes and effects	• complete an outline • complete a survey	• discuss effects of technological advances • discuss effects of new devices in the workplace
eight	• what to do when you know the words but still don't understand	• use techniques suggested for clarification • summarize to check understanding • compare notes	• discuss complex processes • practice using techniques for clarification

Language Functions	Listening Exercises	Speaking Activities
• requesting the main point	• identify polite vs. impolite expressions	• complete conversations with appropriate expressions
• saying "yes" and "no"	• identify various expressions for "yes" and "no"	• complete a "risk taker" test using appropriate expressions
• extending congratulations and condolences	• identify expressions of congratulations and condolence	• share expressions across cultures • role-play situations of congratulations or condolence
• admitting lack of knowledge	• identify expressions for admitting lack of knowledge	• respond to difficult questions • convey feelings with tone of voice
• making negative statements or comments politely	• note introductory expressions and negative statements/comments	• role-play expressing negative statements with various tones/intentions
• expressing the positive view	• note positive sides to a situation	• debate the positive and negative sides of an issue
• persuading and giving in	• identify expressions for persuading and giving in • make inferences	• debate various work issues • role-play scenarios requiring persuading and giving in
• giving and receiving compliments	• listen for opportunities to give compliments • listen for compliments	• share receipt of inappropriate compliments • role-play situations requiring compliments

Chapter	Learning Strategies	Listening Exercises	Speaking Activities
nine	• distinguishing between fact and opinion	• note facts and opinions • justify responses	• critique artwork expressing facts and opinions • summarize facts and opinions of classmates
ten	• dealing with cohesion and reference	• fill in blanks with referential information • listen for reference words	• practice asking rhetorical questions to clarify reference
eleven	• predicting exam questions	• decide which information is likely to appear on an exam	• discuss types of questions on various exams • practice making up questions
twelve	• critical thinking	• distinguish between facts, opinions, and questionable concepts	• discuss validity of various statements • create interviews and discuss response validity

Language Functions	Listening Exercises	Speaking Activities
• expressing doubt or disbelief	• note facts or opinions that are doubtful • note appropriate expressions of response	• share unusual stories or make up stories • use appropriate expressions of doubt/disbelief
• taking the floor and keeping the floor	• listen for appropriate moments to take the floor	• role-play standing on a "soapbox" • practice keeping and taking the floor
• acquiescing and expressing reservations	• note and respond to situations with appropriate expressions	• role-play situations requiring expressions of reservations or acquiescing
• speculating about the future and reminiscing about the past	• note moments to introduce speculation and reminiscent expressions	• role-plays and discussions: speculate about the future and reminisce about the past

CHAPTER one

Language and Learning

The lecture in this chapter is called "To School or Not to School." This lecture was prepared for students planning to become teachers. It discusses the issue of whether or not all children should be required to attend school.

Skill A—Learning Strategy: Listening for the Main Point

Skill B—Language Function: Requesting the Main Point

DID YOU KNOW?

- **High school students in the United States spend an average of 38 hours per week in the classroom. In Russia the figure is 52 hours, and in Japan it's 59 hours.**
- **In the United States, reading, writing, and arithmetic are considered the most important school subjects for young children. These three skills are often referred to as "the three Rs"—reading, 'riting, and 'rithmetic.**
- **The number of children currently being taught at home in the U.S. is over 375,000 and is growing.**

Getting Started
Sharing Your Experience

 **activity**

As a class, or in smaller groups, discuss the following questions. Think back to the time when you were in elementary school and share your recollections with your classmates.

1. Who was your favorite teacher? What grade were you in then? How old were you? Why was he or she your favorite? Can you recall a specific incident that explains why you liked that teacher so well?
2. Who was your least favorite teacher? Why? How old were you? What grade were you in? Can you tell an anecdote that explains why you disliked this teacher?
3. In what ways has school been exciting? Disappointing? Do you feel you would know less, the same amount, or more if you had not gone to school? Why? If you hadn't gone to school, how would you have learned? From your parents, your parents' friends, your friends, siblings, television, radio, movies, books, computers?
4. Do you think everyone should be required to go to school? If so, why? If not, why not? Who shouldn't be required to go to school? Should those children who don't go to school be required to fill their days with special or supervised activities? If so, what kind of activities?

Vocabulary

exercise

Following is a list of adjectives that the speaker uses in the lecture. After the list are six statements that teachers might make to describe students. Fill in the blank in each statement with the appropriate word from the list.

disciplined	*sticking to a routine, having good behavior*
gifted	*very capable and inventive, talented*
inconsiderate	*not thoughtful about people's feelings*
moody	*frequently appearing disagreeable, unpleasant, or sad to others*
obedient	*law abiding, follows orders*
self-centered	*concerned primarily with oneself*

1. In nursery school, Rudy Thomas could sing his ABCs on key without missing a note. He played the piano without being taught. He made up beautiful songs by himself. By the time he was six, he must have spent six hundred hours at the piano. He probably will be a great composer or performer one day, because he's musically _____.

2. Sometimes Barbara Michaels is happy, but more often she seems sad or grumpy. She is so _____ that it is difficult for her to make any friends.

3. When people are talking about someone else, Toby Harrison always manages to bring the conversation around to himself. If you ask him about himself, he is very interested in the conversation and never changes the subject. Toby Harrison is very _____.

4. When Frances Paulson finishes her lunch at school, she always leaves the empty plastic wrappers and milk cartons at her place instead of throwing them away. Then the next person must clean up after her. Frances is very

   _____.

5. "I think George Redfern is the kind of student that many teachers like. He does whatever he is told without asking any questions. He always obeys the teacher and never gets into trouble. I, myself, find this kind of student difficult. I don't like students who are so _____. They are so dull. I much prefer students who challenge me."

6. One reason Patsy Harold turns in excellent work is because she plans ahead and leaves plenty of time for each project. She never leaves her homework for the last minute. She knows how to take good notes, and she always copies them over after each class and puts them in her notebook. She is certainly a _____ student.

SKILL A

Listening for the Main Point

In most lectures, several main ideas are presented. These are the concepts the speaker wants the audience to remember. Most often the lecturer also provides a general statement that is like an umbrella that includes all the main concepts.

The Model Lecture Has Three Parts

1. Introduction

Sometimes all of the main ideas as well as the umbrella statement are included in the introduction. Often, however, this is not the case.

2. Body

The main concepts are always presented here.

3. Conclusion

Traditionally this section contains a summary of all the main ideas. The umbrella statement will be repeated, or it may be introduced here for the first time.

When a lecture is well organized, with a clear-cut beginning, middle, and end, the main ideas are usually easy to pick out. When a lecture is not well organized, getting the gist of what is being said can be challenging. Some lecturers are "long-winded," taking a long time to come to the point. Others ramble on and never seem to come to the point at all.

Listen In

exercise 1

To practice listening for the main ideas in the three parts of a lecture, do the following:

Step 1 Listen to the lecture once all the way through.

Step 2 Listen to the lecture again. This time raise your hand when you think the introduction ends and the body of the lecture begins.

Step 3 Stop the tape and discuss with your classmates how you know this.

Step 4 Start the tape again. Raise your hand when you think the body ends and the conclusion begins.

Step 5 Stop the tape and discuss how you know this.

Step 6 Finish listening to the lecture. Write down what you think the umbrella idea is.

Step 7 Compare your answer with those of your classmates.

exercise 2

Listen to the lecture again. This time, listen for the main ideas in the body of the lecture. Stop the tape after you hear the sentences given in the following four items. Write down the main idea of the portion of the lecture that you have just heard. When you are finished, discuss your answers with your classmates.

Stop 1 *"Mark Twain, Charlie Chaplin, and Vincent van Gogh are examples of what we expect to find."*

_____

_____

Stop 2 *"Wordsworth was a curious child who was interested in the fresh and the new, and he found his teachers to be sympathetic and kind."*

_____

_____

_____

Huck Finn and Tom Sawyer, two of Mark Twain's characters, frequently stayed away from school.

Mark Twain was not a very obedient student and had very negative experiences in school.

5

Stop 3 *"Even though these scientific giants experienced great conflict between the demands of school and the development of their own minds, we should not jump to conclusions."*

_____

_____

_____

Stop 4 *"He passed his medical school entrance examinations with the highest marks that any student had ever received."*

_____

_____

_____

 Discuss the following questions about the lecture with your classmates:

1. Do you think the lecture was well organized? Poorly organized? Why?
2. Was the lecturer long-winded, taking too much time to get to the point? Did the lecturer *ever* get to the point?
3. Did you find it easy or difficult to pick out the main ideas? Why?

Speak Out

 **Step 1** Think about the variety of experiences you've had as you've acquired English (or another language). Begin with the point at which you didn't know a single word in the new language and continue up through the present time. Consider the following:

1. When were you first exposed to the language? How old were you? Have you been learning the language continuously since then, or were you interrupted for some reason?
2. Where were you? Were you in your native country or some other country?
3. Did you study this language in school? If so, where and when? What approaches or methods did your teachers use? Were any of your teachers native speakers of the language? Do you think this made a difference? Why or why not?
4. Have you had opportunities to speak this language outside the classroom with friends or family? Have you had a close boyfriend or girl-friend or perhaps a husband or wife who spoke the language?
5. Were you exposed to more than one dialect of the language? Do you think this helped or hindered your language acquisition? Why?

Step 2 Break into small groups and present this information as your "English autobiography" (or other language autobiography) to the members of your group. Speak for two to three minutes. As you listen to your classmates' autobiographies, note the main points.

Step 3 As a class, share some of the main points of these autobiographies. Did some of you have similar language-acquisition experiences, or were they all quite different? In what ways? Were the main points dealing with personal feelings similar, or were they different? In what ways?

 With some speakers, it's easier to determine the main points than with others. And in everyday interactions with friends, family, or co-workers, there are times when we all have difficulty getting to the point.

To research this, choose three people from the following list and find an opportunity to listen to each one speak without interruption for several minutes. Many of them can be heard on the radio or TV every day on their own shows or on talk shows.

artist   newscaster   teacher
businessperson   politician   three-year-old child
close friend   scientist   used car salesperson
minister

As you listen, make note of the main points and then consider these questions:

- Which of the three speakers was the most long-winded?
- Which one was the most succinct— that is, got to the point in the shortest time?
- Did any of the speakers ramble so much that you felt they never got to the point? If so, which one(s)?
- With which speaker was it easiest to get the gist of what was being said?
- With which speaker was it hardest to get the gist of what was being said?

Share your responses to these items with your classmates and give brief descriptions of your three subjects, including approximate age and educational background. Did you notice any patterns? For example, did you and your classmates discover a relationship between profession and long-windedness? Or perhaps between age and rambling? Were there any particular topics that most subjects tended to "beat around the bush" about?

Requesting the Main Point

Why Speakers Don't Get to the Point

Some speakers are intentionally long-winded. For example:

- A United States senator who does not want a bill to be passed may filibuster, talk on and on, day and night, to delay the vote on the bill.
- Someone who is shy and timid about a particular issue might "beat around the bush," talking all around the subject, to delay having to face it.

Other people are unintentionally long-winded and will talk for a long time and then ask a question such as "Am I talking too much?" or "Does this make any sense?" Still others ramble on and on, never coming to the point at all.

How to Request the Main Point

If a speaker is long-winded or rambles, you may want to ask for the main point. If the speaker is a friend or family member, you might use one of the following informal expressions.

Requesting the Main Point (Informal)

Get to the point, will (would) you please?
I don't get it. What are you talking about?
Oh, come on! Stop beating around the bush and get to the point.
So, what are you trying to say?
So, what's the (your) point?
What are you driving at?
What are you getting at?

If the speaker is not a close friend, but is an acquaintance—a supervisor or a teacher, for example—you must be careful how you ask for the main point so that you don't offend the person. In these or other sensitive situations, when you wish to be more polite, use one of the following more formal expressions.

Conversations

In the following conversations you will hear the expressions used appropriately and inappropriately. Sometimes the intonation is what makes the difference. Listen to the speakers and answer the questions. When you are finished, compare your answers in small groups.

conversation 1  Randy tries to tell Sandy some interesting news.

    1. Was this conversation friendly or unfriendly? _____

    2. Was it formal or informal? _____

conversation 2 Professor Draper is talking about the midterm exam.

    1. Was the student's request for the main point polite or impolite?_____

    2. What would you have said in the same situation? _____

    _____

conversation 3 Professor Werner and Richard discuss an upcoming field trip.

    1. Did Richard handle the situation well?_____

    2. Was he polite or impolite?_____

Listen In

Now listen to another version of the lecture "To School or Not to School." In this version, some of the main points have been omitted. During the lecture, your instructor will stop the tape so that you can ask for the main point. Each time your instructor stops the tape, several of you should practice requesting the main point by using an appropriate expression from Skill B.

Physicist Marie Curie loved school and was a star pupil.

Speak Out

activity

Look at the following incomplete conversations. Only Speaker A's first turn in the conversation is provided.

Step 1 Choose a partner and decide who the speakers are and complete each of the conversations. Speaker B will probably ask for the main point on his/her first turn. Speaker A can choose to answer right away or to continue the conversation for a while before giving the main point.

Step 2 Take turns being Speaker A and Speaker B, varying the conversation as you wish.

Step 3 Try making up a few conversations of your own, using these as models.

Step 4 Select the conversation that you and your partner enjoyed most and present it to the class.

CONVERSATION 1

A: Good morning, professor. Did you hear about that terrible accident on the highway last night? The traffic was backed up for hours. I hope everyone was okay. I'll bet a lot of people were late getting home, too. Probably a lot of people couldn't do some of the things they'd planned to do 'cause they got home so late. You know, almost everything closes by nine o'clock—like the public library and everything and . . .

B:

A:

B:

Etc.

CONVERSATION 2

A: Yes—about your art project—well—oil paint is an interesting medium; the variety of textures one can achieve with oil paints is remarkable. And paper cups—yes—paper cups *do* have some interesting possibilities. And these coat hangers—it never occurred to me to use them like this. So—your sister told me you're not sure whether you're going to major in art or not. Fred Carlson went through the same thing. Have you ever met Fred? He works over in the career counseling center now.

B:

A:

B:

Etc.

CONVERSATION 3

A: Dad, I'd like to talk to you about something. I went over to the registrar's office yesterday. And, you know, Joan works over there. The line was really long—all the way out the door and around the building. I hadn't decided which classes to sign up for yet, but I figured that I had plenty of time to do that while I waited in line. And then I bumped into Joan and we started talking. You know, she's had the most interesting life, and she never even went to college!

B:

A:

B:

Etc.

Albert Einstein at 26

CONVERSATION 4

A: Do you remember that book you loaned me last week? The biography of Albert Einstein? Well, I was reading the chapter about how he developed the theory of relativity, and the phone rang. It surprised me because it was so early. No one usually calls before eight o'clock. I didn't want to get up to answer it because the chapter was so interesting. Did you know that he was only a patent clerk—he wasn't even a professor yet—when he developed that theory?

B:

A:

B:

Etc.

Understanding spoken English on standardized listening comprehension tests (such as the TOEFL) is more difficult than in other contexts. For example, during standardized tests you cannot interact with the speaker to get clarification or rewind the tape to listen again. You get only one chance to listen for important information. The Focus on Testing exercises in this book will help you practice this skill.

You will hear a short presentation. After the presentation, you will be asked some questions. After you hear a question, read the four possible answers and decide which one is the best answer. Circle the letter of the best answer.

QUESTION 1

A. Language and learning.
B. Artificial intelligence.
C. The human brain.
D. Intelligent behavior.

QUESTION 2

A. Intelligent behavior.
B. A machine.
C. The human brain.
D. The environment.

QUESTION 3

A. When there is a lot of information to remember and process.
B. When questions need to be answered.
C. When primitive reasoning is needed.
D. When intelligent behavior is needed.

QUESTION 4

A. The mysteries of the human brain.
B. Logical rules.
C. Intuition.
D. Language and learning.

CHAPTER two

Danger and Daring

in this chapter

The lecture in this chapter is called "Hooked on Thrills." It is the kind of lecture you might hear in an Introduction to Psychology course and describes why certain people are drawn to dangerous situations.

Skill A—Learning Strategy: Noting Specific Details

Skill B—Language Function: Saying "Yes" and "No"

DID YOU KNOW?

- On June 20, 1986, Daniel Goodwin, a Californian, climbed 1,125 feet up a vertical face of the CN Tower in Toronto, Canada, without any climbing aids or safety equipment.
- On May 16, 1986, Ian Ashpole, an Englishman, performed on a trapeze suspended from a hot air balloon over three miles above the ground.
- On August 28, 1978, Donald Vesco achieved a speed of more than 318 miles per hour on his superpowered motorcycle, *Lightning Bolt,* at the Bonneville Salt Flats in Utah.

Getting Started
Sharing Your Experience

In small groups, discuss the following items. Then share the highlights of your discussions with the rest of the class.

1. Do you know of any people in your native culture who seek thrills by facing unnecessary danger? If so, what type of thrill-seeking activity is most common?

An ice skater jumps through a flaming hoop at a holiday ice show.

2. Many thrill seekers claim that they engage in dangerous activities only for personal satisfaction. They are concerned only with increasing their self-esteem. Some critics say, however, that money is the real motive behind the most daring of these activities, and that if there were no publicity to bring fame and fortune, there would be no daredevils to perform dangerous stunts. Why do *you* think people do dangerous daredevil stunts?

3. Discuss which groups you think are more likely to engage in thrill-seeking activity and why:

   - men or women?
   - young children or teenagers?
   - young adults or middle-aged people?
   - rich people or poor people?
   - optimists or pessimists?
   - a person visiting a new country or a person living in his/her native country?

Stunt Jump Thwarted

A police helicopter and emergency services officers yesterday prevented **Tony Vera,** who described himself later as a stunt man and magician, from leaping off the Manhattan tower of the Brooklyn Bridge.

Clad in a loincloth and a straitjacket, Mr. Vera, who had climbed to the top of the tower, stood on top for several minutes, having trouble fastening the straitjacket. A police helicopter hovered close to the bridge, preventing him from making a wide leap, while emergency services officers made their way to the top.

The officers grabbed Mr. Vera and led him down to safety, and he was hustled off by the police. But before they did, Mr. Vera said: "I want some excitement in my life. I'm going to do it again. I just want to jump."

New York Times, September 13, 1980.

Vocabulary

exercise The following words are used in the lecture in this chapter, but the speaker does not define them. Read the definitions and fill in the blanks on the next page with the correct forms of the words.

bizarre	*extremely odd or unusual, fanciful*
daredevil	*one who fears nothing and will attempt anything*
dominance	*power or authority*
extroversion	*interest in the world outside oneself more than in oneself*
impulsiveness	*the inclination to act suddenly, unexpectedly, or without thinking*

irresistible	*too strong to oppose or withstand*
nonconformity	*the refusal to act in accordance with generally accepted customs, beliefs, or practices*
sociopath	*a person with a personality disorder, often involving aggressive and sometimes violent antisocial behavior*
schizophrenic	*a person who has a disorder of the mind, involving a complete withdrawal from reality, that disturbs both emotional and intellectual functions*

Evil Knievel broke his ankle on this leap.

1. Are you willing to take great risks? Do you seek out extremely dangerous situations? If so, you are a(n) _____.

2. Do you reject going along with the crowd? If everyone's hair is short, do you grow yours long? If so, you are a(n)_____.

3. Have you read in the newspaper about people who kill others without any apparent reason? These people are _____.

4. Do you prefer to spend time with other people rather than alone? If so, you are a(n) _____.

5. Do you know of anyone who loves climbing mountains? To such a person, an offer to be a member of an expedition to Nepal to climb Mount Everest would probably be _____.

6. Do you love to do things on the spur of the moment without taking much time to think them through? If so, you are _____.

7. Do you know someone who likes to manage all situations and be the one in charge? That person likes to show his or her _____.

8. Do you know of a man who wears makeup, dresses in Japanese kimonos and baggy pants, and wears his hair in long braids with ribbons? Some people would say this person is rather _____.

9. Have you ever heard about people who see things that are not really there, hear voices, or imagine that someone or something is trying to harm them? These people are _____.

Noting Specific Details

How Is the Lecture Organized?

Once you have learned to pick out the main ideas in a lecture, your next step is to note the specific details. You will need these details later to answer questions on all types of exams: multiple choice, short answer, and essay. To listen for and note specific details, it is helpful to notice if the lecture is organized in the standard way, containing three sections: introduction, body, and conclusion. If so, listen for and note the main ideas in each of these sections. This will help you decide which specific details you should write in your notes.

- If the introduction to the lecture is a recap, or summary, of what you learned in the previous class session, take notes on this material again. These notes will be an added reminder of what the lecturer thinks is important.
- If the introduction to the lecture is just a general introduction or an attention getter (a fact, a saying, a story, or a joke), you don't need to write this down unless you might like to use it later in a paper or on an exam to illustrate a point.
- Next, listen for information in the body of the lecture. You will probably hear the most details in this section. Write down as much information as you can in your notes, but don't worry if you can't get everything. Just put a question mark in the margin and ask a question of the lecturer or another student later.
- As you listen to the conclusion, continue to make your notes as complete as possible. Most conclusions won't contain any new information, but be ready in case the instructor has forgotten to include an important detail earlier and decides to mention it in the conclusion.

Which Outline Form Should You Use?

What are some good ways to organize the main points and specific details as you write them down? One way is to use a formal outline. Look at the examples on the next page. The one on the left is more commonly used, but many note takers find the one on the right easier to use because they don't need to remember when to use the capital and lowercase letters or Roman and Arabic numerals.

OUTLINE USING ROMAN NUMERALS, ARABIC NUMERALS, AND LETTERS	OUTLINE USING ONLY ARABIC NUMERALS

OUTLINE USING ROMAN NUMERALS, ARABIC NUMERALS, AND LETTERS

I. Introduction
   A. Main point
   B. Main point
   C. Main point

II. Discussion/body
   A. Restatement of main point A
     1. Specific detail
     2. Specific detail
     3. Specific detail
       a. Further detail of A3
       b. Further detail of A3
   B. Restatement of main point B
     1. Specific detail
       a. Further detail of B1
       b. Further detail of B1
     2. Specific detail
   C. Restatement of main point C
     1. Specific detail
     2. Specific detail
       a. Further detail of C2
       b. Further detail of C2
     3. Specific detail

III. Conclusion
   A. Summary of IIA
   B. Summary of IIB
   C. Summary of IIC

OUTLINE USING ONLY ARABIC NUMERALS

Introduction
(in paragraph form, a paraphrase of the lecturer's introductory remarks)

1. Main point
   1.1 Specific detail
   1.2 Specific detail
   1.3 Specific detail
      1.3.1 Further detail of 1.3
      1.3.2 Further detail of 1.3

2. Main point
   2.1 Specific detail
      2.1.1 Further detail of 2.1
      2.1.2 Further detail of 2.1
   2.2 Specific detail

3. Main point
   3.1 Specific detail
   3.2 Specific detail
      3.2.1 Further detail of 3.2
      3.2.2 Further detail of 3.2
   3.3 Specific detail

Conclusion
(in paragraph form, a paraphrase of the lecturer's concluding remarks)

Alternative Note-Taking Strategies

Of course, formal outlines such as these work best for note taking when the lecturer carefully organizes the material into introduction, body, and conclusion, uses one of these types of outlines as speech notes, and then sticks to the outline during the talk. But many lecturers may not do this. Some add bits of information here and there as they think of them during the lecture. Other lecturers do not use an outline format when preparing their talks. In these cases, you will need alternatives to the formal outline in order to note main points and specific details well.

Here are five different ways to organize your notes. See which one feels the most comfortable and useful to you in your field of study.

1. This method of note taking is most useful when the main points and details are long phrases and sentences.

> Main point
> Detail
> Detail
> Detail
>
> Main point
> Detail
> Detail
> Etc.

2. This method of note taking is most useful when details are symbols, statistics, single words, or very short phrases.

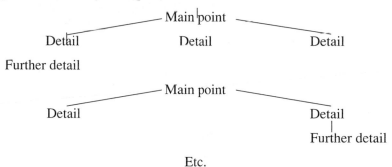

3. The following method is especially useful when the lecturer tends to "back up" and give specific details on points mentioned earlier in the lecture. If you leave enough space to add more details later, this type of lecture should not be problematic.

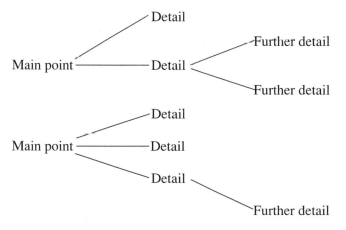

Etc.

4. This method is useful when the details precede the main point.

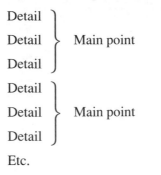

5. This method is especially useful if the lecture is not well organized or if the lecturer does not state the main points clearly or digresses frequently. By putting all the main points on the left and details on the right, you can match them up with arrows later and double check to see if something you thought was a main point was really a detail, and vice versa.

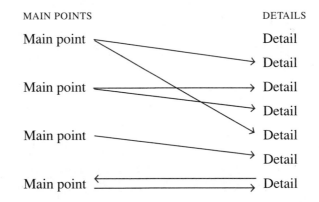

Adding Visual Cues to Your Notes

You may, of course, find it necessary to try each of these systems until you become accustomed to a lecturer's style. In addition to using these basic systems of note taking, many note takers find it helpful to set things off visually by using different-colored inks or by framing certain items in boxes or circles.

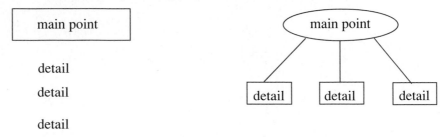

George Willig, "the human fly," is chased by police as he climbs one of the World Trade Towers.

Phillipe Petit balanced on a cable between two buildings 1,350 feet above the street for 45 minutes.

George Willig pays his fine (1 cent per floor) to the mayor of New York City.

Using a parachute, Owen I. Quinn jumped from the World Trade Towers.

Chapter Two • Danger and Daring

Listen In

The presentation in this chapter discusses the types of people who choose to face danger and what it means to be "hooked on thrills." It could be a typical psychology course lecture.

Listen to the lecture and decide whether you should take notes on the introduction.

Your decision: I should _____ should not _____ take notes on the introduction because _____

Listen to the lecture again. This time take notes using one of the two lecture outline forms on page 18 or one of the five alternative note-taking methods shown in Skill A on pages 19 and 20. Note as many specific details as you can.

_____
_____
_____
_____
_____
_____
_____
_____
_____
_____
_____
_____
_____
_____
_____
_____
_____
_____
_____
_____
_____

_____

_____

_____

_____

_____

_____

_____

_____

_____

_____

_____

_____

_____

_____

_____

_____

_____

_____

exercise 3   Did the note-taking method you chose work well for this particular lecture? If not, choose another method and listen again as many times as necessary to get down the main points and specific details.

exercise 4   Compare notes with your classmates and share your feelings about the note-taking methods you used.

Speak Out

activity    Prepare a brief talk on a daredevil stunt that you heard about or read about. (You may need to make a trip to the library.) Present your talk to the class.

- Use notes that you have made in outline form.
- Have your classmates take notes in outline form.
- After you have finished speaking, compare the notes you spoke from with the notes other students made. Do you and your classmates have the same main points and details? If not, discuss the differences and why you think they occurred.

Saying "Yes" and "No"

When we are asked if we would like to do or have something, we have three basic ways to respond: *yes, no,* and *maybe.*

- *Maybe* is a neutral word meaning that at a later time your answer may be *yes* or *no. Maybe* is exactly in the middle of the scale between *yes* and *no,* and there are no ways of saying *maybe* that are either stronger or weaker. Some alternative expressions for *maybe* are *perhaps* and *possibly.*
- *Yes* and *no* can be expressed in a variety of ways. Depending on how close to or far away from *maybe* your feelings are, you may choose either a weaker or stronger expression to say *yes* and *no.* Consider the following expressions.

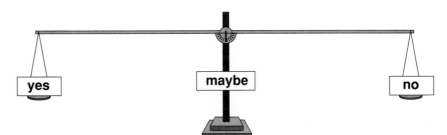

STRONGER YES	**WEAKER YES**
Absolutely!	I think so.
Definitely!	I'm considering it.
For sure!	I'll think about it.
Great!	Most likely I will.
I'll say!	Okay. (with unenthusiastic intonation)
Okay. (with excited intonation)	
Sure thing!	Okay, if you really want me to.
You bet!	Probably.
	That might be a good idea.

STRONGER NO	WEAKER NO
Are you kidding?	I don't think so.
Forget it!	I doubt it.
Never!	I'd rather not.
No way!	Not likely.
Not on your life!	Probably not.
Nothing doing!	That's probably not such a good idea.
Not for all the tea in China!	

Conversations

Listen to the following conversations and note the various ways in which the speakers say *yes* and *no*. Fill in the blanks in each conversation. When you are finished, compare your answers in small groups.

conversation 1   Ted and Paul are discussing their plans for the weekend.

TED: . . . . You wanna go with us?

PAUL: _____

TED: . . . . Take it and you'll be ready to go with us.

PAUL: _____

TED: . . . . I know lots of people who've done it.

PAUL: _____

TED: . . . . The course is only twenty bucks.

PAUL: That's not too bad. _____

TED: . . . . You've got the money don't you?

PAUL: _____

Terry and Lynn are discussing vacation possibilities.

TERRY: . . . . Wouldn't that be great? Let's go!

LYNN: _____

TERRY: . . . . Think how strong and brave you'll feel at the end.

_____

LYNN: . . . . But not me!_____

TERRY: . . . . You'll be a better person for it.

LYNN: I won't climb a mountain!_____

_____

LYNN: . . . . Wanna go out to dinner?

TERRY: _____

Listen In

exercise 1

Listen to the conversations from Skill B again. This time write down as many of the expressions used for saying *yes, no,* and *maybe* as you can in the spaces provided under the following five categories.

STRONGER YES

_____

_____

_____

_____

_____

WEAKER YES

_____

_____

_____

_____

_____

STRONGER NO

_____

_____

_____

_____

_____

WEAKER NO

_____

_____

_____

_____

_____

MAYBE

_____

_____

_____

_____

_____

In the lecture there are four statements from Marvin Zuckerman's "Sensation-Seeking Survey." Listen to the lecture again. As you hear each of these statements, write down the expression that best indicates how strongly you agree or disagree with it. Discuss your answers with your classmates.

Skydivers in ring formation

1. _____
_____

2. _____
_____

3. _____
_____

4. _____
_____

Speak Out

Are you very adventuresome? Do you like to take risks and try new things? Or are you more cautious and not particularly interested in new adventures?

activity 1

First work with a partner. Take turns giving and taking the test on the following two pages. Then share your results with your classmates.

- The test giver reads each item to the test taker.
- The test taker responds to each item (see expressions, pages 24 and 25).
- The test giver puts a check in the appropriate column for each answer.
- When you both have completed the test, look in the appendix for scoring instructions.
- Add up your scores and see how you each "measure up" on the risk-taker ruler on page 30.
- Share your ratings with the class—if you dare!

Risk-Taker Test

question	response				
Would you ever . . .	**Strong yes**	**Weak yes**	**Maybe**	**Weak no**	**Strong no**
1. try a new restaurant?	_____	_____	_____	_____	_____
2. try a new popular, but rather unusual, haircut?	_____	_____	_____	_____	_____
3. try a very unusual food with a familiar name (for example, chocolate-covered ants)?	_____	_____	_____	_____	_____
4. try a very unusual food with an unfamiliar name?	_____	_____	_____	_____	_____
5. explore a recently discovered island?	_____	_____	_____	_____	_____
6. try a new laundry detergent?	_____	_____	_____	_____	_____
7. try a new auto mechanic?	_____	_____	_____	_____	_____
8. volunteer to be the first passenger in a newly designed two-seater airplane?	_____	_____	_____	_____	_____
9. volunteer to test a car with an experimental braking device?	_____	_____	_____	_____	_____
10. try to climb a 15,000-foot mountain?	_____	_____	_____	_____	_____
11. try to climb Mount Everest?	_____	_____	_____	_____	_____
12. parachute from a plane onto a beautiful, sweet-smelling meadow?	_____	_____	_____	_____	_____
13. parachute from a plane onto the top of a sky-scraper?	_____	_____	_____	_____	_____

Mosaic Two • Listening/Speaking

Would you ever . . .	Strong yes	Weak yes	Maybe	Weak no	Strong no
14. try skydiving stunts?	_____	_____	_____	_____	_____
15. sail across the Pacific Ocean from San Francisco to Taiwan in a boat without a motor?	_____	_____	_____	_____	_____
16. dive off a forty-foot cliff in Hawaii into the cool blue water below?	_____	_____	_____	_____	_____
17. go out on a blind date?	_____	_____	_____	_____	_____
18. go to a small party where you know only two of the seven people there?	_____	_____	_____	_____	_____
19. go to a party of sixty people where you know only the host and hostess?	_____	_____	_____	_____	_____
20. drive a race car at 150 miles per hour?	_____	_____	_____	_____	_____
21. volunteer to take part in an experiment to test the effects of a new drug on humans?	_____	_____	_____	_____	_____
22. go to a country where you could not read, write, or speak the language at all and where you did not know anyone?	_____	_____	_____	_____	_____
23. cross the street against a red light?	_____	_____	_____	_____	_____
24. eat a dessert for breakfast?	_____	_____	_____	_____	_____
25. take part in a ritual dance while visiting a tribal village in the hills of Thailand?	_____	_____	_____	_____	_____

Risk-taker ruler

1–30	30–60	60–100	100–130	130–160
No risk-taker. You don't even like to sleep on the other side of the bed.	Low risk-taker. You'll leave the house now and then.	Moderate risk-taker. You might do something if your best friend does too.	Risk taker. You're just waiting for someone to dare you.	Hooked on thrills! You can't live without risks!

activity 2

Now make up a few of your own risk-taker test questions to ask each other. Begin your questions with these or similar phrases:

Would you ever . . . ?
How would you like to . . . ?
How about . . . ?

Answer the questions, using the expressions that best represent your immediate reactions to the questions. Share your questions and answers with your classmates.

focus on testing

You will hear a short news program feature. After the news feature, you will be asked some questions. After you hear a question, read the four possible answers and decide which one is the best answer. Circle the letter of the best answer.

QUESTION 1
A. A popular sport among all young people in California.
B. A very dangerous sport in France.
C. A sport for young daredevils and thrillseekers.
D. A sport that requires a lot of special training.

QUESTION 2
A. They jump feet first from high places.
B. They jump from bridges, cranes, and balloons.
C. They jump into the water below.
D. They jump up into the sky.

QUESTION 3

A. Hot-air balloons.

B. Parachutes.

C. Special suits.

D. Cords that are like giant rubber bands.

QUESTION 4

A. To show courage and ensure a good crop of yams.

B. To test the strength of the vines.

C. To test the strength of their ankles.

D. To be daredevils and thrillseekers.

CHAPTER three

Man and Woman

in this chapter

The lecture in this chapter is called "Becoming a Man, Becoming a Woman." It is the kind of lecture you might hear in an anthropology course, and it describes the transitions children in several different cultures go through as they pass from childhood to adulthood.

Skill A—Learning Strategy: Abbreviating—When and How

Skill B—Language Function: Extending Congratulations and Condolences

DID YOU KNOW?

- In 1909 the Flemish anthropologist, Arnold van Gennep, introduced the term *rites of passage* to describe the rituals that mark important transitions in people's lives.
- Public ceremonies such as weddings and funerals are familiar examples of rites of passage. But smaller, less formal moments, such as a child's first steps or the head-shaving of an army recruit, can also be seen as rites of passage.
- The Dyaks of Eastern Malaysia separate girls at puberty from the rest of society for a whole year. During this time they dress all in white, live in a white cabin, and eat only white foods.

Getting Started

Sharing Your Experience

Do you remember entering adolescence? What was that time like for you? In small groups of three or four, discuss the following questions.

(*Left*) Native American teenagers at a traditional dance; (*right*) Latino teenagers at a school dance

1. Did you participate in any ceremony marking the change from childhood to adulthood (for instance, a graduation ceremony, a religious ceremony, or a social event)? If so, describe it to the class.

2. Have you ever participated in such a ceremony for someone else? If so, describe the ceremony.

3. What changes in responsibilities and relationships do you remember occurring after you reached puberty? For example, did you have greater responsibilities in your home? What were they? What about the community? Did your relationships with your friends or neighbors change? If so, how?

4. Did you change school levels at this time?

5. What new interests did you develop?

6. Were you called by any new name or nickname?

7. Did you learn to drive? Did you feel there was an association between driving and adulthood?

Vocabulary

exercise

The definitions of the words in the list below reflect how they are used in the lecture. Study the list and use these words to fill in the blanks in the following letter from Pam to Nancy below and on the next page.

confirmation	*a religious rite marking admission as an adult into a church or synagogue*
deprivation	*the act of taking something away; loss*
equilibrium	*the state of being in balance*
fasting	*abstaining from food*
humiliating	*lowering the pride or dignity of a person*
infected	*the condition of being diseased with a germ or virus*
isolation	*the state of being alone*
navel	*location on the body where the umbilical cord was attached to the fetus*
ordeal	*an act that tests character or endurance; a difficult experience*
suitor	*a male who courts a female*
tribal	*characteristic of a tribe or group having a common ancestor or leader*

Thursday, October 16

Dear Nancy,

Well, here I am at home, sick in bed. All I've got is a sore throat, but the way

Mom is acting, you'd think I was _____ with the plague

or something. I don't think keeping me in _____ ,

away from everybody else, is really necessary. Nobody will catch what I have if I don't kiss them—ha! ha!

I hate just lying around. I'm getting so fat it's_____ just to look in the mirror. Man! Ever since I turned thirteen, I just look at a piece of cake and I gain weight. Guess I'd better give up junk food and maybe even stop eating for a week or so. But _____ is such an _____ . It's really tough to stop eating for a whole week. I wonder if I can make it. I don't think you can die from food _____ in only a week, though!

We have a foreign exchange student from Africa living with us for a month. Her name is Desta. She's very nice and has been telling me about customs of the various tribes in her country. In one _____rite of passage, girls our age are separated from everyone for a period of time, and then there is a ceremony to celebrate the girl's becoming an adult. Desta says this helps adolescents adjust to the physical and emotional changes in their lives. The puberty rites help them to maintain their _____instead of becoming unbalanced as they go through all these changes.

Desta has made some interesting African dishes, and she taught me some words in her language—like the words for boyfriend and girlfriend. And guess what! I've got a _____ , a real boyfriend! Herman asked me out! And he calls me every day. He's even invited me to his sister's _____ceremony and the party after- wards. But I'm not sure my Dad will let me go to the party, because it goes too late. Sometimes he treats me like I'm still attached to Mom and him by a cord at my _____or something. Oh, well. Maybe next year!

Well, got to split now. Still have homework to do. (Yuck!) Write soon!

Love,

Pam

Abbreviating—When and How

Creating Your Own Abbreviations

When you are taking notes in lectures, you want to record the lecturer's ideas accurately. The best way to do this is to use the same words the lecturer uses as often as possible. (Later, when you are writing exams or papers, you will, of course, need to put the information into your own words.)

Writing down every word the lecturer says is almost impossible. *To abbreviate* means "to shorten." Knowing when and how to abbreviate will help you to quickly and accurately take down the information you will need later.

Four Main Ways to Abbreviate

1. Change word order.
2. Leave out whole words, word endings, vowels, or other letters.
3. Use only the first letter, or first two or three letters, of a word.
4. Use symbols to replace words or letters.

For example, if the instructor says, "You will be expected to learn all about many ceremonies, perhaps over fifty, by the end of the term," you might write:

know ~ 50 ceremonies by end of term.

or

learn > 50 ceremonies.

Or, if the instructor says, "A greater number of males than females are born to the Yuma tribe each year," you might shorten the sentence to:

Yuma tribe : males born > females each year.

or

Yuma tr. : m. born > f. ea. yr.

If you prefer using symbols as much as possible, the previous example might look like this:

> # ♂ than ♀ / yr. for Yuma.

Can you guess what the instructor must have said from the following example?

Rts of pass. impt. in all cults.

When you abbreviate, you must be careful not to use the same abbreviation for two different things. For example, if the instructor is talking about *transitions* in life and *transmissions* of knowledge, you wouldn't want to use *trans.* as the abbreviation for both words. Write two abbreviations you could use instead:

_____ and _____

Similarly, you would not want to use *ord.* as the abbreviation for both of the words *ordeal* and *order.* Write two abbreviations you could use instead:

_____ and _____

Here's a further example. Instead of writing *boy, male,* or *man,* you can usually use the symbol ♂ and instead of writing *girl, female,* or *woman,* you can usually use the symbol ♀ . But if an anthropology lecturer is discussing particular differences between what boys and men in the tribe are allowed to do, for example, it wouldn't be helpful to use ♂ for both. Write two abbreviations you could use instead:

_____ and _____

Naturally, you will develop your own system of abbreviations as you go along. But some systems seem to work well for most everyone. For example, some students use a small raised *g* to shorten all *-ing* words such as:

fast^g_____ (fasting)

humiliat^g_____ (humiliating)

depriv^g_____ (depriving)

Some students also like to keep a key to their abbreviations at the top of the page. For example:

m. = married   M = males _____

_____

unm. M go off w. tribal elders to spend time fast^g. _____

_____

_____

Some Useful Abbreviations

Here are three lists of abbreviations. The first contains symbols; the second includes some of the most common word-level abbreviations; the third features items that are particularly useful for taking down homework assignments. Even if you don't use any of these abbreviations in your own note taking, examining the list can help you develop your own system.

Mathematical and Other Symbols

one	1	because	∴ -, bec., b/c	means, causes	→
two	2, etc.	before	b/4	is caused by	←
first	1st	equal to	=	plus, over	+
second	2nd	not equal to	≠	minus	−
third	3rd	identical to	∫	money	$
fourth	4th, etc.	hence, therefore	∴	percent	%
about, approximately	~	intersection	∩	question	?
and	& or +	more than	>	there is	∃
at	@	less than	<		

Commonly Used Abbreviations

a.	answer	dept.	department	n.b.* (from	note well
alt.	altitude, alternate	doz.	dozen	Latin *nota bene*)	
		Dr.	doctor		
Amer.	American	ea.	each	no(s).	number(s)
Amers.	Americans	e.g. (from	for example	pd.	paid
atm.	atmosphere, atmospheric	Latin *exempli gratia*)		pop.	population
				re.	regarding, concerning
av.	average	ff.	following pages		
ave.	avenue			rel.	religion
b.	born	fr.	from	ret.	retired, returned
b.p.	boiling point	ft.	feet		
¢	cents	g.	gram	riv.	river
c. (from Latin *circa*)	about	gal.	gallon	s.	son
		id. (from	the same,	sc.	science
cf. (from Latin *confer*)	compare	Latin *idem*)	identical	sr.	senior
		i.e. (from	that is	stat.	statistics
co.	company	Latin *id est*)		terr.	territory
ct.	count	jr.	junior	yr.	year
cu.	cubic	m.	married		
d.	deceased, died	mod.	modern		

*N.b. is a good abbreviation to use as a note to yourself, indicating something important.

Abbreviations for Homework Assignments			
ch.	chapter	p.	page
ev. #'s	even numbers	pp.	pages
1	learn	q.	question(s)
od. #'s	odd numbers	st.	study

Listen In

exercise 1

Listen to the lecture and take notes as you would for a regular classroom lecture. Abbreviate whatever you can. You can use abbreviations introduced in this chapter and create a few of your own. If you wish, stop the tape after the lecturer asks the students to write down the ceremonies that mark important life transitions in the United States and Canada. Then you can discuss these ceremonies first, before listening to the rest of the lecture.

A teenager from Taos Pueblo, New Mexico

exercise 2

Compare your notes with those your classmates took. If you see any abbreviations your classmates used that you think would be useful, put them on the blackboard, perhaps in alphabetical order. Use these new abbreviations as you listen to the lecture and take notes a second time.

Speak Out

activity 1

We encounter abbreviations and symbols in a variety of situations every day. As a class, decide what these abbreviations stand for.

1. ASAP (on a business memo)
2. FYI (on a business memo)
3. RGH RIDR (on a license plate)
4. ANML DOC (on a license plate)

5. SOS
6. Marge cd. @ 7:00, call bk.
7. H_2O
8. thanx

9. 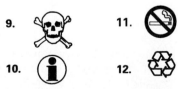   11.

10.   12.

activity 2

Look for examples of symbols and abbreviations in your daily life. (You'll probably need to spend a couple of days looking.) Bring them to class, put them on the blackboard, and let your classmates guess where you found them and what they mean.

activity 3

People sometimes have abbreviated messages on their license plates (see above). In groups of three, write messages for license plates. Use only the number of letters allowed in your state or area. Have your classmates guess their meanings. Then create two messages that you could use on a T-shirt. Put these on the board and have your classmates guess what these T-shirt messages are.

SKILL B

Extending Congratulations and Condolences

Many rites of passage are happy occasions such as birthdays, graduations, and weddings. At these times we offer *congratulations* to those involved. In contrast, when someone you know loses a job or suffers the death of a parent, spouse, child, or close friend, you may wish to offer your *condolences* for the loss.

Extending Congratulations

When you wish to congratulate someone, you can say "Congratulations" and add a phrase expressing good wishes appropriate to the particular occasion.

Congratulations! (plus one of the following)

For something new, for example, a baby; job; car; an award; a raise; an engagement:

> I'm so happy for you!
> I'm so pleased for you!
> I'm thrilled for you!
> I'm tickled for you!
> That's wonderful (terrific, great)!
> That's great news!
> It couldn't have happened to a nicer person!

For birthdays:

> May you have many more.
> May you have a hundred more.
> Many happy returns (of the day).
> I wish you all that you wish for yourself.

For weddings:

> (I wish you) All the best in the years to come.
> All the best to you both.
> May you have a long and prosperous life together.

For graduation:

> I'm sure you'll have much success in the years to come.
> I know you've got a great future ahead of you.

Extending Condolences

On occasions of loss and grief, you will want to choose the most appropriate and sensitive words with which to express your feelings and offer comfort. If you don't feel comfortable with any of the expressions of condolence, just be honest and put it this way:

> I'm sorry. I just don't know what to say.
>
> or
>
> I can't express how sorry I am.

Conversations

When you extend congratulations or condolences, you must be aware of the tone of voice as well as use the right words. For example, if your tone of voice expresses indifference, your enthusiastic words of congratulation will never convince listeners that you are truly happy for them.

Step 1 Listen to the following short conversations. In each conversation, the second speaker offers congratulations to the first. In some conversations, the second speaker is sincere (his or her tone of voice is enthusiastic) and in others he or she is indifferent (not enthusiastic). Listen to each conversation and circle the word that best describes the *second* speaker. When you are finished, compare your answers in small groups.

CONVERSATION 1

sincere   indifferent

CONVERSATION 2

sincere   indifferent

CONVERSATION 3

sincere   indifferent

CONVERSATION 4

sincere   indifferent

CONVERSATION 5

sincere   indifferent

CONVERSATION 6

sincere   indifferent

Step 2 Listen to the following conversations in which congratulations and condolences are made as part of longer on-going conversations. In the spaces provided, write down all the expressions of congratulation you hear in the first conversation. For the second conversation, write down all the expressions of condolence you hear.

CONVERSATION 1

_____

_____

_____

CONVERSATION 2

_____

_____

_____

Listen In

exercise

During the first portion of the lecture, the instructor and students mention a variety of occasions for which congratulations or condolences might be appropriate. During the rest of the lecture, the instructor mentions a few more. Listen to the lecture and note as many occasions as you can that might require either congratulations or condolences. Compare notes with your classmates. Then, as a class, choose expressions from Skill B that would be appropriate for each of the situations in your notes.

OCCASIONS REQUIRING CONGRATULATIONS OR CONDOLENCES	APPROPRIATE EXPRESSION
_____	_____
_____	_____
_____	_____
_____	_____
_____	_____
_____	_____
_____	_____
_____	_____

Speak Out

activity 1 — For the following occasions, think of the expressions of congratulations or condolence that you would say in your native language. Then translate these expressions into English and share them with your classmates. How similar are these expressions to each other and to the English ones listed in Skill B?

1. An engagement _____

2. A wedding (to the newly married couple) _____

   _____

3. A pregnancy _____

4. The birth of a baby _____

5. A graduation _____

6. A job promotion _____

7. A new purchase (a car or a house) _____

   _____

8. A retirement party _____

9. A job loss _____

10. The death of a friend _____

11. The death of a relative _____

12. A serious accident _____

activity 2 — Choose a partner and together work out dialogues for a few of the following congratulations and condolences. In each situation, you must decide what might be said before and what might be said after the congratulations and condolences. Change partners if you wish and work out a few more. Present your favorite conversation to the class.

1. Congratulations! I'm so happy for you. When do you expect the new arrival?
2. I'm so sorry. How did it happen?
3. I'm so sorry. How sad you must feel. Is there anything I can do?
4. Congratulations! Who's the lucky person?
5. Congratulations! And what are your future plans?
6. Congratulations! What's his/her name?
7. I can't tell you how sorry I am. How's your mother doing?
8. Congratulations! I'm so pleased for you! When do you start?
9. Congratulations! That's great news! What time?
10. I'm sorry. I just don't know what to say. Please call me if you need anything.
11. Oh, that's terrible. I'm so sorry. Do you have any other possibilities?

You will hear a short conversation. After the conversation you will be asked some questions. After you hear a question, read the four possible answers and decide which one is the best answer. Circle the letter of the best answer.

QUESTION 1

A. A professor.
B. A doctor.
C. A student.
D. A friend.

QUESTION 2

A. He thinks they are too much.
B. He thinks they sound like a good idea.
C. He thinks they are a strange idea.
D. He thinks that climbing mountains is fun.

QUESTION 3

A. What seems normal is all a matter of what you're used to.
B. What seems okay is based on your cultural perspective.
C. Cultural norms never change.
D. Western rites of passage may seem strange to a tribal culture.

QUESTION 4

A. Their first date.
B. Their next date.
C. His driver's license.
D. Cars.

CHAPTER four

Mysteries Past and Present

The lecture in this chapter is called "The Origins of Our Solar System." It is the kind of lecture you might hear in a science course, and the lecturer will describe several traditional theories about how our solar system got started.

Skill A—Learning Strategy: Using Illustrations in Note Taking

Skill B—Language Function: Admitting Lack of Knowledge

- In the early 1980s, a U.S. scientist, Alan Guth, proposed the "big bang" theory of the origin of the universe. According to Guth, the universe came about when a pocket of extremely condensed matter exploded and expanded to millions of times its previous size.
- The reason that the length of a month ranges from 28 to 31 days has its origins in early theories about the universe. Ancient peoples created the calendar of months using a system based on the apparent movements of the moon and the stars.
- The star closest to Earth, Alpha Centauri, is 260,000 times farther away than the sun is.

Getting Started

Sharing Your Experience

activity 1

In groups of three or four, discuss the following questions. If possible, try to include people from different cultures in each group.

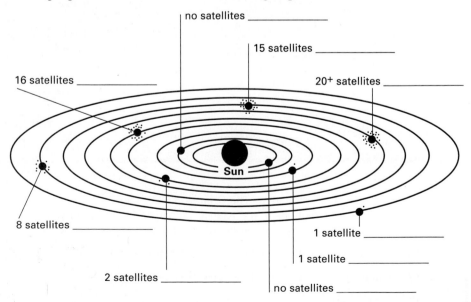

no satellites _____

15 satellites _____

16 satellites _____

20+ satellites _____

8 satellites _____

1 satellite _____

1 satellite _____

2 satellites _____

no satellites _____

Sun

1. Refer to the diagram on the opposite page. How many planets can you name? Which planet is closest to the sun? Which one is farthest away? Which one is closest to the earth? Label the diagram as well as you can. If you know the names of the planets in English, write them in English. If you don't, write them in your native language. The number of moons or natural satellites is written as a numeral next to each planet.

2. Share stories, myths, or folktales that you have heard about the origin of the solar system. What similarities and differences are there among the creation stories from various cultures?

3. Share with group members any scientific theories about the origin of the solar system that you learned in school. Did you all learn the same ones?

1. As a whole class, compare the names for each planet in several different languages. What similarities do you notice?

2. Share with the class any similarities among the creation stories from various cultures.

3. Summarize the scientific theories about the origin of the solar system from the small-group discussions and list them on the board.

Vocabulary

exercise

Look over the following vocabulary words and phrases and discuss them with a partner. Then read the sentences in items 1–11 below. The sentences in each item give a context which helps define a word or phrase. Fill in your own definitions. Compare your answers with those of your classmates.

(to) bear in mind	electromagnetic field	lump
bottom line	elements	mass
contraction	(to) get right down to it	to speculate
dense	hypothesis	sphere

1. Most scientists say that the universe is in a state of expansion—that it is getting larger. However, there are a few scientists who argue that some regions of the universe are not in a state of expansion, but rather a state of *contraction*.

   Contraction means _____

   _____

   _____

2. A magnet is a piece of metal that can attract iron. When a piece of metal is made into a magnet by using an electric current, the magnet is called an electromagnet. In outer space we find places where there are entire *electromagnetic fields*.

   An *electromagnetic field* is _____

   _____

   _____

3. To demonstrate to the class the relative sizes of the planets, the instructor took balls of different sizes and placed them at various distances from a very large ball, which represented the sun. These *spheres* were of many different colors, and the students were very interested in what the colors indicated about the planets.

Sphere means _____

_____

_____

4. When we study objects in space, we are often concerned with the size or volume of the object and what it is made of. We want to know, for example, if the *mass* is a solid or a liquid.

Mass means _____

_____

_____

Modern astronomers, Edwin P. Hubble (*left*) and Carl Sagan (*right*).

5. Astronomers who work on developing theories of the origin of the planets seem to enjoy their work, which mainly involves sitting and thinking. They take certain ideas and theorize about what the results would be *if* these ideas were true. These results or conclusions then need to be tested to see if the ideas are actually true. Unfortunately, it is often difficult for the astronomers to get enough money to test their *hypotheses*. They may struggle for years before they are given the necessary money.

Hypothesis means _____

_____

_____

6. "Take these small pieces of clay," the instructor told the students, "and put the *lumps* together to build your own model of the solar system. Of course, you don't have to use clay. You could use lumps of dough or papier mâché if you prefer."

   Lump means _____

   _____

   _____

7. Another question astronomers ask about objects in space is this: How *dense* is the object? They need to know how close the molecules in the object are to each other. Often they use special photography to find the answer.

   Dense means _____

   _____

   _____

8. Scientists make guesses about what objects in space are made of. They *speculate* based on what they already know about the frequency of certain *elements* in the universe. They have a good idea ahead of time how much iron, hydrogen, or mercury will be found in objects in space.

   To speculate means _____

   _____

   _____

   Examples of *elements* are _____

   _____

9. *"Bear in mind,"* said the professor as a reminder to the students, "that we'll have an astronomy quiz each Thursday from now to the end of the term."

   To bear in mind means _____

   _____

   _____

10. "You must have a passing average to complete this course," he went on. "The *bottom line* is that no one with less than a 70 average passes." (See item 11 for an additional example of the use of *bottom line*.)

    Bottom line means _____

    _____

    _____

11. "You know," said the astronomy professor, "you'll learn a lot about astronomy in this course. Astronomers have learned an enormous amount in the last hundred years. But when you *get right down to it,* what we've learned is that what we don't know is far greater than what we do know. The *bottom line* is that our ignorance is greater than our knowledge."

To get right down to it means _____

_____

_____

SKILL A

Using Illustrations in Note Taking

A major problem for many students is accurately remembering important information given in a lecture. The best solution to this problem is to take notes. Research has shown that students who take notes using the lecturer's own words as much as possible do better than students who take notes using their own words.

To take good notes, however, you don't need to write down every single word the lecturer says. For example, you can abbreviate. (See Chapter Three, Skill A.) You can also use diagrams and pictures to illustrate what the lecturer says. There is a saying, "A picture is worth a thousand words," and a quick sketch can often effectively replace several sentences in your notes.

A good time to take down a lecturer's words as pictures is when the lecturer is speaking about the relationships between two or more objects or ideas. For example, a lecturer says, "Consider two stars. The second one is about twice as big as the first. Now think about the smaller one rapidly approaching the larger one." In this case, you might draw something like this:

☆ ← ✬

Or you might draw it this way:

◯ ← ○

Later, the lecturer may add, "Now, let's call the larger star LS and the smaller star SS." You then label the stars. Your drawing would now look like one of these drawings.

Label drawings carefully in order to avoid confusion later. The circles in the second drawing, for example, could be stars, planets, satellites, novas, or snowballs. When you reread your notes, you want to feel secure that you can tell the planets from the stars.

For example, if the lecturer says, "According to Tycho Brahe, planets travel in concentric circles around the sun, but then travel as a unit around the Earth," you might draw and clearly label a diagram like this one.

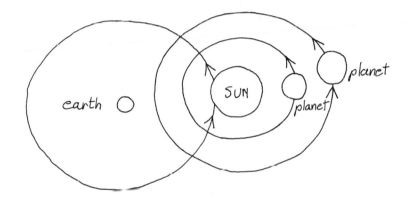

Note: In addition to making your own drawings and diagrams, you should always copy drawings and diagrams your instructor uses into your notes.

Listen In

exercise

Listen to the lecture once through to become familiar with the scientific concepts introduced. Next look at the hypotheses on the next page, some of which have been illustrated for you as examples. Then listen to the lecture again (as many times as necessary) and fill in the missing illustrations and labels.

1. Descartes's vortices theory
   a. Hot cloud of dust and gases

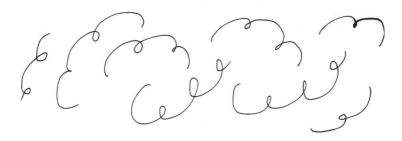

   b. Cooling cloud becomes central body with smaller bodies revolving around it

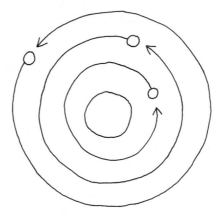

2. Kant and Laplace's nebular hypothesis

3. Jeans and Jeffries's gravitational attraction hypothesis

4. Alfvén's plasma-nebular hypothesis
  a. Rotating protostar sets off thermonuclear reaction

  b. At first, disk rotates more slowly than center sphere

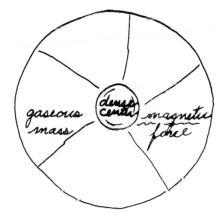

  c. Later, disk rotates faster than center sphere, and cooling causes lumps to form, which eventually become planets and moons

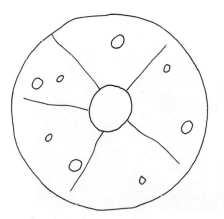

d. Planet and moons formed according to chemical composition of the lumps

Speak Out

activity

Make up a description of an uncharted, new solar system.

Step 1 In pairs, imagine that you and your partner are traveling in a space capsule toward a new solar system. When you arrive, describe what you see out the window of the space capsule as you pass through this new solar system. Be sure to include the following:

- the size of the sun in relation to the planets
- the number and size of planets in relation to each other
- the distance of each planet from the sun
- the number of moons each planet has (if any)
- any unusual characteristics of any of the planets (for example, any planet that always faces the sun so that half the planet is in darkness)
- any other objects, such as spaceships and meteors

In a simulated weightless atmosphere, astronauts Sharon Christa McAuliffe (*right*) and Barbara R. Morgan practice an experiment planned for the *Challenger's* space flight.

Step 2 Using illustrations, your partner should take notes on everything you describe. (To make this activity more interesting, put a barrier of some sort between you and your partner, or sit back-to-back, so you cannot see and try to correct what he/she draws as you go along.)

Step 3 When you have finished your description, look at your partner's drawings and discuss how well they match what you tried to describe. Also, name the planets if you like.

Step 4 Now switch places. It is your partner's turn to describe an uncharted solar system, while you draw. Repeat steps 1–4.

activity **2** Report to Mission Control. As in Activity 1, put a barrier between you and your partner or sit back-to-back.

Step 1 In pairs, imagine that you are a space explorer and your partner is your contact at Mission Control. Choose one of the planets of the uncharted solar system you described in Activity 1 and report to Mission Control what you see on both sides of the planet as you circle it in your spaceship. You will need to give enough information so that your partner at Mission Control can help you decide on the best place to land. For example: "On one side of the planet I see three large bodies of water, and the funny thing is that they are all shaped like letters of the alphabet. The first, at the upper left, is shaped like an E. The second, right below it, is shaped like an R, and the third, in the upper right, is shaped like a G. The land masses all have mountains in the middle that seem to be made entirely of some sort of shiny metal. All around the mountains are meadows of crystal. There are seven cities, all on the plains. . . ."

Step 2 When your partner taking notes at Mission Control has a good "picture" of the planet, change roles and do the activity again.

Step 3 When everyone in the class has finished, a few pairs of students can give their descriptions of their planets to the entire class. As the descriptions are given, class members can take turns drawing the various features of the planets on the board.

SKILL B
Admitting Lack of Knowledge

In the United States and Canada, a person's ability to admit lack of knowledge is a valued trait. Students often criticize an instructor who is unwilling to admit ignorance and compliment an instructor who *is* willing to admit ignorance. The same holds true for how students view one another.

Formal Ways to Admit Lack of Knowledge

ONE OF THESE:	FOLLOWED BY ONE OF THESE:
I'm afraid . . . I'm sorry but . . .	I don't know. I can't/couldn't tell you. I'm not sure. I don't remember. I can't remember. I forget. It's slipped my mind. I have no idea.

If you add a reason for your lack of knowledge, your words will sound more polite. For example:

A: Can you tell me where the post office is?
B: No, I'm afraid I couldn't tell you. I'm new here myself.

Informal Ways to Admit Lack of Knowledge

The following expressions are used frequently among friends, but may sound rude in other contexts.

Beats me.
(I) Can't/couldn't even begin
  to guess.
Don't ask me.
(I) haven't (got) a clue.
(I) haven't the foggiest (idea).

How do I know?
I give up!
I have no idea.
I'm sure I don't know.
It's beyond me.

Conversations

Listen to the following conversations in which one person admits a lack of knowledge. In some conversations, the second speaker is polite and in others he or she is rude. Listen to each conversation and circle the word that best describes the *second* speaker. When you are finished, compare your answers in small groups.

CONVERSATION 1

polite   rude

CONVERSATION 2

polite   rude

CONVERSATION 3

polite   rude

CONVERSATION 4

polite   rude

CONVERSATION 5

polite   rude

Listen In

Listen to the lecture and write the expressions the lecturer and students use to express lack of knowledge.

_____

_____

_____

_____

_____

Speak Out

Step 1 Think of an unexplained phenomenon or mystery that you know about and write down ten questions about it. Try to have five questions that people will probably be able to answer and five that they won't.

Stonehenge

examples: Where is Stonehenge? (England)
How did the Druids move the rocks at Stonehenge? (No one knows.)

Step 2 Choose a partner and take turns asking and answering the questions. Answer the questions if you can, but when you can't, admit your lack of knowledge by using an expression from Skill B. Use a variety of expressions.

Step 3 When you finish, change partners and do the activity again. Then change partners several more times if time permits. You may want to eliminate some of your questions and add a few others for variety as you go along.

Now think about some less mysterious questions such as:

- Where's the cap for the toothpaste?
- Where are the car keys?
- Why are some fire engines painted red and others green?
- When will they fill that big hole in the street in front of the school?

Jot down ten questions of this type and ask and answer questions with a partner as you did in Activity 1. Practice responding in various tones of voice from polite to irritated to downright rude.

focus on testing

You will hear a short tale. After the tale you will be asked some questions. After you hear a question, read the four possible answers and decide which one is the best answer. Circle the letter of the best answer.

QUESTION 1

A. Coyote.
B. Silver Fox.
C. Coyote and Silver Fox.
D. Coyote, Silver Fox, and the rest of the animals.

QUESTION 2

A. They decided to make things.
B. They decided to dance.
C. They decided to make the world.
D. They decided to whirl around.

QUESTION 3

A. They sang and hopped.
B. They danced and ran.
C. They ran and jumped and hopped and skipped.
D. They sang and danced and jumped and skipped.

QUESTION 4

A. The Story of a Traveler.
B. The Story of How the World Was Made.
C. The Story of How Not to Become Lonely.
D. The Story of a Silver Fox.

CHAPTER five

Transitions

in this chapter

The presentation in this chapter is called "The Stages of Life—A View from Shakespeare." This lecture takes place on an educational radio program. You will hear a professor of English literature talk about Shakespeare's views on some of the transformations we all go through during our lifetimes.

Skill A—Learning Strategy: Understanding and Making Analogies

Skill B—Language Function: Making Negative Statements or Comments Politely

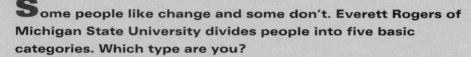

DID YOU KNOW?

Some people like change and some don't. Everett Rogers of Michigan State University divides people into five basic categories. Which type are you?

- "Innovators" are adventurous and eager to try new things. They are usually young and don't care too much what others think. ($2\frac{1}{2}$% of the population)
- "Early Adopters" are often respected leaders within the established social system. Others check with them before adopting new ideas. ($13\frac{1}{2}$%)
- "Early Majority" people are followers rather than leaders. They make changes only after a lot of their friends have done so. (34%)
- "Late Majority" people are skeptical of change and cautious about adopting new ideas. They have little influence on the actions of others. (34%)
- "Resisters" are very suspicious of new ideas and generally think things were better in the past. They are not curious and do not take risks. (16%)

Getting Started
Sharing Your Experience

activity

As a class or in small groups, discuss the following questions.

1. Everyone has experienced at least a few major transitions in life. These might include changing schools, losing someone close, or just getting another year older and facing the responsibilities and privileges that come at a particular age. Share at least two such transitions that you've faced and what they meant to you. When you were going through these transitions, did you feel "in control" or did you feel caught by the circumstances and events surrounding these times?

2. Do you think people have much influence over their own growth and development (physical, mental, and emotional)? Or do you think that "free will" does not exist and that human beings are like puppets whose strings are pulled by forces beyond their control? Why?

3. Assume for the moment that you *do* direct your own life or "pull your own strings," as the expression goes. What do you personally want to achieve to feel successful? (Give at least one example.) What are the steps you plan to take to make this happen?

4. Consider the following analogies about time. What do you think they mean? Does any one of them hold any particular significance for you? Why? If you can, tell about an event or time in your life when one of these quotations might have been significant. Let your classmates guess which quotation best applies to the situation you describe.

Time wasted is existence, used [it] is life. —*Henry Wadsworth Longfellow*

I recommend you take care of the minutes, for the hours will take care of themselves. —*Lord Chesterfield*

Unhappy is he who trusts only to time for his happiness. —*Voltaire*

Vocabulary

exercise 1 — Find a word on the right that defines each italicized word on the left, and put the letters of the correct words in the blanks.

1. _____ An *inflated* self-image is something like a balloon *inflated* with hot air.

2. _____ People who believe that we are like puppets and have little control over our lives may feel that our efforts in life will produce only "sound and *fury*" and in the end will not mean anything.

3. _____ Many politicians have been found to be extremely *corrupt* individuals who are interested only in money and power, not in the public welfare.

4. _____ Some people believe that *passion* is the cause of much suffering in life, while others believe that *passion* is the only thing that makes life worth living.

5. _____ Extremely confident and strong-willed people can easily *intimidate* others who are shy and less confident.

6. _____ The man was so *driven* by ambition that he rarely went home from work until ten or eleven at night.

a. compelled to do something
b. blown up, enlarged
c. anger, rage
d. to frighten
e. dishonest
f. intense emotion

exercise 2 — As a class or in small groups, discuss the following questions.

1. Did you ever feel as if you were *in a rut* and want to make a major change in your life? If so, when? Why?

2. Do you think it's important *to make a name for yourself* in life? Why or why not?

3. What are some of the things you would do *at the drop of a hat?* (For example: Help a friend in trouble? Eat a piece of chocolate cake? Go for a swim in the ocean?)

4. There's a fine line between honesty and rudeness. But sometimes you have to speak out and say something in a straightforward manner, in other words, *put it bluntly.* When was the last time you had to do this? What were the circumstances? What did you say?

5. Sometimes it seems that certain laws of irony operate in the universe. For example, Jeremy called Susan to invite her to a party and left a message about the party with her roommate. When Susan called back two hours later, Jeremy rushed to answer the phone and fell and broke his arm. It was bad enough that he had broken his arm, but *to add insult to injury,* it turned out that Susan was planning to go to the party with someone else instead. What have been some of the ironies in your life, or cases in which insult was added to injury?

SKILL A
Understanding and Making Analogies

Life is like a river, always changing yet ever the same. This expression is an example of figurative language—that is, language used to create an image and not meant to be taken literally. An analogy is one type of figurative language. It is a comparison, showing the logical relationship between two things. Some examples:

1. An idea is like a seed.
2. History is merely gossip. — *Oscar Wilde*
3. Love is food for the soul, but jealousy is poison.
4. Life is a disease. The only difference between one man and another is the stage of the disease. — *George Bernard Shaw*

If you can paraphrase a statement as an equation, it is an analogy. For example, the four analogies given as examples can be represented by the following equations:

1. idea = seed
2. history = gossip

3. love = food for the soul
4. life = disease

Analogies make language more interesting and vivid and are powerful conveyors of meaning. They do not have to be complex; in fact, they can be quite simple. It is common for people to use analogies to help others understand what they are trying to say. Therefore, it is important for you to be able to recognize analogies and to know the difference between literal and figurative language as you develop your listening skills.

Expressions Often Used in Making Analogies

about the size of a . . .	as (big) as . . .	mean(s) . . .
are almost like . . .	is the same as . . .	seem(s) like . . .
are similar to . . .		

Listen In

Listen to the lecture once all the way through and note the main ideas. Then play it again, stopping the tape when you come to each new section of the speech the lecturer is about to discuss. Discuss what you are about to hear and then go on and listen to what the lecturer has to say. Make a mark in the box on the opposite page each time you hear an analogy and add up the total number at the end. Discuss your results with your classmates. How many of the analogies can you remember?

Public Radio Newsletter

Transitions in Literature Series
Program 6

Jacques' Speech from *As You Like It*

Jacques from Shakespeare's
As You Like It.

All the world's a stage,
And all the men and women merely players.
They have their exits and their entrances,
And one man in his time plays many parts.
His acts being seven ages. At first the infant,
Mewling and puking in the nurse's arms,
Then whining schoolboy, with his satchel
And shining morning face, creeping like a snail
Unwillingly to school. And then the lover,
Sighing like a furnace, with a woeful ballad
Made to his mistress' eyebrow. Then a soldier,
Full of strange oaths, and bearded like a pard,
Jealous in honor, sudden and quick in quarrel,
Seeking the bubble reputation
Even in the cannon's mouth. And then the justice,
In fair round belly with good capon lined,
With eyes severe, and beard of formal cut,
Full of wise saws and modern instances,
And so he plays his part. The sixth age shifts
Into the lean and slippered Pantaloon,
With spectacles on nose and pouch on side,
His youthful hose, well saved, a world too wide
For his shrunk shank, and his big manly voice,
Turning again toward childish treble, pipes
And whistles in his sound. Last scene of all,
That ends this strange eventful history,
Is second childishness and mere oblivion,
Sans teeth, sans eyes, sans taste, sans everything.

exercise 2

Listen to the lecture a third time. As you listen, complete the analogies listed below. Use the lecturer's words if you can. Otherwise, complete the ten analogies in your own words.

examples: A Buddhist would probably see transformation or change as <u>an opportunity for spiritual growth.</u>

_____

A business executive may see change as <u>financial loss or gain.</u>

_____

1. Planning, working, and struggling for success are like _____
   _____

2. One disturbing vision is the idea that we are just _____
   _____

3. Or even worse than this idea is the notion that we are just _____
   _____

4. The seven stages of life are _____
   _____

5. The schoolboy creeps to school like _____
   _____

6. When the lecturer says the hero burns with desire, he means that desire is
   like _____
   _____

7. The young hero thinks that becoming a man is _____
   _____

8. The young soldier grows a beard so he will look as fierce _____
   _____

9. As the man grows older, he loses the clear voice of youth. Now his voice

_____

10. Reaching old age, the man has almost come full circle. He is now like

_____ again.

Speak Out

activity 1

In small groups, think of as many analogies as you can for each of the following items. One way to do this is to "free associate"—that is, to see what pops into your head when you hear each item. Then make an analogy comparing the item with the idea that just came to you. Or, you may prefer to be more deliberate and analytical in devising your analogies.

example: time
            time = change
            Time is like a river, constantly changing yet always the same.

1. love	**6.** sorrow	**11.** youth
2. infatuation	**7.** life	**12.** old age
3. passion	**8.** death	**13.** a friend
4. a realist	**9.** a woman	**14.** imperfection
5. a man	**10.** perfection	**15.** ambition

activity 2

Share some of your group's analogies with the rest of the class by playing the following guessing game. Consider all the analogies your group created and, as a group, select a few favorites. Now substitute the pronoun _it_ for the subject of each of these analogies and see if the rest of the class can guess which item you are talking about.

example: _It_ is like a river, constantly changing yet always the same.
            Question: What is _it_?
            Answer: Time.

SKILL B

Making Negative Statements or Comments Politely

Many times there is only a fine line between honesty and rudeness. This is especially true when what is being said is negative or critical. The negative comment may be based on accepted fact, or it may be just a personal opinion, in which case the thin line between honesty and rudeness becomes even thinner. Therefore, when you find yourself in a situation in which you feel compelled to make a negative statement, but you don't want to offend the listener, you can use one of the following expressions with a sympathetic tone of voice.

Polite Expressions for Making Negative Comments
Actually, I hate to say this, but . . .
Frankly, I don't like saying this, but . . .
I'm sorry to tell you . . .
Let's face It . . .
Not to beat around the bush . . .
This is difficult/hard to say, but honestly . . .
To be frank . . .
To be honest with you . . .
To put it bluntly . . .
To tell the truth . . .

If the expression and the negative statement following it are not delivered in a sympathetic, sincere tone, they will not have the desired effect. For example, if your voice sounds sarcastic, angry, or impatient, your words will convey only these feelings and you will sound rude.

Conversations

You will hear three pairs of conversations. Each pair of exchanges uses exactly the same words, but each version conveys a different meaning because of the tone of voice used by one of the speakers. Listen to each conversation and answer the questions. When you are finished, compare your answers in small groups.

conversation **1A**

1. Is Gloria really concerned about Ted?

_____ Is Mickey? _____

2. How do you know? _____

_____

3. How would Ted feel if he overheard

this conversation? _____

_____

1. Is Gloria really concerned about Ted now? _____ Is Mickey? _____

2. How do you know? _____

3. How would Ted feel if he overheard this conversation? _____

   _____

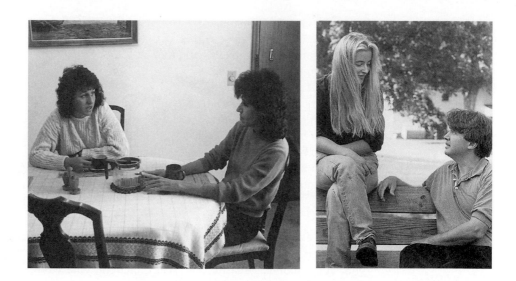

 *conversation* **2A**

1. How does the father feel about not going to his daughter's wedding? _____

   _____

2. How do you know? _____

3. What reason might he have for not going? _____

   _____

 *conversation* **2B**

1. How does the father feel about not going to his daughter's wedding? _____

   _____

2. How do you know? _____

3. What reason might he have for not going? _____

   _____

**conversation 3A**

1. Does Jane like Paul's artwork? _____

2. How can you tell? _____
   _____

3. Does Jane like Paul? _____

4. How can you tell? _____
   _____

conversation 3B

1. Does Jane like Paul's artwork? _____

2. How can you tell? _____
   _____

3. Does Jane like Paul? _____

4. How can you tell? _____
   _____

Listen In

**exercise 1**

In the lecture, the instructor uses various expressions to introduce negative statements or comments. As you listen to the lecture, jot down an introductory expression on the first line after each number on the next page. What can you tell about the lecturer's attitudes from the tone of voice used with each one? Share your responses with the class. (The second and third lines after each number will be used for Exercise 2.)

All the world's a stage . . .

1. <u>Let's face it. (for Exercise 1)</u>

   <u>Time and change inevitably bring decline and death. (for Exercise 2)</u>

   _____

2. _____

   _____

   _____

3. _____

   _____

   _____

4. _____

   _____

   _____

5. _____

   _____

   _____

6. _____

   _____

   _____

7. _____

   _____

   _____

exercise 2

Listen to the lecture again. This time write the negative statement that follows each of the introductory expressions you wrote for Exercise 1. You may paraphrase these negative statements if you wish. Share your responses with the class.

Speak Out

activity 1

Step 1 Choose a partner and together select one of the situations on the opposite page as the basis for a dialogue you will perform.

Step 2 Invent two characters who might find themselves in this situation and decide which of you will play each one.

Step 3 Select an attitude and tone of voice for each character from the list below. The characters can use the same tones of voice or different ones.

Step 4 Role-play a dialogue in which the characters talk about the situation they find themselves in. Practice introducing negative comments using the expressions from Skill B. (See the sample dialogue below.)

Step 5 If time permits, choose another situation, another set of characters, and new tones of voice and do a new role-play.

SITUATIONS

1. the birth of a baby
2. a child's first day at school
3. a child skipping class
4. a child pretending to be sick so he or she won't have to go to school
5. graduating from school
6. cheating on an exam
7. being interviewed for a job
8. getting offered a job you don't want
9. getting fired
10. retiring
11. falling in love with someone who doesn't love you
12. getting divorced
13. getting married
14. changing careers
15. becoming a widow or widower
16. a situation of your choice

TONES OF VOICE

1. sad	8. hurt	15. nervous
2. angry	9. vengeful	16. passionate
3. depressed	10. shy	17. confused
4. delighted	11. sarcastic	18. envious
5. excited	12. guilty	19. mean
6. frightened	13. powerless	20. amused
7. loving	14. powerful	

SAMPLE DIALOGUE

Here is a sample dialogue for Situation 1, the birth of a baby. Terry speaks in a depressed tone, and Francis is amused.

TERRY: Did you hear what happened after Jennifer's baby was born?
FRANCIS: No! What happened?
TERRY: Well, after seeing the baby, Jennifer's husband went home and cried.
FRANCIS: You're kidding! Why?
TERRY: Well, to put it bluntly, their baby is really ugly. Isn't that depressing?
FRANCIS: No, not particularly. Let's face it: All newborn babies are ugly.
TERRY: To tell the truth, I agree with you. It's a wonder more fathers don't go home and cry after they see their babies for the first time.
FRANCIS: Well, why waste tears so soon? By the time they're teenagers, the parents will really have reasons to cry!

 **activity 2** With your partner, present a dialogue to the rest of the class, but do not tell your classmates which situation or emotions you have selected. After you've finished, let them guess.

focus on testing

You will hear a short presentation. After the presentation you will be asked some questions. After you hear a question, read the four possible answers and decide which one is the best answer. Circle the letter of the best answer.

QUESTION 1

A. 5%
B. 40%
C. 8%
D. 85%

QUESTION 2

A. The first stage.
B. The second stage.
C. The third stage.
D. The fourth stage.

QUESTION 3

A. Hindu women are considered to be both divine and inferior.
B. Hindu women are expected to go through the same Dharma stages as men.
C. Hindu women are traditionally expected only to serve their husbands.
D. Hindu women are traditionally expected to have no interests outside the home.

QUESTION 4

A. Samnyasa
B. Brahmacarya
C. Dharma
D. Vanaprasthya

CHAPTER SIX

The Mind

in this chapter

The lecture in this chapter is called "Dreams and Reality." It uses some of the ideas presented in Ursula LeGuin's *The Lathe of Heaven* in a discussion of how dreams may shape our lives and how they may even help determine the future of the world as a whole.

Skill A—Learning Strategy: Listening for Comparisons and Contrasts

Skill B—Language Function: Expressing the Positive View

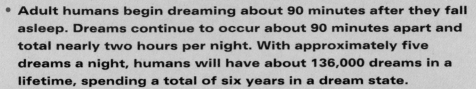
- **Adult humans begin dreaming about 90 minutes after they fall asleep. Dreams continue to occur about 90 minutes apart and total nearly two hours per night. With approximately five dreams a night, humans will have about 136,000 dreams in a lifetime, spending a total of six years in a dream state.**
- **The dream state is called REM (rapid eye movement) sleep because when they dream, most people's eyes move rapidly as if they were watching an exciting movie.**
- **REM sleep is a combination of very light sleep and very deep sleep. The person in a REM state is sleeping lightly enough so that he or she can respond to light and noises in the room. However, the REM sleeper is not able to move any part of the body at will.**

Getting Started

Sharing Your Experience

activity

As a class or in small groups, discuss these questions.

1. Do you usually remember your dreams?
2. When do you remember your dreams? After you've eaten a large meal? After seeing an exciting movie? At the end of a stressful day?
3. Do you believe dreams help you cope with daily life? If so, how?
4. Have you ever dreamed about something that later actually happened? For example, you might have dreamed about receiving a gift or seeing a car accident and then had the exact same thing happen in real life.

Le Libérateur by René Magritte

Hand with Reflecting Sphere by M. C. Escher

Time Transfixed by René Magritte

Vocabulary

exercise 1

You may already know the meanings of some of the following words. However, the words you know may be different from the ones your classmates know. Working together in small groups, match the definitions on the right with the words on the left.

1. _____ chaotic

2. _____ to cling

3. _____ conceptualization

4. _____ fleeting

5. _____ flexibility

6. _____ to manipulate

7. _____ perception

8. _____ trivial

9. _____ in tune with

10. _____ visualization

a. unimportant, ordinary
b. formation of mental images
c. ability to bend; ability to adjust to new situations
d. to hold on tightly
e. disorderly, in a state of confusion
f. vanishing quickly
g. insight gained through the senses; observation
h. to manage (people, numbers, stocks, and so forth) skillfully for one's own profit
i. in harmony with, in agreement with
j. formation of theories, ideas, or concepts

exercise 2

Work with a partner. First choose roles and read the telephone conversation on the next page together. Then read it a second time, pausing to replace the italicized words with the expressions introduced in Exercise 1.

STACY: Hi, Hank. What's up? How's the psych course going? Is it interesting?

HANK: Yeah. The unit this week is pretty good.

STACY: Oh yeah? What's the topic?

HANK: It's a unit on dreams.

STACY: What's so interesting about dreams?

HANK: Well, for one thing, it's hard to come up with new theories about dreams. The *making of theories* is difficult because there are so many current theories.

STACY: Like what?

HANK: Well, for one thing, there's the theory that dreams reflect reality.

STACY: What do you mean by that?

HANK: Some philosophers argue that there is no way to prove that those *quickly disappearing* images we have in our sleep may be just another form of this crazy, *unorganized* world we live in. They say that our *view* of the world, which we get through sight, sound, touch, taste, and smell, may actually be changed through dreams.

STACY: That sounds like it might not be *unimportant*. What else did you learn?

HANK: Well, that in some cultures the *formation of an image* that comes in a dream is considered to be no different from reality. And people in those cultures *hold on* so strongly to this belief that they react in waking life as though the dream were true. They seem to have no *willingness to adjust or change their minds* on this matter. For example, a Zulu man reportedly broke off a friendship after he dreamt that his friend intended to harm him.

STACY: I wonder how that would work in our culture. People would try to *control and guide* their dreams so they could make their waking hours happier, don't you think?

HANK: I guess so. You'd really have to understand the workings of the mind to be so *in harmony with* your dreams like that, wouldn't you?

STACY: Yeah, I guess you would.

HANK: Hey, listen. Enough about school. You want to catch a movie Thursday night?

STACY: Sure. What did you have in mind?

HANK: Renoir's <u>The Grand Illusion</u> is playing at the Fine Arts. Want to see it?

STACY: Sure, come by for me at 6:00.

HANK: Okay, see you then. 'Bye.

STACY: 'Bye.

SKILL A

Listening for Comparisons and Contrasts

In the previous chapter, you learned about using analogies for comparison—that is, looking at the similarities between two things. English speakers commonly use analogies both in formal and informal situations. For example, in a lecture on the nature of dreams you might hear:

Dreams are like smoke. You can't quite get a hold on them, and they go away so quickly that you can barely remember them.

In a friendly conversation a friend might say:

In my dream last night the clouds were like human heads, each one smiling and wearing a funny hat. I woke up laughing.

Another way of looking at the relationship between two things is to point out the differences between them, that is, to contrast them. In this chapter we will look at how analogies can be used for both comparison and contrast. Such analogies are often used to call attention to characteristics or points that might otherwise be overlooked. Because comparison and contrast are used so frequently, it is important for you to recognize them.

Comparisons and contrasts are indicated in four main ways: (1) through the use of words that signal comparison, (2) through the use of words that signal contrast, (3) through the use of pairs of antonyms within a single statement, and (4) through the tone of voice you use. Below are some examples of each type of indicator.

Words That Signal Comparison

again	in a similar way
also	likewise
and so does	similarly
equally important	the same way (as)
in a like manner	too

Words That Signal Contrast

although / though / even though	meanwhile
but	nevertheless
by (in) contrast	on the contrary
conversely	on the other hand
however	whereas
instead	yet

Pairs of Antonyms

Antonyms can be used to show contrast when the speaker is talking about one topic or idea.

Fortunately . . . Unfortunately . . .
The advantages are . . . The disadvantages are . . .
The best part is . . . The worst part is . . .
The positive features are . . . The negative features are . . .

> **Tone of Voice**
>
> Word stress and intonation can also indicate comparison and contrast.
> For example, in the following sentence, comparison is indicated by
> stressing the words *mind* and *body* and by using rising intonation at the
> end of the first sentence and falling intonation at the end of the second.
> Try it.
>
> The *mind* repairs itself during sleep.
> The *body* repairs itself during sleep.

Conversations

You will hear some conversations that illustrate the informal use of comparison
and contrast. Listen to the conversations once and discuss them with a partner.
Then listen a second time and list which indicators of comparison and contrast
were used by the speakers. When you are finished, compare your answers in small
groups.

conversation **1** **Otto and Henry**

_____

_____

conversation **2** **Judy and Paula**

_____

_____

conversation **3** **A Teaching Assistant and Students**

_____

_____

Listen In

exercise

Listen to the lecture to get the main ideas. Then
listen again and jot down any words or phrases that
might signal a comparison or a contrast.

_____

_____

_____

_____

Photo from the movie version of Ursula LeGuin's
novel *The Lathe of Heaven*

 **exercise 2** The chart here and on the next page lists some of the comparisons and contrasts in the lecture. Listen to the lecture again and fill in the chart as you listen. Replay the tape as many times as necessary. The first item has been done for you.

dreams vs. reality

	Comparison	Contrast
1. Dreams and waking life	Both waking images and dreams are inspirations for scientists, artists	Dream images are more subtle than waking experiences
2. Two types of dreams		
3. Dr. Haber's reaction to George and other people's reaction to George		

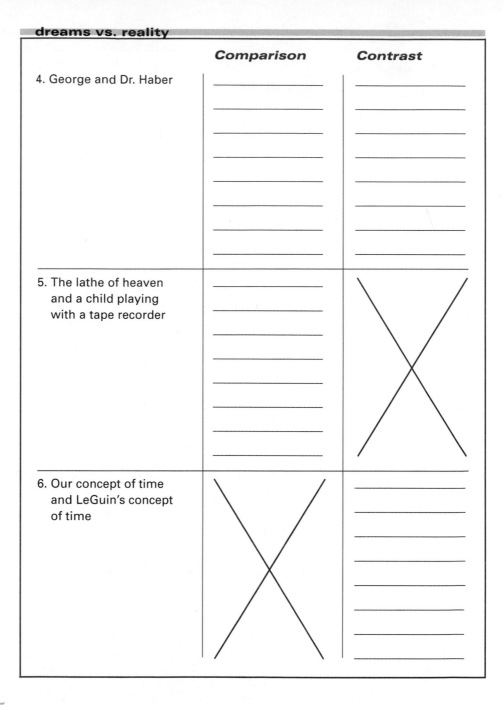

	Comparison	Contrast
4. George and Dr. Haber	_____	_____
5. The lathe of heaven and a child playing with a tape recorder	_____	
6. Our concept of time and LeGuin's concept of time		_____

At what points in the lecture are comparisons and contrasts *not* introduced by the usual signal words? Which comparisons are marked by intonation changes? Discuss your responses with your classmates.

Speak Out

activity 1

Ursula LeGuin suggested that reality cannot be fixed or held still in order to be controlled. Similarly, dreams cannot be controlled, which may be one reason we can learn about our hopes, beliefs, and feelings from our dreams. Some dreams are symbolic; others are more straightforward representations of actual events.

In this activity you will be comparing and contrasting two dreams triggered by the same event. First read Situation 1 and the two dreams. Then discuss your reactions as a class. Continue in this way for Situations 2 to 5.

1. How are the dreams similar?
2. How are the dreams different?
3. Which one is more symbolic and which is more related to actual events? Why do you feel this way?

Situation 1   You and a friend read the following story in a newspaper: The Hotel Ritz has been robbed. Three professional gunmen, posing as doctors, entered the hotel in Dallas. Because there was a medical convention in the hotel at the time, the gunmen were undetected and made a clean getaway.

> *Dream 1:* A doctor is examining you, but instead of being in an office, you are in your car. All of a sudden, the doctor pulls out a gun.

> *Dream 2:* You have invited a few friends for dinner. You are making the final preparations in the kitchen. As you reach for the butter, it turns into a pistol.

Situation 2   The atmosphere at school has been chaotic because final examinations will be given next week. Of course, students are studying frantically. You're especially worried about your economics final because your instructor is hard to understand and reminds you of a rhinoceros.

> *Dream 1:* While you are in the library with your economics book, you notice a giraffe chewing a textbook on the table next to yours. Nobody but you seems to notice.

> *Dream 2:* You are reading a paperback in bed with your stereo blaring. Everything is fine. All at once, your normally well-behaved dog jumps on the bed and begins howling and will not stop.

Situation 3   A quarrel between two men in the office stems from administrative policies. Jim, who has worked there longer, wants the promotion, but the offer was made to Michael, a newer employee who has been working for Jim. No seniority system exists.

> *Jim's dream:* A rock band is playing in the cafeteria, and everyone is eating pink and green food with stars on it. Jim asks the band to play some folk music, but the band members ignore him. He tries to buy some of the pink and green food with stars on it, but the young man at the cash register says he's too old to eat this food and asks him to leave.

> *Michael's dream:* Michael has a conversation with Jim and apologizes for the argument. Jim forgives him and announces that he has a new job at twice the salary at a Japanese company just opening down the street.

Situation 4   You have read in the newspaper about a group of skiers who have been missing for two weeks. Rescue teams fear the worst because avalanches have been occurring daily this winter.

> *Dream 1:* You are jogging in shorts and a T-shirt. The weather changes drastically, and it begins to rain. To make matters worse, you are eight miles from home.

> *Dream 2:* You are walking in the snow thinking about how fresh and clear the air is. Your warm clothing feels too heavy and tight all of a sudden. Soon you are having trouble breathing. Your hat keeps falling down over your eyes, and your collar creeps up over your mouth. You wake up gasping for air.

Situation 5   Tom reads in the paper that since it is the last Sunday in October, he must set his clock back one hour.

> *Dream 1:* He dreams that he wakes up in the morning and everything is backwards. He walks backwards to the bathroom to brush his teeth and sees the back of his head in the mirror. He feels like he is putting on his clothing correctly, but when he looks down it is all backwards. The car goes in reverse to work, and at the end of the day when he climbs into bed he finds his head where his feet usually rest.

> *Dream 2:* Tom dreams that he is an hour early for a major appointment with a man named Mr. Timekeeper. Mr. Timekeeper is very impressed that Tom is so early and gives Tom four million dollars' worth of business.

activity 2

GROUP ACTIVITY

In this activity you will be doing some more dream analysis, this time as part of a team of "psychoanalysts" analyzing patients' dreams. Work in groups of three or four. Then discuss your findings with the other groups.

1. How are each group of dreams alike and how are they different?
2. Which dreams represent a single major issue and which deal with several different issues in the person's life?
3. What does each dream mean?

Patient 1   Peter is a thirty-eight-year-old used-car salesman who has recently filed for bankruptcy. His wife has threatened to leave him unless he gets out of debt.

Dream 1: He jumps off the Eiffel Tower but is picked up by a stork and carried to the Caribbean.

Dream 2: He is at his bank making a night deposit when two female outlaws hold up the bank and leave him tied up and bound with a scarf so that he cannot talk.

Dream 3: He flies to Italy to order lasagna, but can find only pizza. As he enjoys the pizza, a helicopter lands across the street and two men get out and offer him $77,000.

Patient 2   Martin, from Denver, Colorado, marries Françoise, from Lyon, France, and lives and works in Lyon for three years. Then they move back to Denver.

Dream 1: Martin dreams he is back in Lyon at their apartment talking to the neighbors.

Dream 2: Martin dreams he is alone in an airplane, and all the signs and control indicators are labeled in French. He picks up an equipment manual, which is written in French, and realizes he can't read it.

Dream 3: Martin goes to the office in Denver and finds that all of the people there are his co-workers from France. None of them speaks English, and all of them need his help. He speaks French perfectly and easily arranges housing for his co-workers. When he finishes, everyone cheers and they pick him up on their shoulders and carry him around the office.

Patient 3   An elderly man, Mr. Hill, describes these dreams.

Dream 1: Mr. Hill dreams he is in college taking courses and living in the dorms. Although he does very well, no one notices or sees him.

Dream 2: Mr. Hill is a young man working on his father's ranch. Everyone is looking at the blue sky and hoping for rain.

Dream 3: Mr. Hill meets his first grandchildren. They are twins, a boy and a girl. The boy looks like him and the girl looks like his deceased wife.

Patient 4   Tina is a freshman at Santa Barbara City College, majoring in computer science.

Dream 1: Tina is in a computer store selecting a word processor. As she walks up to look at one, it changes into an ice cream sundae. The second one changes into a bicycle, the third into a small swimming pool, the fourth into a refrigerator, and the fifth into a sculpture of a dancer. She leaves the store feeling worried that she'll never find a computer that will stick around.

Dream 2: Tina walks into class feeling very good, confident about the exam she is about to take. She sits down, and the instructor passes out the exam. She takes one look at it and can't remember anything.

Dream 3: Tina is at a party and three men come up to her and ask her to dance. She can't decide whom to dance with.

activity 3

Ask three native speakers of English about a dream they remember.

1. Find out as much as you can about the dream.
2. Share your findings with your classmates.
3. Discuss whether anyone could have had this dream or only a native speaker of English? Why?

SKILL B

Expressing the Positive View

People often need others to listen to their complaints. It is quite common, for example, to find ourselves listening to the complaints of family, friends, or colleagues about something that has gone wrong at home, at school, at work, or at a shop.

To console or "cheer up" the unhappy person, we can suggest ways to look at the problem as though it were "all for the best." This ability to look at the bright or positive side of an issue is useful in both informal conversations and formal discussions.

Statements that demonstrate a positive point of view are often introduced in one of three ways: (1) by expressions that signal contrast, (2) by expressions that present a positive view, and (3) by comparing this situation with one that is even worse. Below are some examples of each type of indicator.

Expressions That Signal Contrast	
although/though	nevertheless
but	on the contrary
by (in) contrast	on the other hand
conversely	whereas
however	yet
meanwhile	

Conversations

You will hear several conversations. Answer the questions you hear after each one. Then discuss your responses as a class or in small groups.

conversation 1   Gary and Julius

1. What expression does Gary use to help Julius "look at the bright side"?

_____

2. Is Gary's suggestion amusing?_____

Why or why not?_____

_____

 **conversation 2** **Christine and Eric**

1. What does Eric suggest doing instead of going to the picnic?_____

_____

2. What expression does he use to introduce this suggestion?_____

_____

3. Do you think Eric was glad the picnic was rained out?_____

Why or why not?_____

 **conversation 3** **Clara and Joyce**

1. What is Joyce's complaint?_____

_____

2. What does Clara suggest?_____

3. What expression does Clara use to introduce her suggestion?_____

_____

4. Was Clara able to convince Joyce to see the bright side?_____

How do you know this?_____

_____

Listen In

 **exercise**

Listen to the lecture as you complete this exercise. Listen specifically for situations that might be considered negative or unpleasant.

Step 1 Read through the eight statements below. They are paraphrases of parts of the lecture.

Step 2 After each statement, write a summary of the positive response to the situation given in the lecture. When the speaker uses one of the optimistic Skill B expressions (in items 2, 3, 4, and 7), include it in your response. When the speaker doesn't use one of these expressions (in items 1, 5, and 6), add it at the beginning of your response. The first two have been completed for you.

Step 3   Compare your answers with those of your classmates.

    1. Dreams are very mysterious.

        <u>Yes, but look at it this way. It's these kinds of mysteries that</u>

        <u>make life interesting.</u>

        _____

    2. Dreams can be irrelevant to waking life, even silly.

        <u>On the other hand, many breakthroughs in science and</u>

        <u>inspirations in the arts came through dreams.</u>

        _____

    3. After Coleridge's writing was interrupted by a visitor, he could not remember the rest of the poem he had created in a dream.

        _____

        _____

        _____

    4. And one night last week I dreamed about hot dogs piled up on a bridge—no useful images for scientific discoveries or artistic creations there that I can figure out.

        _____

        _____

        _____

    5. Every time George dreams a new reality, each person in the world forgets who they once were and acquires a new set of memories to fit this new reality.

        _____

        _____

        _____

    6. Dr. Haber has been trying to use George's dreams to change the world.

        _____

        _____

        _____

7. Dr. Haber dreams that everything is gray—the people, the buildings, the animals, and the plants.

_____

_____

_____

8. Time is moved forward or backward in response to George's dreams.

_____

_____

_____

Speak Out

activity **1**

In this activity, you will have a chance to become an eternal optimist, looking only on the bright side, or an immovable pessimist, who can see only the dark side. You will be forming teams and debating the positive and negative sides of the topic you choose. Your instructor can serve as moderator. Each team gets a point for each good argument it presents for or against a particular point of view.

Step 1   Form teams of three or four persons. Then find another team to be your opponents in a debate.

Step 2   Work with the other team to choose one of the topics from the list to debate. Decide which team will take the positive point of view and which will take the negative.

Step 3   Spend 10 minutes preparing for the debate. Imagine what the other team's position will be and come up with arguments against their point of view.

Step 4   During the debate, take turns with the other team in presenting and then defending your point of view. (Those presenting the positive side can use expressions from the Skill B section of this chapter. Those presenting the negative side can use the Skill B expressions from Chapter Five.)

Step 5   If time permits, stay on the same teams, choose a new topic, but take the opposite point of view. This time around, pessimists become optimists and optimists become pessimists.

TOPICS

1. hypnosis
2. mind-altering drugs such as LSD
3. telepathy
4. memorization as a method of study

5. many years of intense study on a particular subject, excluding all other areas of study
6. controlling anger at all times
7. being totally honest at all times
8. daydreaming
9. treatment of mental illness with drugs
10. experimenting with mind-altering situations such as sleep deprivation or total sensory deprivation

activity 2

A conversation that degenerates into one complaint after another is called a "gripe session." A gripe session can be a good thing because it helps everyone get feelings out into the open. Participants may also feel better because of the support and sympathy they receive. Sometimes, however, a gripe session may go on for a long time without producing positive results. At times like this, we welcome the "eternal optimist" who helps everyone see the bright side and get back on a positive track.

Step 1 In small groups, choose a topic from the list below.

Step 2 Complain all you want. Say all the negative things you can about the topic.

Step 3 After a few minutes, try offering a more optimistic view of the situation using some of the expressions from the Skill B section of this chapter.

Step 4 Choose another topic and begin again. Cover as many different topics as time permits.

SUGGESTED TOPICS

1. dormitory or cafeteria food
2. bureaucracies / red tape
3. politicians / politics
4. traffic / parking
5. roommates
6. single life / married life
7. final exams / writing papers
8. going to the dentist
9. music / art
10. people who . . .
11. the high cost of . . .
12. the quality of . . .

You will hear a short conversation. After the conversation you will be asked some questions. After you hear a question, read the four possible answers and decide which one is the best answer. Circle the letter of the best answer.

QUESTION 1

A. Dreaming.
B. Studying.
C. Losing touch.
D. Reading.

QUESTION 2

A. He's been reading a boring book.
B. He's been losing touch with reality.
C. He's been drifting off.
D. He's been up late studying.

QUESTION 3

A. She sat with Brian in the garden.
B. She gave Brian a pink rose.
C. She brought Brian some refreshments.
D. She said that Brian looked rested and refreshed.

QUESTION 4

A. Because he didn't like cookies.
B. Because he wasn't sure who brought the cookies.
C. Because he was losing touch with reality.
D. Because the girl in the dream brought the cookies.

QUESTION 5

A. To share refreshments with the girl in the dream.
B. To share refreshments with Kelly.
C. To share refreshments with Freud.
D. To share refreshments with a lovely lady.

Working

in this chapter

The Downlink discussion in this chapter is called "Japanese and American Business Management." In it we hear two management consultants talk about some of the differences between Japanese and American business practices.

Skill A—Learning Strategy: Listening for Causes and Effects

Skill B—Language Function: Persuading and Giving In

DID YOU KNOW?

W. Edwards Deming, who died in 1994 at the age of 93

An American business consultant, W. Edwards Deming, played an extremely important role in the economic growth of Japan after World War II. His principles, which American businesses were slow to adopt, are as follows:

* Quality is defined by the customer.
* Quality comes from improving the production process, not by sorting out and eliminating defective products.
* Long-lasting quality improvement comes from working "smarter" rather than from working longer or harder or faster.
* Change and improvement must involve *everyone* in the organization.
* On-going training of all employees is the key to continuous improvement of processes and products.
* Replacing warnings and slogans with education and self-improvement programs for employees leads to greater productivity.

Getting Started
Sharing Your Experience

activity

What images does the term *work* bring to mind? Do you imagine bored people watching the clock? Or do you picture an excited group of people working cooperatively on a project that will profit all of them? The following questions are designed to give you a chance to hear your classmates' attitudes toward work and to clarify your own. Answer the questions in small groups.

1. Have you or anyone you know ever had a job that you thought was wonderful? What made it so good?
2. Have you or anyone you know ever had a terrible job? What made it so bad?

94

3. What do you think the "perfect job" would be? Create a fantasy job in your mind and share it with your group. What is it? Where is it? What are the hours? How much do you earn? With whom do you work?

4. Under what conditions do you think it is important for workers to cooperate and rely on each other? Under what conditions is an interdependent work situation better than one in which each person does a separate task?

5. Each person has a slightly different definition of job satisfaction. Read the items in the following list and rank them from 1 (for most important) to 10 (for least important) according to your criteria for job satisfaction. Add some new criteria if you wish. Compare your answers with those of your classmates. What new criteria did students add? What category did most people rank first? Last?

_____ mental challenge

_____ good pay

_____ health and hospital care

_____ long paid vacations

_____ opportunities for advancement

_____ individual recognition

_____ flexible working hours

_____ cooperative decision-making involving both workers and management

_____ friendly co-workers

_____ other _____

6. How do you think most Americans would rank the categories in Question 5? To find out, interview three to five people who work in a variety of situations. Then combine your results with those of the rest of the students in your class and find out how each item ranked overall.

Vocabulary

exercise 1

Some of you may already know the meanings of several of the following words. However, the words you know may be different from the ones your classmates know. Pool your knowledge and match the definitions on the right with the words on the left.

1. _____ to assemble
2. _____ consensus
3. _____ consultant
4. _____ dispute
5. _____ imperative
6. _____ individualism
7. _____ innovation
8. _____ interdependence
9. _____ quota
10. _____ to slump

a. the belief that the interests of the individual should come before the interests of the group
b. to put together
c. disagreement
d. necessary, mandatory
e. newly introduced idea, method, or device
f. collective opinion
g. person who gives expert advice in a particular field
h. maximum number (especially of people allowed to enter a place)
i. mutual reliance or support
j. to fall or sink suddenly

 **exercise 2** Fill in the blanks with the appropriate forms of the words from the vocabulary list.

American companies often find themselves in economic trouble. Their stockholders become uneasy, and quick action is imperative. It is common practice for specialists or consultants to be called in to help find a solution to the company's problem. In fact, this has just occurred at a major corporation. A _____ has been hired by XYZ to find out why sales have _____ in recent months. In order to learn more about the company's problems the consultant has arranged a meeting with company managers. This consultant believes that it is _____ that he understand the existing philosophy before he introduces any _____ or makes any changes.

According to the company philosophy, each worker is expected to take the initiative on a new idea; workers are not led by the hand. However, once the individual devises the idea, a _____ , or collective agreement, is needed before the idea can be carried out. Once there is agreement about an idea, costs are carefully analyzed to judge whether the idea fits with the general plan. Then, if the project is determined to be worthy of company effort, a team is _____ . This cooperation, or _____ , among workers makes the company's managers proud. The company's cooperative policies have been working well up until the past few months; workers have been content, and few _____ have occurred among the workers. Because the working conditions are so favorable, the sales slump must be caused by other factors. At least that is the assumption the consultant will start with.

SKILL A
Listening for Causes and Effects

When businesspeople and researchers look at successful companies, they often ask themselves: What factors make the company successful? To answer this, they examine various factors to decide which ones seem to be related. Then they determine if the relationship is one of cause and effect rather than mere coincidence.

For example, one automobile dealership sells more Oldsmobiles than any other Oldsmobile dealer. The other dealers wonder why. They look at many factors: loca-tion of the showroom, business hours, prices of the cars, and the amount of commission paid to sales-people.

When the dealers discover that the showroom location of each dealership is similar, the business hours are similar, and the prices of the cars are similar, but that the commission paid to the salespeople is greater at the most successful dealerships, they suspect a cause-and-effect relationship.

Seeing cause-and-effect relationships can help us find solutions to problems in all aspects of life, from business to academic life, from social situations to solitary ones. It's not surprising, therefore, that instructors present causes and effects as they lecture. In explaining cause-and-effect relationships, lecturers generally use two approaches.

Method 1: The Straightforward Approach

Method 1 is a straightforward approach. The instructor explicitly lists the causes and the effects that are involved in a given situation. If a lecturer uses Method 1, you may find the best note-taking system is to put all of the causes on one side of the page and the effects on the other. For example, consider the following notes on the garbage collectors' strike in New York City from a lecture on labor unions and management.

Labor Unions and Management: NYC Garbage Collectors' Strike

CAUSES		EFFECTS	
1a.	low wages	1.	workers strike
1b.	long hours		
1c.	dirty working conditions		
2.	strike	2a.	city looks ugly
		2b.	areas smell bad
		2c.	tourist business is lost
		2d.	disease breaks out
3.	picketers throw rocks at "scab" workers	3a.	twenty-five persons are arrested
		3b.	bad feelings increase between management and employees

Method 2: Implied Connections

Method 2 is less obvious. Causes and effects are presented as a series of facts with implied connections rather than explicitly stated ones. It is the student's job to recognize the implications and make the connections. If a lecturer uses Method 2, it may be more difficult to make the connections between causes and effects. Becoming familiar with cause and effect expressions can help you find the connections. However, if you don't catch on right away, you can go back to your notes later and determine which bits of information are causes and which are effects. You can then show connections between causes and effects with numbers, arrows, or any other system you'd like to use. Causes, effects, and their relationships are frequently signaled by the following expressions.

Expressions Signaling Causes
- because
- for
- since

Expressions Signaling Effects
- as a consequence
- as a result
- consequently
- hence
- so
- therefore
- thus

Expressions Signaling a Cause/Effect Relationship
- as a consequence of . . .
- as a result of . . .
- due to the fact that
- due to this
- due to this fact
- for this reason
- if . . . then
- when . . . then

Listen In

exercise 1

Listen to the discussion all the way through, pausing when indicated to fill out the audience survey.

audience survey

How Would *You* Run a Doorbell Company?

For each item circle either a or b.

1. Supervision of production; wages
   a. Use a supervisor. Have a supervisor record the number of doorbells each worker assembles; pay each person according to how many he or she produces.
   b. Don't use a supervisor, but do have a team of workers assemble the doorbells. Record the number of doorbells assembled by a production

team of several workers without a supervisor and provide equal bonuses for each member of the team when more than a specific number are produced.

2. Raises and promotions
   a. Give frequent raises and promotions to workers who work fastest. Give frequent raises and promotions to workers who work hardest. Give fewer rewards to the others.
   b. Give few but regular promotions and raises to everyone on the basis of age and number of years with the company.

3. Slow work periods
   a. Hire many workers during periods when the demand for doorbells is heavy; fire unnecessary workers when business slows down. Don't reduce pay of those who remain employed.
   b. Give all employees life-long employment guarantees. Reduce pay and hours for both labor and management, but fire no one when business slows down.

4. Quality control
   a. Have an outside inspector responsible for quality control. The outside inspector is someone who is not involved in the production process.
   b. Make the work team responsible for quality control. Give extra money or time off for excellent records. Encourage team workmanship by giving awards and public praise.

5. Changes and improvements in the system
   a. Use outside consultants to get new ideas for improving electronic doorbells. Reward individual workers who make usable suggestions. To avoid disagreements among workers, let management decide on all changes.
   b. Use work teams to get new ideas. Have regular discussion meetings of the work team. Make changes slowly, only after workers and management agree.

exercise 2

Listen again. This time take notes by filling in the outline on pages 99–102 listing causes and effects. Some of the information is provided for you. When you are finished, share your answers with the class.

CAUSES

1a. Japanese products are easy to get.

1b. Japanese products are

_____.

1c. Japanese products are

_____.

EFFECTS

1. Americans buy many Japanese products.

Japanese workers doing their daily gymnastics

The assembly line at a Japanese automobile plant appears to be similar to assembly lines at American companies. So what's the secret?

CAUSES	EFFECTS
2. _____ _____ _____	**2.** American companies are losing business.
3. _____ _____ _____	**3a.** Some leaders in business, labor, and government want protective taxes and _____ _____.
	3b. Other leaders say the United States should _____ _____.
4. U.S. manager encourages individual initiative.	**4a.** Separate people moving up from _____ _____.
	4b. Keep clear division between _____. _____.
5. Japanese manager encourages group efforts.	**5a.** _____ _____.
	5b. _____ _____.

CAUSES	EFFECTS

6a. Japan is a small country.

6b. Japan is isolated.

6c. Japan is _____

_____

6. _____

_____

_____.

7a. The United States is

_____

_____.

7b. The United States has

_____

_____.

7c. The United States has

_____

_____.

7d. The people in the United

States like _____

_____.

7. Business practices that are competitive and free from roles that may not be as good for modern industrial production as Japanese practices.

8a. William Ouchi says the United States should strengthen the bond between workers and their companies by providing

_____

_____,

8b. _____

_____,

8c. _____

_____,

8d. and _____

_____.

8a. Then United States productivity will _____

_____.

8b. And in the long run, these reforms will lead to

_____

_____,

8c. _____,

8d. _____,

8e. and _____.

CAUSES	EFFECTS

9a. IBM, Intel, Procter and Gamble, and Hewlett-Packard have _____

_____,

9b. _____

_____,

9c. and _____

_____.

10. U.S. companies adopt the Japanese philosophy of business organization.

9a. Decrease in _____

_____

_____

9b. and _____

9c. Increase in _____

_____

9d. and _____.

10. U.S. citizens _____

_____

_____.

Speak Out

activity 1

The items in the following three pictures are available through mail-order catalogs in the United States. Each one represents a technological advance that has had a noticable effect on the work we do. Can you think of any other technological "toys" that have had an important effect on how work is accomplished? Share your ideas with the class.

EPSON ACTION PRINTER 3250.
Get a big-time printer at a home office price. Quiet operation, effortless paper handling, and 24-pin dot matrix printing make this vertical or horizontal position printer a steal! Prints at 200 characters per second (cps) at 12 character per inch (cpi). Has Epson ESC/P2 emulation with two scalable fonts. Includes 60 page paper cassette.
Epson Action Printer 3250 .... **$209**

CALL NOW!
800 677-5380

activity **2**

Look in some current magazines, mail-order catalogs, and business or scientific journals. Cut out or copy a few pictures and descriptions of high-tech items that are used in the workplace. Bring these pictures to class and use them to do this activity.

Step 1 In small groups read the descriptions aloud and talk about the benefits of using this device.

Step 2 Decide whether or not this device could have a major effect on our lives. If so, would it be a positive or a negative effect?

Step 3 Decide which of these devices might cause the most dramatic effect on society as a whole. Why do you think so?

activity **3**

In small groups, share your answers to the following questions.

1. If you could design something to make your work (at school, at home, or on the job) easier, what would it be? Describe it.
2. How would it affect society as a whole?

Share a few of your group's most beneficial or most imaginative designs with the whole class.

SKILL **B**

Persuading and Giving In

Persuading

The most effective way to persuade someone to adopt your point of view is to present a strong argument. A persuasive argument may be purely logical and reasonable, or it may have an emotional component. However, in both cases you will need to give reasons why this particular argument or point of view is a good one.

You might want to start off with a strong cause-and-effect statement. This can then be followed by additional support for your point of view. As you make additional points, you can take advantage of certain expressions to emphasize that you are introducing additional facts in support of your argument.

A Persuasive Statement of a Cause-and-Effect Relationship

More companies in this country should adopt Japanese-style management practices. A company in my town did this and doubled both productivity and sales.

Additional Points

Not only that, but the employees are much happier, so they are generally healthier and don't have to take so many days off because of illness. What's more, the food in the employee cafeteria is really terrific, so the employees don't have to eat in expensive restaurants or take time to make their own lunches.

Expressions Used to Strengthen Arguments

Along with that . . .	Moreover . . .
And another thing . . .	Not only that, but
And I might add . . .	Not to mention the fact that . . .
Besides . . .	Plus the fact that
Furthermore . . .	What's more . . .
In addition to that . . .	

Giving In

Now what do you do when someone has managed to persuade you to come over to his or her point of view? How can you let this person know that he or she has presented a convincing argument and you're ready to "give in"? In this case, the following expressions will be useful.

Expressions Used When Giving In

Okay plus one of the following expressions:

If you really insist.	Maybe you're right.
(I guess) You're right (after all).	Perhaps in this case (you're right).
(I guess) You've convinced me.	You may have a point there. (You've
I'll buy that.	got a point there.)
I'll go along with that.	You've sold me.
I'm sold.	

Freely Accepting an Offer

Persuading and giving in can take place in settings other than intellectual discussions. For instance, someone may try to persuade you to actually do something for them, not just to agree with their point of view. They may even add an incentive to give you a stronger reason to go along with their request. In the following example a person is making an offer to a fellow employee.

> Could you help me out? I'd really like to go to San Francisco for the weekend, but I've been scheduled to work on Saturday. Will you fill in for me on Saturday if I work for you on a day you want to take off to visit your mother?

When someone has been persuaded to accept an enticing offer, one of several expressions is commonly used.

Expressions Used When Freely Accepting an Offer

Come to think of it . . .	On second thought . . .
If you insist . . .	That's an offer I can't refuse!
I'm sold!	You've sold me!
In that case . . .	You've talked me into it.
Now that you mention it . . .	When you put it that way . . .

Reluctantly Accepting an Offer

Sometimes people will try to persuade you to do something for them by presenting the negative consequences that will result if you do not do what they are asking. In the following example a worker describes what will happen if a fellow employee doesn't go along with a request.

> Do you think you could work on Saturday? We all have to put in some extra time this week. If we don't, the project won't be finished on time and the company might lose the contract.

When someone reluctantly accepts an offer, one of the following expressions is commonly used.

Conversations

Step 1 Listen to the conversation, which involves persuading and giving in. Then answer the questions you hear following the conversation.

1. Where is the company executive from? _____

2. What does he want to do? _____

_____

3. Who is he trying to persuade? _____

_____

4. Who will work for the company? _____

5. Who will manage the company? _____

6. What does the company executive say about pollution problems? _____

_____

7. What is the mayor concerned about? _____

_____

8. What enticing offer does the executive make? _____

_____

9. Is the mayor persuaded? _____

Step 2 Listen to the conversation a second time and write down all the expressions you hear for persuading and giving in. When you are finished, compare your answers in small groups.

PERSUADING   GIVING IN

_____   _____

_____   _____

_____   _____

Listen In

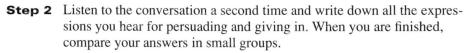

Listen again to the discussion comparing Japanese and American business customs. As you listen, make a list of the expressions the speaker uses to introduce persuasive reasons. Then compare your list with your classmates' lists.

_____

_____

_____

_____

_____

The three speakers share a particular point of view. In one or two sentences, state their point of view. Did the speakers persuade you to agree with them? Why or why not? Share your answers with your classmates.

_____

_____

_____

Speak Out

activity 1

As a class or in smaller groups, form teams to represent opposing sides in debates on work-related issues. Choose from the following topics or devise your own topics for debate. Use the techniques and expressions described in Skill B to persuade your opponents to accept your point of view and to give in each time they present a convincing argument.

DEBATE TOPICS

1. Trade unions are / are not the best means of solving problems in the workplace.
2. Industrial spying is / is not justifiable.
3. White-collar jobs should / should not have more prestige than blue-collar jobs.
4. Women should / should not be allowed to do *any* job they choose if they meet the basic qualifications.
5. Robots in the workplace are a help / hindrance to the welfare of workers.
6. Management should / should not involve itself in the personal life and well-being of its employees.
7. Selecting children at a young age and training them for certain professions is / is not best for these individuals and for society as a whole.
8. Companies should / should not be responsible for the costs of continuing education for employees.

A carpenter at work

activity 2

In pairs, choose one of the following scenarios to role-play. Use the expressions for persuading and giving in as your characters express their views to each other. If time permits, change partners one or more times and do the activity again. Then present one of the role-plays to the class.

SCENARIOS

1. You love to ski and try to go to the mountains on the weekends as often as possible. Therefore, you support the idea of a four-day, ten-hour work week. A fellow employee, on the other hand, likes to play tennis every afternoon after work and wants to continue working five days a week for eight hours a day. The matter will be voted on by the employees tomorrow. Try to persuade the other employee to vote for the four-day work week.
2. You are waiting for a plane at the airport. You start a conversation with a friendly Japanese woman sitting next to you. She works for an American camera company, perhaps Eastman Kodak, in Japan. You work for a Japanese camera company, perhaps Nikon, in Chicago. Each of you is happy with your work situation and tries to convince the other person that your company is the best.
3. You are interviewing for a management job with an American company. The interviewer is impressed with your background and seems to want to hire you. There have been problems in the relationship between workers and management at the company in recent years. When you start to suggest some changes based on Japanese management style, the interviewer says

he doesn't think they need to change so much. Try to convince him that the company really does need to make some changes.

Japanese-style loyalty to the company is catching on at General Electric.

activity 3

There is a cynical saying: "Everyone has a price." This means that if someone initially does not want to do something, his or her services can be "bought" if he or she is presented with the right enticement. For fun, try the following activity as a class or in small groups.

1. Ask another student in the class (or your instructor) to do something unusual or something that would very likely elicit a *no* response. For example:

   Will you pay for my trip to Paris next week?
   Will you marry my brother tomorrow?
   Will you do my homework for me?

2. When the student responds negatively (see p. 25 for ways to say *no*), do not take *no* for an answer. Try to persuade your classmate by presenting various positive or negative consequences. For example:

   Well, would you pay for my trip if I gave you a 1 percent interest in my company?

   If you don't marry my brother, he will be heartbroken.

3. If your classmate still refuses to do what you've asked, you must continue to present consequences that are more and more positive or negative until your classmate finally gives in. For example:

   If you don't pay for my trip, I will probably lose my entire business because I can't get to Paris to negotiate a big contract.

   If you marry my brother, you will be married to the richest, kindest, and most handsome man in my country. He will be devoted to you all your life.

4. Then change roles so that your partner is now making a request of you.

5. If you work in small groups, let other students in on the laughter by sharing a few of your group's conversations with the rest of the class.

You will hear a short segment from a radio interview. After the interview, you will be asked some questions. After you hear a question, read the four possible answers and decide which one is the best answer. Circle the letter of the best answer.

QUESTION 1

A. Small and large businesses that want to improve.
B. Small and large organizations that want to do a job well.
C. Small and large families that have a problem to solve.
D. All of the above.

QUESTION 2

A. Gracie.
B. June.
C. The children.
D. All of the above

QUESTION 3

A. The garbage was disturbed every day.
B. The garbage was disturbed when everyone was home.
C. The garbage was disturbed when they ate meat.
D. The garbage was disturbed almost every day.

QUESTION 4

A. Understand the reasons for the problem.
B. Plan and implement a solution to the problem.
C. Collect data on the current situation.
D. Make plans for further improvement.

QUESTION 5

A. They took Gracie out right away.
B. They stopped eating meat.
C. They gave Gracie a little of the garbage.
D. They gave Gracie some meat in her bowl.

QUESTION 6

A. Staying home with the dog.
B. Collecting data about the dog.
C. Taking out the garbage and rewarding the dog.
D. Cleaning up the mess in the kitchen.

CHAPTER eight

Breakthroughs

DID YOU KNOW?

- The word *physics* comes from the Greek word *physis,* which means *that which shows itself and becomes observable.* So physics is the study of the observable world and what makes it work. It is the science of matter and energy.

- In 1993, two major theories that seem contradictory, but are really just different sides of the same coin, emerged to explain how the world works.

  1. Chaos theory says that certain things, even seemingly small events, involve so many factors that they are inherently unpredictable. For example, a scientist might be able to predict the pattern of a clock pendulum, but cannot predict just how far apart two leaves will be after they go through a waterfall, or how the movement of butterfly wings in South America will affect the wind in Australia.

  2. Complexity theory examines systems that lie in the middle ground between the predictable and the chaotic. These systems are not entirely predictable, but they are not exactly unpredictable either. They seem to resist chaos through a process called critical self-organization. That is, when the system reaches a certain point, it breaks down and then builds itself up again to be similar to, but not exactly the same as the way it was before. Examples of these types of middle ground systems are sand dunes, the stock market, and even the biological systems of extinction and creation. Complexity theory explains how a species can suddenly become extinct or how a new one can appear. It seems that biological evolution takes place at the boundary between order and chaos.

Getting Started
Sharing Your Experience

As a class, or in smaller groups, discuss the following questions.

1. In what ways did you learn in school about the laws of physics? For example, did you learn about these laws through textbooks? Lectures? Class discussions? Laboratory experiments? Which way worked best for you?

2. In your everyday life, what have you learned about the physical laws of nature? Share what you have learned and how you learned it.

3. Have you ever known anyone who made a scientific breakthrough? Share with your classmates who this was and what they discovered.

4. Breakthroughs or discoveries can happen in all areas of life, not just in science. Share with your classmates a non-scientific breakthrough that you (or someone you know) has made in his or her life.

5. Briefly share your understanding of the following concepts:

energy	motion
gravity	space
light	time
matter	

6. Select the concept in Question 5 that you understand best. Do you think that your understanding of this concept is more correct than the understanding of a student five years ago? Fifteen years ago? Fifty years ago? Two hundred and fifty years ago? Twenty-five hundred years ago? Share why you feel this way.

7. Herman von Helmholtz (1821–1894), a German physiologist who contributed to the development of the principle of conservation of energy and the theory of electricity, said: "The originator of a new concept . . . finds, as a rule, that it is much more difficult to find out why other people do not understand him than it was to discover the new truths." In what ways do you think this statement is true or not true? Give specific examples if you can.

Vocabulary

Many English words have more than one meaning. Sometimes the meanings are quite similar, but often they are very different. The words in the following list are defined as they are used in the lecture. Look over these words and definitions. Then choose the sentences in the following exercise that use the words as they are defined in the vocabulary list.

contemporary	*person of approximately the same age as another person living at the same time*
cosmos	*the universe considered as an orderly system*
matter	*that which is material, physical; not mental or spiritual*
relative	*not absolute, dependent on something else*
divine	*sacred, holy, having the nature of a deity*

example: matter

    a. The brain is made up of both grey and white matter.

    b. It doesn't matter.

    c. It's only a matter of time.

1. Contemporary
    a. I love contemporary painting.
    b. Einstein was a contemporary of Niels Bohr.
    c. Have you read any contemporary books on the subject of energy?

COSMOGRAPHIE.

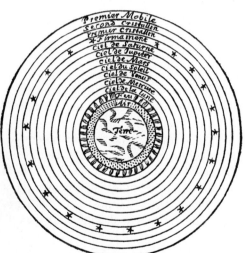

Ptolemaic planetary system

2. cosmos
    a. He likes to read *Cosmos* magazine.
    b. The cosmos she planted in the garden came up late this year.
    c. He often wondered about the nature of the cosmos.

3. relative
    a. My cousin Pete is my favorite relative.
    b. Time and space are relative to each other.
    c. He finished the exam with relative ease.

4. divine
    a. "You look divine tonight, my dear!" he exclaimed.
    b. Many cultures have places that they regard as divine.
    c. To divine water, you hold a Y-shaped stick and walk around until the end of the stick points suddenly toward the ground.

exercise 2

The following words used in the presentation do not have multiple meanings. Look over these words and their definitions. Then pick out the sentences in the exercise that use the words correctly.

manifestation	*form, aspect*
metaphysical	*having to do with the branch of philosophy that deals with the nature of truth and knowledge in the universe*
such and such	*a condition, person, place, thing, or time not specifically mentioned*
wild-goose chase	*unfruitful attempt*

1. manifestation
   a. She met a manifestation at the party.
   b. One manifestation of electrical energy is lightning.
   c. The manifestation he wrote was not acceptable to his contemporaries.

2. metaphysical
   a. He had a metaphysical at the doctor's office.
   b. She metaphysicals on her way back to work.
   c. They were both interested in metaphysical ideas.

3. such and such
   a. The instructor gave this example to illustrate the theory: If you were going at such and such a speed for such and such an amount of time through space, the amount of time that seemed to pass on earth might be quite different.
   b. He was such and such a difficult instructor that the student wondered if she should wait until someone else taught the physics course.
   c. They were not interested in metaphysical ideas such and such as these.

4. wild-goose chase
   a. During the mating season for geese, we often see one wild-goose chase another goose.
   b. The quest for a unified field theory encompassing all the laws of nature may turn out to be a wild-goose chase.
   c. It was their first wild-goose chase, and they were proud of their success.

SKILL A

What to Do When You Know the Words But Still Don't Understand

Have you shopped for a computer, a VCR or some other high-tech machine lately? If so, you may have found it difficult to follow exactly what the salesperson was saying. Maybe you thought you should understand because you knew all of the words the salesperson used, but somehow, in the end, you just didn't get it.

If this has happened to you, don't worry. This happens to everyone, even native speakers of a language. Anyone who is trying to understand a complex new subject or concept may have a problem with understanding even when every word is familiar. For example, when you listen to the presentation in this chapter, "Discovering the Laws of Nature," you may find that some of the concepts are difficult to comprehend, even though the words are not.

Additionally, the length of the sentences and the speaker's rhythm and intonation can sometimes cause confusion. For example, the speaker in the presentation may use exceptionally long sentences that would be a challenge for *anyone,* or the speaker may pause and hesitate and change the rhythm in a way that confuses you.

What to Do When You Just Don't Understand

1. Don't panic. Remember that you're not alone. Your classmates are probably having difficulty, too.
2. Continue to take notes even though they may not be perfect. Any nouns and verbs you manage to write down will be useful later when you start asking questions to determine exactly what you missed.
3. Don't give up. Continue to concentrate on the topic. Try not to let your mind wander. Thinking about something you *do* understand about the topic usually helps.
4. When you feel lost, listen for key nouns and verbs in the next few sentences. These words carry most of the meaning.
5. Also jot down any negative terms such as *never* and *not*. Without these words, your notes may appear to say the opposite of what the speaker intended.
6. Try repeating to yourself the sentence or sentences you can't seem to understand. If this does not help, try punctuating the sentence differently or changing the rhythm, stress, or intonation patterns as you repeat it to yourself. Sometimes this is all it takes to jump from the muddle of incomprehension to the "Aha!" of understanding.
7. Familiarize yourself with the speaker's topic ahead of time. If this is an academic class, complete the assigned readings before the lecture. If there are no assigned readings or if the readings are very difficult, try to find some general information on the topic from an encyclopedia, a magazine, or a textbook from a lower-level course.

Listen In

exercise 1

Listen to the lecture once through. Then listen again. As you listen the second time:

- Take notes, keeping in mind the suggestions of things to do when you're just not getting it.
- Afterwards, discuss with your classmates which of the suggestions worked best for you.
- Also look at the areas in your notes that may be incomplete. Use whatever you did manage to write down to help you form questions to ask a classmate or your instructor in order to complete your notes.

Johann Kepler

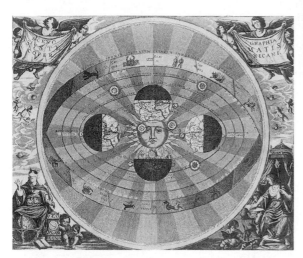

Copernican planetary system

Sir Isaac
Newton

Listen to the lecture again. Fill in any gaps in your notes as necessary. Then look over your notes and paraphrase and/or summarize each of the major ideas to make sure that you really understand everything you wrote down. Compare your oral summaries with your classmates.

Galileo

Speak Out

Earlier in this chapter, the example of the computer salesperson was given to represent ordinary situations in which you may understand the individual words someone uses, but you do not get the whole idea. In small groups, discuss the following:

1. What situations have you experienced where you understood each word but missed the main point of what someone was saying? What did you do? What was the result? Did you devise a strategy you could use in the future (for example, asking for repetition, asking the speaker to give you an example or analogy, making eye contact with the speaker and raising your eyebrows or shrugging your shoulders)?

2. What techniques do instructors use to help you understand? Do they, for example, use study guides, charts, diagrams, or outlines?

3. What techniques do you use during conversations to present concepts that may be difficult to understand? For example, do you gesture with your hands? Do you draw diagrams?

As a class or in small groups, take turns describing what happens to energy and matter in the following everyday situations. Most of the vocabulary should be familiar, but the concepts may be a bit tricky. Use a basic physics book as a reference, if you wish, but don't make your explanations too technical.

1. blowing out a candle
2. riding a bicycle
3. grinding food in the garbage disposal
4. reflecting sunlight with a mirror onto a piece of paper
5. starting a car engine
6. planting a seed in a sunny garden
7. baking a cake
8. slipping on ice
9. rowing a boat
10. shooting an arrow
11. the turning of a windmill
12. the rising tides during a full moon

SKILL **B**

Giving and Receiving Compliments

Giving Compliments

Flattery

Flattery is the kind of compliment that sounds insincere. There is an old saying, "Flattery will get you everywhere." It means that some people like receiving compliments so much that if you flatter them a lot, they will do just about anything for you. Sometimes people say, "Flattery will get you nowhere with me." They mean that whatever it is you want, you won't talk them into it by giving them lots of compliments.

Sincere Compliments

People are often suspicious of flattery. Therefore, giving genuine compliments can be tricky. The keys to offering compliments appropriately are timing, number, and phrasing.

Timing

The person receiving the compliment will be more likely to feel it is sincere if it's deserved. Compliments are generally deserved when:

* a person has accomplished something special.
* a person is discouraged and you are reminding them of their good efforts and steady progress.

Number

How many compliments can you give at one time without overdoing it?

One's okay, and two are fine;
But stop at three, and draw the line.

Exception: If you give more than one compliment at a time to a superior at work or someone else in a position of authority, it may look like you are flattering them to gain favor or approval.

Phrasing

Take care to use adjectives and analogies that the person is pleased to identify with. For example:

Hank, you're really a *special* person. You have *a heart as big as the ocean.* Even though you're trying hard to complete your research, you still made time to raise money for the Homeless Children's Fund.

Expressions Used to Introduce Compliments

I don't mind saying . . .
I don't mind telling you . . .
I'd like to compliment you on . . .
If you ask me . . .

I've been meaning to tell you . . .
Just between you and me . . .

Receiving Compliments
Undeserved Compliments

Sometimes you may receive a compliment that you feel is undeserved. In this case, you may wish to be humble and say that the compliment is not true. However, do not deny or protest the compliment more than once or twice before you give in and accept the compliment graciously. Otherwise:

- It might seem like you think the compliment is worthless.
- People might think you are "protesting too much" which could mean that you are really looking for even more compliments.

Inappropriate Compliments

Sometimes you may receive a compliment that you feel is inappropriate.

- If the compliment is not offensive you may either say a simple "thank you" or you may ignore it.
- If the compliment is offensive, you should consider telling the person so and/or reporting the incident to a friend or superior.

Expressions Used to Receive Compliments

A simple "thank you" is always an appropriate and gracious response to a compliment. If you feel this is not enough, add one of the following expressions:

Coming from you, that's a real compliment.
Coming from you, that means a lot.
Do you really think so? How nice (sweet, kind) of you to say that.
I appreciate you saying that.
I'm really glad (pleased) you think so.
I'm really glad (pleased) you feel that way.
I'm very flattered.
That (Your opinion) means a lot to me.
That's nice to hear.
That's very kind (nice, sweet) of you.
Thanks, I needed that!
You've made my day!
What a nice (lovely, sweet) thing to say!

To show modesty you can say:

Oh, I can't take all the credit for that.

or

_____ deserves as much credit as I do.

Conversations

You will hear four conversations; the first two involve an instructor and some students, and the last two include several senior citizens. These conversations contain examples of both appropriate and inappropriate ways of giving compliments. After listening to each conversation, answer the questions you hear in the spaces provided. When you are finished, compare your answers in small groups.

conversation 1 Ron and Mr. McGovern are in the hall after class.

1. Ron's compliments to Mr. McGovern are inappropriate. What's wrong with Ron's timing? _____

_____

2. What's wrong with the number of compliments? _____

_____

3. What's wrong with the phrasing? _____

_____

conversation 2 Sandra and Mr. McGovern are in the professor's office during office hours.

Are Sandra's compliments to Mr. McGovern appropriate? _____
Why or why not? _____

_____

conversation 3 Helen, Larry, and Martin are chatting at a retirement home.

1. How does Larry first compliment Helen? _____

_____

2. What is Helen's response? _____

_____

3. Why do you think she says this? _____

_____

4. How does Martin compliment Helen? _____

_____

5. How does Helen respond this time? _____

_____

6. What do Helen and Larry tell Martin about his dancing? _____

_____

7. Who looked beautiful on the dance floor? _____

_____

8. How does Martin feel about the compliments from Helen? _____

_____

conversation 4   Later in the day at the retirement home Helen, Martin, and Larry continue chatting.

1. What's wrong with Martin? _____

_____

2. Is the compliment Martin gives Helen appropriate? _____

_____

3. How does Helen accept this compliment? _____

_____

4. How does Larry try to cheer Martin up? _____

_____

5. What does Helen say to encourage Martin? _____

_____

6. Does it work? _____

7. How does Martin respond? _____

_____

8. What does he mean by this? _____

_____

Listen In

exercise 1

Choose a partner for this activity.

1. Listen to the presentation again. This time stop the tape each time you hear the speaker mention a "breakthrough" or other accomplishment.

2. Pretend that your partner is the person the speaker is talking about. Imagine that you now have the opportunity to compliment this person on his or her achievements. Take this opportunity to really flatter him or her.

3. Let your partner respond to your compliments. Then continue listening to the tape.

4. When you stop the tape next time, change roles with your partner. This time *you* will pretend to be the person who made the "breakthrough" and your partner will compliment *you*.

5. Continue taking turns in this way as you listen to the rest of the tape.

exercise 2 Listen for compliments.

1. Listen to a TV soap opera or comedy.

2. Each time you hear a compliment, jot it down. Also note the context, the situation, and the response.

3. Listen until you hear at least three compliments.

4. Bring your notes to class. Describe to your classmates the situations, compliments, and responses you noted.

Did you or your classmates hear any inappropriate compliments? If so, list them.

_____

_____

_____

_____

What made them inappropriate? _____

_____

_____

Speak Out

activity 1 Have you ever received an inappropriate compliment? If so, share this with your classmates as a class or in small groups.

- What was the situation?
- What was the compliment?
- How did you respond?
- If you could do it all over again, would you respond differently?

activity 2 Be part of a "cutting edge" team on the verge of a real "breakthrough."

1. In groups of three to five, imagine that you are a team of scientists living in the year 2200. You have recently made some important discoveries about the relationship of energy and matter.

2. It is now your team's task to put these theories to practical use. You must design a device that converts energy into matter. As you brainstorm your ideas, make whatever drawing or diagrams you need to illustrate your ideas to your teammates.

3. As you work together, there should be opportunities to compliment your teammates on their ideas and to receive a few compliments yourself.

4. When your team has finished the task, make a drawing or diagram of the device.

5. Plan how you will make a group presentation to describe this device.

activity 3

Present your "breakthrough" invention from Activity 2 to the world!

1. Imagine that your research team is at an international conference. As a group, present your device to the other "scientists" (your classmates) assembled in the main conference hall.

2. Use the diagram your team developed to help explain the principles of the device.

3. After each group has presented its work, be sure to compliment them on their presentation.

activity 4

Try this activity for fun! Take turns "buttering each other up"—that is, giving an excessive number of compliments because you want something very much and don't want to be refused. You may want to role-play one or more of the following small-group situations, or you may choose just to be yourselves.

SUGGESTED SITUATIONS

1. a Hollywood party with producers, directors, actors, and actresses
2. a company Christmas party
3. a reception for a famous visiting physicist
4. a reception at the White House
5. a dinner party with your future in-laws

activity 5

Research the language around you.

1. For the next day or two, pay particular attention to any compliments that you give, receive, or overhear.

2. Note the circumstances in which these compliments were given:

   • What was the relationship of the people involved?
   • What were their attitudes towards each other?
   • What expressions did they use to give or receive compliments?

3. Answer the following questions. Then share the results of your research with your classmates.

   • Were any expressions used that were new to you? _____

- If so, what were they? _____

  _____

  _____

  _____

- How many compliments did you give in one day? _____

- How many compliments did you receive? _____

- Describe any situations in which you thought the compliments were

  inappropriate. _____

  _____

- Describe any situations in which you thought someone refused a

  compliment and "protested too much." _____

  _____

- Do you think that consciously observing the behavior of giving and
  receiving compliments caused you to give more compliments than
  usual, fewer compliments than usual, or had no effect on the number of
  compliments you usually give? _____

  _____

focus on testing

You will hear a short presentation. After the presentation, you will be
asked some questions. After you hear a question, read the four possible
answers and decide which one is the best answer. Circle the letter of the
best answer.

QUESTION 1

A. In the 1930s.
B. In the 1950s.
C. March 14, 1879.
D. April 18, 1933.

QUESTION 2

A. Because Einstein had reached the age of fifteen.
B. Because Einstein had not completed secondary school.
C. Because he was failing his exams.
D. Because the family business failed.

QUESTION 3

A. Electrical engineer.
B. Patent office clerk.
C. Secondary school teacher.
D. Mathematician.

QUESTION 4

A. Wrote scientific papers.
B. Read a lot of books on physics.
C. Talked to other physicists.
D. Taught mathematics and physics.

QUESTION 5

A. The Kaiser-Wilhelm Gesellschaft in Berlin.
B. The German University of Prague.
C. The University of Zurich.
D. The Swiss Federal Institute of Technology.

QUESTION 6

A. In the United States.
B. In Germany.
C. In Switzerland.
D. In Italy.

CHAPTER nine

Art and Entertainment

in this chapter

The presentation in this chapter is called "The Rise of Rock 'n' Roll." The speaker is on a radio program discussing the history of rock 'n' roll and provides samples of some famous rock songs.

Skill A—Learning Strategy: Distinguishing Between Fact or Opinion

Skill B—Language Function: Expressing Doubt or Disbelief

Aretha Franklin

- Aretha Franklin sang the United States' national anthem, *The Star Spangled Banner*, with "a touch of soul" at President Clinton's 1994 inauguration.
- The Rolling Stones started playing together in 1965. In 1994, when they were all over 50 years old, they made $58 million on their *Voodoo Lounge* concert tour.
- The biggest selling album of all time is the rock 'n' roll classic, *Thriller,* by Michael Jackson. This record sold over 40,000,000 copies by May 1990 and continues to sell even today.
- The most successful group in the history of rock 'n' roll was the Beatles (shown on the preceding page). From the time they started playing in the early 1960s until May 1985, they sold over 1 billion records.

Michael Jackson

Getting Started
Sharing Your Experience

activity

As a class or in smaller groups, discuss the following questions.

1. What kinds of music are most popular in your native country?
2. What kinds of music are most popular among your friends?
3. What are your favorite types of music and who are your favorite musical performers?
4. How often do you listen to music at home? Do you listen to music while you study? Cook? Clean? Exercise? Entertain?
5. Have you attended a live concert? If so, describe who you heard and where you went.
6. Do you like rock 'n' roll? Why or why not?
7. Do you play any musical instruments? If so, describe what type of music you like to play and why. If not, discuss what you would like to learn to play and why.

Vocabulary

The following list of words has been taken from the presentation in this chapter. Fill in the crossword puzzle with the correct forms of the words on the list. See the appendix for the answers.

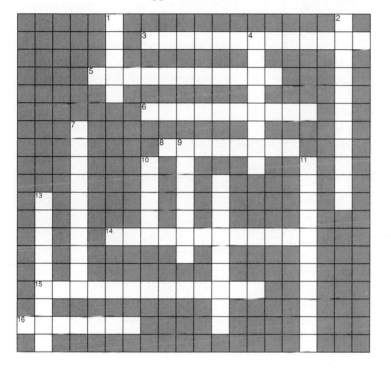

ROCK 'N' ROLL CROSSWORD PUZZLE

accompaniment
acoustic
to backtrack
blues
to boo
cellist
censorship
to enhance
harmonies
hillbilly
indifferent
musicologist
nostalgically
outrageous
to reaffirm
segregation

ACROSS CLUES

3. music that is played while the principal singer sings
5. the separation of one group from another based on race, class, or ethnic origin
6. the removal of offensive material from communications
8. estate with confidence
14. one who studies music from a historical and scientific standpoint
15. in a manner that shows longing for something out of the past
16. one who plays the cello, the next-to-largest member of the violin family

DOWN CLUES

1. shouted disapproval or contempt
2. having no preference; not interested in anything
4. of or relating to sound; natural sound, not electronic
7. extremely unusual; fantastic
9. make more valuable, beautiful, desirable; upgrade
10. a style of music characterized by sadness
11. moved backwards; backed up
12. a person from a mountainous backwoods area
13. pleasant or congruent arrangements of parts, such as musical chords

SKILL A

Distinguishing Between Fact and Opinion

Suppose a friend of yours made almost $4,500 in two years by buying old records and reselling them. You like music, and you decide to try to make some money, too. You go to a record trade show and find an old recording of "She Loves You" by the Beatles. It is an unusual recording because it was made without drummer Ringo Starr. The salesperson offers to sell it for $1,690 and tells you that the recording will triple in value in the next year, and that if you are smart, you will buy it now and resell it when the value goes up. Is this a fact or only the salesperson's opinion? How do you know?

Some statements about the future are facts. For example:

The sun will rise in the East tomorrow.

Some statements about the future are merely opinions. For example:

This record will triple in value next year.

In everyday life and in academic life, it is important to distinguish fact from opinion. Facts, however, can be "slippery." A rare recording of "She Loves You" may be of great value today, but if someone finds a warehouse with 200,000 copies of this "rare" recording tomorrow, it won't be so valuable.

Sometimes people say things very strongly to make them sound like facts. If, for example, someone said with great assurance, "Elvis Presley was the first rock 'n' roll singer," that would sound like a fact. But it's not a fact. This statement is not true. If you don't know the "fact" yourself, it would be wise to check it for accuracy.

An opinion is someone's feeling, belief, or judgment about someone or something. It is not objective. Personal feelings, biases and attitudes influence opinions. In the presentation in this chapter, many personal opinions that may sound like facts are given.

How to Distinguish Opinions from Facts

1. Look/listen for words and phrases that may signal an opinion:

I believe	often
I feel	personally
In my opinion,	personally speaking
I think	probably
It seems to me that	sometimes
occasionally	usually

Listen In

Step 1 Listen to the presentation at least twice all the way through and ask about anything that you don't understand.

Step 2 Look over the following statements and listen to the presentation once more. This time the teacher will stop the tape from time to time so that you can answer the questions that follow. For each item, mark whether the statement is a fact or an opinion and then tell why. If you decide a statement is an opinion, indicate whether you agree or disagree with this opinion and explain why. Two examples have been provided.

Step 3 When you have finished, discuss your answers with your classmates.

example A: Music is a universal phenomenon.

<u> X </u> Fact _____ Opinion Why? <u>Because</u>
<u>musicologists are probably reliable sources.</u>
_____

_____

_____ Agree _____ Disagree Why? _____

_____

_____

Elvis Presley in concert, Tampa, Florida, 1956

Music has the most meaning for the people from the culture in which it was created.

____ Fact __X__ Opinion   Why? _Because speaker_ _said "I think" and "it seems to me."_

__X__ Agree ____ Disagree   Why? _Personal_ _experience; I don't fully understand music from other_ _countries._

1. The name *rock 'n' roll* comes from Alan Freed.

____ Fact ____ Opinion   Why? _____

_____

____ Agree ____ Disagree   Why? _____

_____

2. The actual beginning of rock 'n' roll music was on April 12, 1954, in New York City when Bill Haley and the Comets recorded "Rock Around the Clock."

____ Fact ____ Opinion   Why? _____

_____

____ Agree ____ Disagree   Why? _____

_____

_____

Bill Haley and the Comets

3. Rockabilly is a mixture of the blues harmonies of black music and the hillbilly sounds of white music.

____ Fact ____ Opinion   Why? _____

_____

____ Agree ____ Disagree   Why? _____

_____

4. The '50s generation was eager to grow up.

_____ Fact _____ Opinion Why? _____

_____

_____ Agree _____ Disagree Why? _____

_____

5. Teenagers in every society have rebelled against or resisted their parents in some way.

_____ Fact _____ Opinion Why? _____

_____

_____ Agree _____ Disagree Why? _____

_____

6. In the '60s there was a mood of confusion and instability.

_____ Fact _____ Opinion Why? _____

_____

_____ Agree _____ Disagree Why? _____

_____

7. Bob Dylan was more a poet than a songwriter.

_____ Fact _____ Opinion Why? _____

_____

_____ Agree _____ Disagree Why? _____

_____

The young Bob Dylan

8. Protest rock condemned the evils of our society.

_____ Fact _____ Opinion Why? _____

_____

_____

_____ Agree _____ Disagree Why? _____

_____

_____

9. The Beatles appeared respectable to adults.

_____ Fact _____ Opinion Why? _____

_____

_____

_____ Agree _____ Disagree Why? _____

_____

_____

10. The Beatles had a good sense of humor.

_____ Fact _____ Opinion Why? _____

_____

_____

_____ Agree _____ Disagree Why? _____

_____

_____

Mick Jagger and the Rolling Stones

11. The Rolling Stones were outrageous compared to the Beatles.

_____ Fact _____ Opinion Why?

_____

_____ Agree _____ Disagree Why?

_____

_____

_____

Soul singer Aretha Franklin

12. Soul music is an expression of black pride.

_____ Fact _____ Opinion   Why? _____

_____

_____

_____ Agree _____ Disagree   Why? _____

_____

_____

Speak Out

activity For this activity, you will be a critic of the arts. Follow the six steps.

Step 1 Choose one of the arts that interests you, such as painting, architecture, dance, music, sculpture, or theater.

Step 2 Find a visual example of the type of art you've chosen. You might find a postcard with a reproduction of a painting, a newspaper ad for a movie, play, dance performance, or opera, or a picture from a book on architecture.

Step 3 Gather as much factual information as you can from the visual example you selected. For example, who painted the picture, wrote the script, or did the choreography? Where is the event taking place? What time? What materials did the artist use?

Step 4 Now critique this art work. Evaluate it and decide whether you like it or not, whether you will give it a favorable review or an unfavorable one.

Step 5 Prepare and present a two-minute review of the work to your classmates. Try to include as many facts and opinions about the work as you can. Your classmates' job is to remember at least three facts and three opinions from your presentation.

Step 6 After each presentation, discuss the various facts and opinions. Which do you and your classmates usually find most interesting, facts or opinions? Why?

SKILL B

Expressing Doubt or Disbelief

People sometimes present statements as facts when actually these so-called "facts" have either not been proven or are only opinions. When people do this, you may want to express doubt or disbelief. If you express doubt or disbelief too formally, you will never be considered rude. However, if you speak too informally, you take the chance of offending some people.

Expressions for Expressing Doubt or Disbelief

FORMAL

Are you sure that's (it's) correct?   Could he (she, they) really think
Are you sure that's (it's) okay?   (believe) that?
Are you sure that's (it's) right?   Do you really believe that?
Could he (she) really do that?   I find that hard to believe.

INFORMAL

Are you serious?   Oh, sure!
Don't give me that!   Really?
Get out of here!   Seriously?
I doubt it (that).   That can't be true!
I'll believe it (that) when I see it.   You're kidding!
No way!   You've got to be kidding!
Oh, come on!

Note: You may wonder why "I don't believe it!" is not on this list. This is because when you use the expression "I don't believe it!" in this context, usually placing strong emphasis on the word *believe,* it shows surprise without disbelief. It really means "I believe you, but I'm very surprised."

Conversations

You will hear four conversations in which people's responses range from very formal to very informal. After listening to each one, answer the questions you hear in the spaces provided. When you are finished, compare your answers in small groups.

conversation 1   Carl discusses a project with Professor Johnson.

1. What expression does Carl use to express doubt? _____

   _____

2. Why do you think he uses that expression? _____

   _____

3. Professor Johnson expresses disbelief twice in this conversation. Is he polite to Carl? _____

4. The first time he expresses disbelief through intonation alone. What words does he use? _____

5. What expression does he use the second time? _____

   _____

conversation 2   Mr. Jones chats with Mr. Smith about his son's band.

1. Is this conversation formal or informal? _____

2. When the second speaker says "Get outta here," does he sound amused or angry? _____

3. How does the second speaker sound when he says, "Oh, sure!"?

   _____

4. When the second speaker says "Yeah, right—and I'm Mick Jagger," does he sound rude? _____

5. Why do you think the second speaker expresses disbelief this way? _____

   _____

conversation 3   Jenny and Al talk about dancing.

1. Are Jenny's expressions of disbelief formal or informal? _____

2. Is she polite or rude? _____

3. What are some expressions Jenny uses? _____

   _____

conversation 4   Rachel attends Professor Starr's music appreciation class.

    1. Are Rachel's expressions of disbelief formal or informal? _____

    2. Is she polite or rude? _____

    3. Does the professor seem impatient with Rachel? _____

    4. What are some expressions Rachel uses? _____

    _____

Listen In

exercise

Listen to the presentation again. When you did the exercises in Skill A, you answered questions about some of the facts and opinions you heard.

Step 1   This time listen for additional statements that you think are not proven facts. When you hear one, ask the teacher to stop the tape and replay the statement.

Step 2   Copy the statement onto the lines below.

Step 3   After each statement, add a response that expresses your doubt or disbelief about it.

Step 4   Share your responses with your classmates.

    1. Statement: _____

       _____

       Response: _____

       _____

    2. Statement: _____

       _____

       Response: _____

       _____

3. Statement: _____

_____

Response: _____

_____

4. Statement: _____

_____

Response: _____

_____

5. Statement: _____

_____

Response: _____

_____

6. Statement: _____

_____

Response: _____

_____

Speak Out

This is a game that you win by fooling your friends. Follow the four steps.

Step 1   Divide into two teams and share interesting or unusual facts about your life that have to do with the arts. These events do not have to involve you directly, but you must be connected to them in some way. For example:

- One of my drawings is on display in the city hall in my hometown.
- My father-in-law is a famous actor.
- I once got a standing ovation for my dancing at a folk-dance festival.
- When I was seventeen, I won third prize in a whistling contest.
- My brother is a well-known graffiti artist.

Step 2   Make up some events that did not actually happen and share these with your teammates, too.

Step 3   With your team, choose some of the real and imaginary events to tell the other team about. Each person can present facts about himself or herself, or about other team members.

Step 4 Take turns presenting these "facts" to the other team. They can choose to believe what you say and respond "Okay, I believe that," or they can respond with expressions of doubt or disbelief. Each time a team is correct in distinguishing fact from opinion, they get a point.

activity 2 Look over the following unfinished conversations.

Step 1 Choose a partner and complete one or more of them together using expressions of doubt or disbelief. A sample is provided for Conversation 1.

Step 2 If you wish, you can create some original conversations using the sample as a model.

Step 3 Choose one conversation (either one from the book or an original one) and present it to the rest of the class.

CONVERSATION 1

A: I went to a terrific concert last night.
B: Oh—which one?
A: It was a John Cage concert, and a woman played the cello underwater.

B: No way!

A: Not only that, but the piano player was underwater, too.

B: Get out of here!

A: Really—John Cage concerts are always far out!

B: Yeah, I know, but I'll believe that when I see it!

CONVERSATION 2

A: Do you remember the contemporary artist, Christo, who wrapped the coast of Australia in canvas and an entire island in pink plastic?
B: Yeah, why?
A: Because his latest project is wrapping the Eiffel Tower in blue silk.

B: _____
_____
_____

A: _____
_____
_____

B: _____
_____
_____

Christo, the artist, wrapped two islands in pink plastic.

Etc.

CONVERSATION 3

A: What a disaster at the theater tonight!

B: Why? What happened?

A: We were trying to rehearse, and first the lights went out, then the scenery fell over, then the leading man was taken to the hospital, and, as if that weren't enough, we put out a fire in a trash can just in time! I think someone is trying to keep the play from opening.

B: _____

A: _____

B: _____

Etc.

CONVERSATION 4

A: Did you hear what your friend David did?

B: No, what?

A: He had a waiter come into the room where he and 300 others were taking their law exams and serve him a three-course lunch.

B: _____

A: _____

B: _____

Etc.

focus on testing

You will hear a short review of a music festival. After the review, you will be asked some questions. After you hear a question, read the four possible answers and decide which one is the best answer. Circle the letter of the best answer.

QUESTION 1

A. It was a large "happening."
B. It was an important sociological event.
C. It was an important political event.
D. All of the above.

QUESTION 2

A. Aquarian Exposition.
B. Woodstock.
C. Music and Art Fair.
D. The Happening.

A. As many as one million.
B. Between 16 and 30.
C. More than 400,000.
D. Thousands.

QUESTION 4

A. Between 16 and 30.
B. Between 30 and 60.
C. Between 13 and 60.
D. Between 16 and 40.

QUESTION 5

A. Because they happened to get stuck in a traffic jam in Bethel.
B. Because they wanted to go on a pilgrimage to Bethel.
C. Because they wanted to reject traditional values and goals.
D. Because they wanted to see the cast of top rock stars.

QUESTION 6

A. An inadequate sound system.
B. An inadequate sanitation system.
C. An inadequate amount of food.
D. An inadequate amount of dry ground.

CHAPTER ten

Ethical Questions

The discussion in this chapter is called "Organ Transplants." This conversation takes place while Richard and his sister, Susan, are spending a few days at home during a college vacation. They talk about ethical issues involved in human organ donation.

Skill A—Learning Strategy: Cohesion and Reference

Skill B—Language Function: Taking the Floor and Keeping the Floor

DID YOU KNOW?

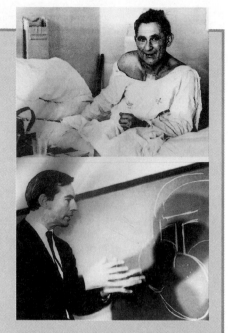

- The first heart transplant took place in Cape Town, South Africa in 1967 and was performed by Christiaan Barnard. The patient, Louis Washkansky, lived for only 18 days after the surgery.
- The longest surviving heart transplant recipient is William van Buuren. He received a heart at the Stanford Medical Center on January 3, 1970. He lived for 21 years, 10 months, and 24 days (after the surgery). He died at the age of 62.
- The longest surviving kidney transplant patient, Johanna Leanora Tempel, received a kidney from her twin sister at the age of 12 in 1960. Both have children of their own now.
- About 78% of Americans say that they are "very likely" to agree to donate the organs of a loved one. However, only 20% of Americans say that they are "likely" to become organ donors themselves

Louis Washkansky a few days after receiving the first transplanted human heart (*top*). Dr. Christiaan Barnard, the surgeon who performed the heart transplant operation, explaining how it was done (*bottom*).

Getting Started
Sharing Your Experience

activity

As a class, or in smaller groups, discuss the following questions.

1. The choices of several famous men and women are described below. In similar circumstances, would you have made the same choices?
   a. Buddha left his family and gave up all his worldly possessions; he vowed to sit in meditation until he achieved enlightenment for the sake of all human beings.
   b. Socrates chose to accept his unjust punishment of drinking poison rather than escape from prison and live in hiding.

Socrates

Joan of Arc

Harry S. Truman

Buddha

c. Harry Truman chose to drop the atomic bomb and face worldwide criticism because he thought that even more people would die if World War II continued.

d. Joan of Arc chose to be burned to death rather than deny her belief that her actions were directly guided by God.

2. Choose someone you know who had to face a difficult ethical choice and describe it to the class. It may be a famous person from your native country, a friend, an acquaintance, or someone you have heard about.

3. What principles do you live by? How did you develop them? Do you ever go against any of them?

Examples of principles:

a. Do unto others as you would have them do unto you.

b. Never lie.

c. Honor your father and mother.

d. Never kill.

e. Never steal.

4. What would you sacrifice to maintain your principles?

5. Medical resources such as doctors, nurses, hospital beds, expensive drugs, and highly advanced medical machines are scarce. In your opinion, should these resources be given to the most needy or to those who can afford them? If too many people need one item, should the person who will receive that item be chosen by lottery, by judges, or by some other method?

6. Do you think people should be allowed to sell their own organs? Why or why not?

FOR SALE: 1 kidney to highest bidder. Call 555-9981. Ask for Harry Highliver.

Out of work family man wants to sell 1 cornea for $50, 000 minimum. Write to Box 791 and make offer.

Potential suicide victim wants to leave large inheritance to children. Selling heart, liver and corneas for $2 million. Call 555-1623 and leave name and phone number on message machine.

Vocabulary

One way to determine the meaning of a word you don't know is to break it down into parts. You can look at prefixes, roots, and suffixes. For example, the word *transportable* can be broken down into these parts:

trans	*a root which means "across"*
port	*a root which means "carry"*
able	*a suffix which means "can be done."*

Therefore you can figure out that the word *transportable* describes something that can be carried from one place to another.

exercise

The following exercise gives you practice figuring out the meanings of words by looking at their prefixes, roots, and suffixes. With a partner:

Step 1 Fill in the meanings of each prefix, suffix, and root. (Some meanings have been filled in for you.)

Step 2 Try writing a short definition of the meaning of the whole word.

Step 3 When you are finished, compare your answers with those of your classmates.

Step 4 Use a dictionary to check the meaning of a word part or a whole word to fill in anything the class could not complete.

1. *a(d)-* = to _____

   loc(are) = place _____

   -at(e)   makes the word a verb _____

   -ion   makes the word a noun _____

   allocation = _____

2. *commod(us)* = convenient or useful _____

   -ity   makes the word a noun _____

   commodity = _____

3. *com-* = with _____

   pati = to feel, sympathize _____

   -ible   makes the word _____

   compatible = _____

4. *de-* = from _____

   gener = _____

   -ative   makes the word an adjective _____

   degenerative = _____

5. *discrimin (discrimen)* = distinction _____

   -ate   makes the noun a _____

   to discriminate = _____

6. *humane* = _____

   -ness   makes the word a _____

   humaneness = _____

7. *immuno-* = exempt from service; not vulnerable _____

   su(b) = _____

   press = _____

   -ion   makes the word a _____

   immunosuppression = _____

8. *in-* = _____

   cur(e) = _____

   -able   makes the word a _____

   incurable = _____

9. *ir-* = not _____

   re- = _____

   verse = to turn _____

   -ible = _____

   irreversible = _____

10. *pro-* = before _____

    gnosis = knowing _____

    prognosis = _____

11. *recipi(ens)* = past participle of to receive _____

    -ent   makes the word a noun _____

    recipient = _____

SKILL A
Cohesion and Reference

Cohesion

For a paragraph to make sense, the individual sentences must fit together. Likewise, for a series of paragraphs to make sense they must also be connected in a logical manner. When sentences or paragraphs are well connected, we say that they cohere, that they are cohesive. This means literally that they stick together.

co (the prefix) = together   *here* (the root) = to stick

Reference

How is cohesion maintained in both spoken and written language? One of the ways is called reference. Reference is the use of nonspecific words to refer back to a specific noun or idea. There are several ways to make sure that the reference is clear.

Option 1: Creating Dependent Relationships

Consider the following sentences:

1. The doctor had to make a choice.
2. The doctor had to decide which of the accident victims to treat first.

These sentences are *independent*. They seem to be related to the same topic, but the meaning of one sentence does not depend on the meaning of the other.

To create a *dependent* relationship between two sentences, connect them so that together they have meaning and one of the sentences alone is ambiguous. For example:

3. The doctor decided to treat the little boy first.
4. He hoped that he had made the right choice.

Sentence 3 establishes that we are talking about the doctor. In sentence 4, *he* refers to the doctor, but this reference would not be clear without sentence 3. Sentence 3 and sentence 4 are dependent and cohesive.

Option 2: Using Personal Pronouns to Create Cohesion

Every language has words that refer to other words. You are already familiar with the use of personal pronouns.

personal pronouns		
Subject and Object Pronouns	**Possessive Pronouns**	**Possessive Adjectives**
I, me	mine	my
you	yours	your
we, us	ours	our
he, him	his	his
she, her	hers	her
they, them	theirs	their
it	its (rarely used)	its

The use of the word *it* deserves special attention. This pronoun can refer to an idea or concept expressed by a phrase, a whole sentence, a paragraph, or perhaps even an entire conversation. For example:

5. The doctor cleaned up the wounds on the little boy's face, ordered some X-rays of his head, and told the nurses to get the operating room ready while the medical assistant checked the rest of the boy's body for other injuries.

6. So far, it was going well.

In sentence 6, *it* refers to the treatment described by all of sentence 5 and perhaps even to the ethical choice the doctor had to make described in sentences 1 through 4.

Option 3: Using Demonstrative Pronouns to Create Cohesion

The words *this, that, these,* and *those* often help create cohesion between sentences. However, it can be difficult to understand exactly what these demonstrative pronouns refer to when they are used to describe something that cannot be named in one or two words. Consider the following sentences:

7. The surgery was taking a long time; the doctor felt tired, hungry, and worried about the other accident victims who still needed to be treated.

8. That was the way it went some days in the emergency room.

Notice that the word *that* in sentence 8 refers to a particular circumstance described and feeling conveyed by sentence 7. However, the word *it* in sentence 8 refers to daily life in general.

Option 4: Demonstrative Pronouns that Come Before their Referent

Sometimes a demonstrative pronoun may come before rather than after the sentence it refers to. For example:

9. This was going to be hard.

10. He never enjoyed making life-or-death decisions.

In this case, the word *this* in sentence 9 does not refer back to something already mentioned. Instead, this refers ahead to "making life-or-death decisions" which is mentioned in sentence 10.

A Final Note

Although reference words allow you to avoid repetition, they can be ambiguous and confusing if not properly used. Consider the following:

11. The little boy smiled at the doctor as he opened his eyes.

Whose eyes are they? Most likely they are the little boy's eyes. However, what if sentence 9 had been this:

12. This was going to be hard; the weary doctor closed his eyes for a moment.

In this case, we could not be certain whose eyes opened, the doctor's or the little boy's.

Bone marrow transplant recipient Stesan Morsh and donor Terrence Bailey

> **Ways to Avoid Confusing References**
>
> When speaking or writing:
>
> **1.** Do not overuse reference words.
> **2.** Restate exactly who or what you are talking about periodically.
>
> When listening or reading:
>
> **1.** For all reference words, ask yourself Who? Whose? What? When? or Where? Immediately try to connect the reference word with its referent.
> **2.** If you do become confused, stop the speaker at an appropriate time and ask for clarification, or put a question mark in the margin of your book or notes and ask for clarification from an instructor or friend later.

Listen In

exercise 1

Listen to the presentation once all the way through. Then listen again and fill in the blanks in each of the following items with the appropriate information. Note that:

Mosaic Two • Listening/Speaking

- In items 1–5, the "clue" question has been provided, and you simply answer it.
- In items 6–19, you must write both the "clue" question and the answer.
- In items 1–10, the reference words are not italicized.
- In items 11–19, you must first find the reference words before completing the rest of the item.

example: Try to imagine this situation.
Question: What situation?
Answer: The entire story about David needing a transplant and finally getting one.

1. *"They had been told that David's only hope was a liver transplant."*
Question: Who had been told?

Answer: _____

2. *"So anyway,* this *boy's parents hoped that their son's liver could help."*
Question: Which boy's parents?

Answer: _____

3. *"The patients needing organs vastly outnumber donors,* those *who can give organs."*
Question: Those what?

Answer: _____

4. *"Because of* this, *each year, thousands of people who could be saved by a routine transplant die."*
Question: Because of what?

Answer: _____

_____

5. *"I heard* it *once, but I've forgotten* it. *How does* it *go again?"*
Question: Heard what once?

Answer: _____

_____

Question: How does what go?

Answer: _____

6. *"As the sea becomes rougher,* it *is clear to all of you in the boat. . . ."*
Question: _____

Answer: _____

7. *"If so, do you trust* his *fairness in making the decision?"*

Question: _____

Answer: _____

8. *"In* that *case, the only fair method of decision would be some sort of lottery."*

Question: _____

Answer: _____

9. *"In other situations like this where the public welfare is affected so dramatically, the government* here *has always intervened."*

Question: _____

Answer: _____

10. *"I thought that recently, laws have been proposed that would make* this *a crime."*

Question: _____

Answer: _____

11. *"And that these laws would place the allocation of this precious commodity entirely in the hands of the federal government."*

Question: _____

Answer: _____

Question: _____

Answer: _____

12. *". . . doctors in that hospital would keep their organs alive artificially until they are needed."*

Question: _____

Answer: _____

_____

Question: _____

_____

Answer: _____

_____

Because we do not yet have the means to keep organs alive outside the human body for long periods of time, organs often must be rapidly delivered to needy recipients.

13. *"I suppose this would be something like harvesting the dead, though."*

Question: _____

Answer: _____

14. *". . . some psychologists believe this might present a greater psychological threat to humanity."*

Question: _____

Answer: _____

15. *"The response to that argument has often been that few people, if any, have the wisdom to see what the social good is now."*

Question: _____

Answer: _____

16. *"Nor can they see what it will be in the future."*

Question: _____

Answer: _____

Question: _____

Answer: _____

17. *"The problem with this position is still the shortage of organs and the large number of needy people."*

Question: _____

Answer: _____

18. *"What if three people are in immediate danger of dying from kidney failure, but there is only one kidney? Then this solution does not help."*

Question: _____

Answer: _____

19. *"At least they would know that no one discriminated against them for any reason."*

Question: _____

Answer: _____

20. *"It's really overwhelming to realize that certain ethical choices can mean that one person will live and others will probably die."*

Question: _____

Answer: _____

exercise 2

Listen to the presentation again. As you listen, make a list of as many of the reference words as you can and who or what each refers to (the referent). Then combine your list with your classmates' lists. How many reference words do you have as a class? Are most of the referents people? Ideas?

REFERENCE WORDS	REFERENTS
_____	_____
_____	_____
_____	_____
_____	_____
_____	_____
_____	_____
_____	_____
_____	_____
_____	_____
_____	_____
_____	_____
_____	_____
_____	_____
_____	_____

exercise 3

As a class or in small groups discuss the following. As you discuss, listen for the reference words. Ask for clarification of references as necessary.

The family of Nicholas Green, who was killed in a robbery attempt in Italy and whose organs were donated for transplant.

1. Do you think the lifeboat analogy is a good one? Why or why not?
2. Do you think an organ transplant lottery is a good idea? Why or why not?
3. Do you think the government should regulate organ transplants? Why or why not?
4. Do you think facilities should be set up that make it easier to harvest the organs of the dead? Why or why not?
5. What do you think is the best solution to the organ shortage problem? Why?
6. Would you want to be a person who decides who gets an available organ and who doesn't? Why or why not?

Speak Out

activity 1

Find a brief article in a magazine or newspaper that deals with some type of ethical choice and bring it to class.

1. In small groups, take turns reading your articles aloud.
2. Whenever those who are listening hear a reference word, they should call out the appropriate question to clarify the reference. Several people may call out similar questions at the same time.
3. Someone in the group who did not ask the question should answer it.
4. The reading of the article then continues.

activity 2

Step 1 Listen to friends, TV and radio commentators, and other English speakers and try to pick out:

- examples of ambiguous reference.
- examples of extended reference in which the thing referred to is described in a whole sentence or paragraph, not just one word.

Step 2 Write down examples and discuss them with your classmates. Consider the following questions:

1. How or why was the reference ambiguous?
2. How could the ambiguity be avoided.
3. What happened because of the ambiguity? Was there a misunderstanding?
4. Were the examples of extended reference hard to find? Why or why not?
5. What did most referents refer to? Things? People? Places? Ideas?

SKILL B

Taking the Floor and Keeping the Floor

In conversation, people take turns listening and speaking. Smooth "turn taking" is a critical part of any conversation.

Even among native speakers of the same language, however, turn taking does not always occur smoothly. For instance, there are many times when what you have to say may be ignored unless you assert your right to say it. More importantly, people may interpret silence as agreement, or they may assume that you have nothing to say if you do not claim a right to say it.

Taking the Floor

Asserting yourself and speaking out is called "taking the floor." As with other functions in English there are appropriate ways to take the floor in both formal and informal situations.

Taking the Floor (Formal Situations)

1. Unless you are specifically asked to save questions until after the speaker is through, you may interrupt in order to:

   - Ask for clarification or repetition.
   - Add pertinent information.
   - Challenge a point.

2. When you interrupt, stick to the immediate topic. Do not raise issues from previous lectures or sources unless they are relevant. If you do, you risk interrupting the speaker's train of thought and annoying other listeners as well as the speaker.

Taking the Floor (Informal Situations)

Interruption and overlap are acceptable. The limits depend entirely on the individuals involved—their relationship as well as their cultural backgrounds.

Expressions and Cues for Taking the Floor

Polite (Verbal)

Can (Could, May) I just say (add) something here?
Excuse me for interrupting, but . . .
I don't think so . . .
If I could interrupt . . .
If I could just come in here . . .
May (Can, Could) I interrupt?
That reminds me . . .
That's true, but . . .
Yes, but . . .

Polite (Nonverbal)—depending on the situation, relative status of speaker, and listener, etc.

Clear your throat.
Move closer to the speaker.
Raise your hand or index finger.
Take an audible breath.

Impolite (Verbal), except among close friends

Enough about . . .
Hold on there . . .
Wait a minute . . .

What about . . .?
Yeah, but . . .

Impolite (Verbal), even among close friends

No, you're wrong!
That's ridiculous!

What a stupid idea!

Impolite (Nonverbal)

Any threatening gesture
Derisive laughter

Fidgeting
Rolling your eyes

Keeping the Floor

Refusing to give up a turn is called "keeping the floor." The rules for keeping the floor in both formal and informal situations are similar to the rules for taking the floor, except in the reverse. Be sure to allow people to interrupt you when it is polite and necessary.

Expressions and Cues for Keeping the Floor
Polite (Verbal)

Can (May, Could) I please just get through (say) this?
I don't want to lose my train of thought.
Just a minute (second), please.
Let me just finish what I was saying (before I forget).
Let me just say this (one more thing).
Let me just tell you . . .
Please don't interrupt just now, okay?

Polite (Nonverbal), depending on the situation, relative status of speaker and listener, etc.

Signal "stop" with hand.
Talk louder.
Talk faster, keeping pauses to a minimum.
Any combination of these three.

Impolite (Verbal)

Don't interrupt me!
Let me handle this!

(Shut up and) let me finish!

Impolite (Nonverbal)

Any threatening gesture

Derisive laughter

Conversations

You will hear two conversations in which people take and keep the floor. After listening to each one, answer the questions you hear in the spaces provided. When you are finished, compare your answers in small groups.

conversation 1 Erik and Sylvia are talking in the cafeteria after class.

1. What nonverbal cue might Erik have used when he said, "That's true, but . . ."? _____

_____

2. What nonverbal cue might Erik have used when he said, "Yes, but . . ."?

_____

_____

3. What nonverbal cue might Sylvia have used when she said, "Let me just tell you the main point he made."? _____

4. What nonverbal cue might Sylvia have used when she said, "Let me finish what I was saying."? _____

_____

conversation 2 A teaching assistant and some students are in class.

1. Was Sally's interruption about youth in Asia polite or impolite? _____
   Why? _____

2. Was Gina's interruption about states allowing for extenuating circumstances polite or impolite? _____ Why? _____

3. Was Fred's interruption about research for a term paper polite or impolite? _____ Why? _____

Listen In

exercise Listen to the discussion on organ transplants once or twice again. As you listen:

- Pretend that Susan and Richard have invited you home with them for the weekend and that you are sitting at the breakfast table with them.
- Signal you wish to interrupt by raising your hand. The teacher will stop the tape. Then use appropriate verbal and nonverbal cues to take the floor and make your point.

- You might wish to interrupt to:
  a. Explain how people in your country feel about an issue.
  b. Ask for clarification or repetition.
  c. Add pertinent information.
  d. Challenge a point.

Speak Out

activity

In this activity, you will have a chance to "stand on a soapbox" and give a two-to-three-minute "spiel" on what you think about a particular ethical question.

- Select a topic from the suggestions below.
- Organize your thoughts before you begin.
- Give your spiel in small groups. (Later you may want to share it with the whole class.)
- When you are the speaker, it will be your task to keep the floor as much as possible. You may, however, want to allow someone to take the floor who has pertinent questions or information.
- When you are listening, it will be your task to interrupt the speaker as many times as possible. Since this is only a game, you may play the role of a rude person, if you wish. But no more than one or two people in the group should do this to any speaker.
- During this activity, practice using a variety of verbal and nonverbal cues for taking and keeping the floor.

TOPICS

1. using live animals for research
2. declaring someone officially dead when the brain stops rather than when the heart stops
3. buying and selling organs
4. pleading insanity for murder
5. euthanasia
6. appropriate versus inappropriate uses of technology (for instance, nuclear fission)
7. genetic engineering (for instance, changing existing organisms or developing entirely new ones)
8. shortening sentences of prison inmates for participating in potentially dangerous medical research
9. respecting the wishes of the dead (wills, informal requests)
10. birth control
11. taking away licenses or putting people in jail for drunk driving
12. placing the elderly in nursing homes
13. using ridicule as a punishment for crime (for example, forcing a person to wear a sign that says, "I stole $50 worth of groceries.")
14. sterilizing child abusers
15. forcing people with contagious diseases to live apart from everyone else

You will hear a short human interest story. After the story, you will be asked some questions. After you hear a question, read the four possible answers and decide which one is the best answer. Circle the letter of the best answer.

QUESTION 1

A. From Marissa's hip.
B. From the medical team.
C. From Marissa's parents.
D. From older sister, Anissa.

QUESTION 2

A. One out of seven.
B. Seventeen out of one hundred.
C. Seven out of ten.
D. Three out of ten.

QUESTION 3

A. The Ayalas could have aborted the fetus if it wasn't a match for Anissa.
B. A body part was harvested from a living body.
C. The baby gave a part of her body without her consent.
D. All of the above.

QUESTION 4

A. In order to receive a bone marrow transplant.
B. In order to receive a heart-lung transplant.
C. In order to receive a liver in exchange.
D. In order to receive a kidney in exchange.

QUESTION 5

A. The United States.
B. China.
C. India.
D. North America.

CHAPTER eleven

Medicine

Laser treatment for cancer of the mouth

in this chapter

The lecture in this chapter is called "Laser Technology and Medicine." It starts with an explanation of how lasers work, and goes on to describe some of the many medical applications of laser technology.

Skill A—Learning Strategy: Predicting Exam Questions

Skill B—Language Function: Acquiescing and Expressing Reservations

DID YOU KNOW?

- Libraries routinely use laser scanners at the check-out desk. Many grocery, drug, and department stores add up your bill using laser-based equipment. Your favorite compact disk was produced through laser technology.
- Police can use a laser-based device at a crime scene to locate fingerprints that may be several years old.
- Doctors are finding new ways to use lasers every day. Starting with a few basic surgical applications, they have developed treatments for such diverse ailments as cancer (photo on the preceding page), detached retinas, kidney stones, and tooth decay (at the right).

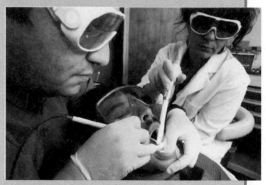

- Laser technology has great potential as both a productive and a destructive force. Through controlled nuclear fusion, lasers could produce enough power to support the energy needs of whole cities. Used in an uncontrolled way, they could just as easily destroy those same cities.

Getting Started
Sharing Your Experience

activity

As a class, or in smaller groups, discuss the following questions.

1. Compare what you know (or imagine) about medical practices and surgery in the 1890s with medical practices and surgery in the 1990s.
2. Consider medical advances in the last 25 years that have benefited friends, relatives, acquaintances, or someone you've read about. Describe the person's medical problem and how a particular medical advance helped that person.
3. Describe all the ways you know of that lasers are used. Have you or anyone you've known ever seen a medical laser in operation? If so, describe the experience to the class.

Vocabulary

Step 1 Break the code to discover the secret phrase. Study the list of words and phrases in the box. Then, use clues *a* through *j* to fill in the corresponding blanks (*a–j*) with the appropriate form of the words from the list in the box. A sample has been completed for you.

---

blockage
blood clots
cholesterol
   deposits
to emit
fiber-optic
local anesthetic
postoperative
   complications
to rupture
suction
trauma

CLUES

a. pulling or sucking in (caused by creating differences in air pressure between interior or exterior space)
b. an obstruction; something that causes closure
c. severe injury to the body
d. referring to a threadlike tool that helps doctors see into the body without cutting it open
e. semisolid masses of a fluid that circulates in the arteries and veins
f. broken or burst open
g. medical problems arising after an operation
h. lumps of a fatlike substance that can stick to artery walls and cause blockages
i. to give out or send forth
j. a substance that produces insensitivity to pain in the area where it is injected

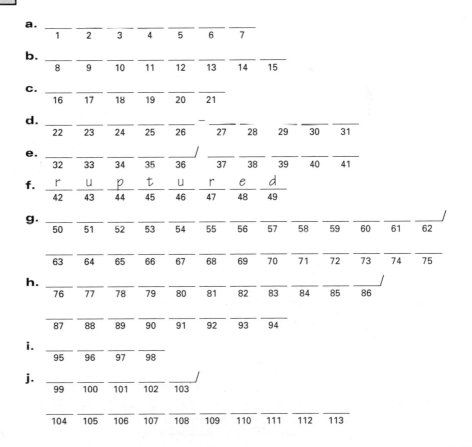

a. __ __ __ __ __ __ __
   1 2 3 4 5 6 7

b. __ __ __ __ __ __ __ __
   8 9 10 11 12 13 14 15

c. __ __ __ __ __ __
   16 17 18 19 20 21

d. __ __ __ __ __ - __ __ __ __ __
   22 23 24 25 26 27 28 29 30 31

e. __ __ __ __ __ / __ __ __ __ __
   32 33 34 35 36 37 38 39 40 41

f. r u p t u r e d
   42 43 44 45 46 47 48 49

g. __ __ __ __ __ __ __ __ __ __ __ __ __ /
   50 51 52 53 54 55 56 57 58 59 60 61 62

   __ __ __ __ __ __ __ __ __ __ __ __ __
   63 64 65 66 67 68 69 70 71 72 73 74 75

h. __ __ __ __ __ __ __ __ __ __ __ /
   76 77 78 79 80 81 82 83 84 85 86

   __ __ __ __ __ __ __ __
   87 88 89 90 91 92 93 94

i. __ __ __ __
   95 96 97 98

j. __ __ __ __ __ /
   99 100 101 102 103

   __ __ __ __ __ __ __ __ __ __
   104 105 106 107 108 109 110 111 112 113

Step 2 Fill in the letters of the secret phrase by matching the number under each letter blank with the corresponding number under the blanks in the Step 1 activity. Note that not all of the letters from Step 1 are used. For example, in the word *ruptured* only the *r* (42) and the *d* (49) appear in the secret phrase. These (and a few other letters) have been written in for you.

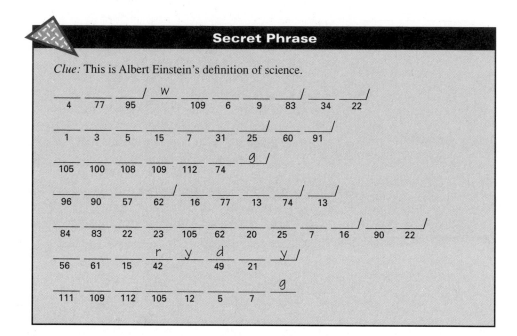

Secret Phrase

Clue: This is Albert Einstein's definition of science.

___ ___ ___/ _w_ ___ ___ ___ ___/ ___ ___/
 4   77   95   109   6   9   83   34   22

___ ___ ___ ___ ___ ___ ___/ ___/
 1   3   5   15   7   31   25   60   91

___ ___ ___ ___ ___ _g_/
105 100 108 109 112 74

___ ___ ___ ___/ ___ ___ ___/ ___/
 96   90   57   62   16   77   13   74   13

___ ___ ___ ___ ___ ___ ___ ___ ___/ ___ ___/
 84   83   22   23   105   62   20   25   7   16   90   22

___ ___ ___ _r_ _y_ _d_ ___ _y_/
 56   61   15   42   49   21

___ ___ ___ ___ ___ ___ _g_
111 109 112 105 12 5 7

SKILL A
Predicting Exam Questions

Most students want to get good grades. One strategy for getting good grades is to predict what questions an instructor will ask on an exam.

Information Likely to Be on Exams

1. Any point the instructor tells you will be on the exam or anything the instructor says would make a good exam question.
2. Information that the instructor repeats directly from the textbook or class readings.
3. Things stated more slowly or more loudly than other things. (Instructors often slow down or speak louder when they want to point out something important.)

Listen In

Step 1   As you listen to the lecture, "Laser Technology and Medicine," imagine that you are a student in the class. Listen several times, using the handouts on the next page to help you understand the new terms you are hearing.

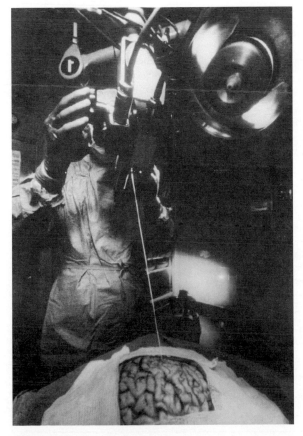

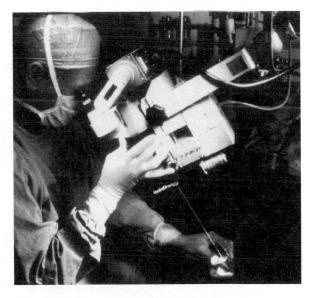

Argon laser being used in surgery on a human ear

CO_2 argon/lasers can be used to vaporize brain tumors.

Engineering 203 HANDOUT 1

Lecture 11: Laser Technology and Medicine

1. Laser = Light Amplification by Stimulated Emission of Radiation

2. Types of lasers used in surgery
   a. YAG = yttrium-aluminum garnet laser: uses a synthetic gemstone as a conductor to produce the laser energy
   b. CO_2 laser: uses carbon dioxide gas
   c. argon laser: uses argon gas
   d. HeNe laser: uses a mixture of helium and nitrogen gases

3. Two laser-assisted surgical processes
   a. photocoagulation necrosis: cuts, burns, or fuses all tissues in its path
   b. photoradiation therapy: uses laser in combination with the drug HpD; destroys only selected tissues
      (e.g., cancer cells)

4. Instruments used in combination with lasers to perform surgery
   a. X rays
   b. fiber optics

5. Type of operation determines type of laser to be used
   a. argon laser, selectively absorbed by tissues and can be passed through fiber optics; therefore
      used for surgery such as:
         repairing small ruptured blood vessels
         reattaching detached retinas
         removing tattoos and birthmarks
   b. YAG laser, not selectively absorbed by tissue and can be passed through fiber optics; therefore good for:
         penetrating blood clots
         repairing large ruptured blood vessels
         reducing the size of tumors
   c. Carbon dioxide laser, cannot easily be passed through fiber optics but is still favored for:
         surgical procedures on the ears, nose, and mouth
         delicate neurological, gynecological, and burn surgery

Engineering 203 HANDOUT 2

Lecture 11: Laser Technology and Medicine

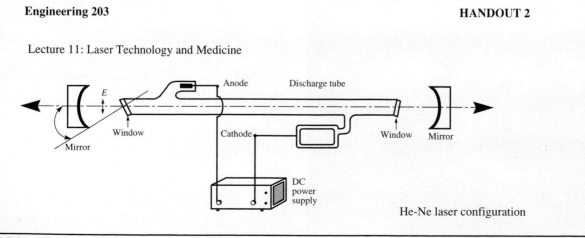

He-Ne laser configuration

Step 2 For each of the questions below, circle *Yes* or *No* to indicate whether or not you think the professor would include this question on an exam. Note your reasons for circling *Yes* or *No* in the spaces provided.

QUESTION | GOOD EXAM QUESTION?

example: The laser is becoming a more and more popular surgical tool. True or false?

Yes   (No)
Reason: *too general,*
too easy

_____

_____

1. What does the acronym *laser* stand for?

Yes   No

Reason: _____

_____

_____

2. How much do lasers cost?

Yes   No

Reason: _____

_____

_____

3. Which hospital recently used the laser to clear away cholesterol deposits in an artery?

Yes   No

Reason: _____

_____

_____

4. What is photoradiation therapy?

Yes   No

Reason: _____

_____

_____

5. What precautions are necessary during laser surgery?

Yes   No

Reason: _____

_____

exercise 2

Listen to the lecture again. This time take notes and indicate which items in the notes you think the instructor is most likely to test you on.

- You can place an asterisk (*) next to probable test items.

  *Most lasers use CO_2, Ar, or a mixture of He and Ne.

- Another way to identify these items is to write *N.B.* (*note bene* in Latin meaning "note well").

  N. B. Most lasers use CO_2, Ar, or a mixture of He and Ne.

Speak Out

activity 1

As a class, discuss the types of questions that can appear on tests: true/false, multiple choice, short answer, and essay. Discuss how the subject matter of the course (math, literature, business, etc.) may influence the kinds of questions the instructor chooses. For instance, when might a literature instructor choose to ask a true/false question? When might a mathematics instructor choose to ask an essay question?

In your discussion, consider the kinds of questions that would be asked in courses such as those in the following list. Add to the list any additional courses that are of interest to you.

biology	marketing
chemistry	operations research
computer science	philosophy
engineering	statistics
English	urban planning
history	

activity 2

Based on your lecture notes:

Step 1 Make a list of 5–10 questions you think might appear on an exam that covers the lecture.

Step 2 Ask a classmate your exam questions.

Step 3 After your partner has answered your questions, answer his or her questions.

Step 4 Change partners and try the activity again. If time permits, do this several more times.

Step 5 As a class, discuss the variety of types of questions you and your classmates predicted would be on the exam.

Acquiescing and Expressing Reservations

We often get the impression that professional people such as doctors, lawyers, or professors are much wiser than the patients, clients, or students they are dealing with. They *seem* to have all the right answers. Therefore, when dealing with professionals, people tend to acquiesce—they yield or submit to the professional person's opinion or judgment without questioning it. However, people sometimes feel angry at themselves for not speaking up when they have a question or reservation about what a professional is telling them. If you have questions or doubts about what a professional says, you should express your reservations.

For example, speak up when you think:

- your doctor has overlooked something important or wants to try a treatment that is risky.

- your advisor doesn't understand a problem you are having.

- your professor didn't see the rest of your answers on the back of the page and thought you didn't complete the exam.

Useful Expressions for Acquiescing and Expressing Reservations

Acquiescing
Do whatever you think is best.
I'm putting myself completely in your hands.
I suppose you must know best.
I trust you completely.
If you think that's best.
Whatever you say.

Expressing reservations
How long do I have to think it over?
I'd like to get a second opinion.
Let me think it over.
One concern I have is . . .
One drawback is . . .
Possibly, but . . .
What bothers me is . . .
What I'm afraid of is . . .
Yes, but the question really is . . .

Conversations

Listen to these conversations between a doctor and two of his patients, in which the patients acquiesce or express reservations. Answer the questions you hear after each conversation. When you are finished, compare your answers in small groups.

conversation 1

1. The patient asks two questions to express reservations. What are they?

_____

_____

_____

_____

2. At the end of the conversation, does the patient acquiesce? _____
What does the patient say?

_____

_____

_____

_____

_____

_____

_____

conversation 2

1. The patient in this conversation also expresses reservations. What are this patient's concerns?

_____

_____

_____

_____

2. At the end of the conversation, does this patient acquiesce? _____
What does the patient say?

_____

_____

Listen In

exercise

Listen to the lecture.

1. After every major operation is described, decide how you would respond if a doctor suggested that you should have that operation.
2. Discuss with your classmates any reservations you would have and how you would tell them to your doctor.
3. Discuss how you would feel if the operation involved some risks, but it was described to you as "the only alternative." Would you believe the doctor? Would you seek other opinions or other forms of treatment? What would you say to the doctor?

Speak Out

activity

With a partner, role-play one of the following situations. If time permits, role-play another situation with the same partner or change partners and do the activity again. Present some of the role-plays to the whole class.

Situation 1   Marcia, twenty, is a pre-med student. She has just gotten back her chemistry mid-term exam with a grade of C+ on it. She looks over the exam and realizes that the professor did not see page three of her six-page exam. This professor, however, had announced on the first day of class that he never changes a grade. Grades are important to Marcia and she decides to speak to the professor about her exam anyway.

Situation 2   Kamal has been sick for quite some time. He is in a foreign country and goes to a doctor who is highly recommended by the student health service at the university. She tells him that his kidneys are failing and that he must be hospitalized immediately and must receive a kidney transplant as soon as possible.

Situation 3   Sam, forty-four years old, has an excellent reputation in the community as a father, a good provider, and a concerned citizen. He is president of one of his city's leading banks, and he generously donates his time to a number of local charities. His doctor, a close friend for many years, has just given Sam a yearly checkup and found that Sam has a serious illness. He is puzzled about what to do. If he tells Sam about his condition, he is afraid Sam will fall apart. He has seen this happen before. Therefore, he decides not to tell Sam the true results of his yearly checkup. Sam, however, has not been feeling well and knows that something must be wrong.

You will hear a short human interest story. After the story you will be asked some questions. After you hear a question, read the four possible answers and decide which one is the best answer. Circle the letter of the best answer.

QUESTION 1

A. 35.
B. 3.
C. 4.
D. 7.

QUESTION 2

A. Rome.
B. Palermo.
C. Naples.
D. Pompeii.

QUESTION 3

A. He slowed down.
B. He argued with the men.
C. He drove faster.
D. He turned around.

QUESTION 4

A. Because the Italians honored the Greens.
B. Because Nicholas's donated organs helped seven people in Italy.
C. Because the robbers shot Nicholas in Italy.
D. Because the Greens still loved Italy.

QUESTION 5

A. The robbers were caught and punished.
B. The Greens received an award.
C. Nicholas helped save the lives of other children.
D. Family and friends came to the funeral.

The Future

The discussion in this chapter is called "The World in the 21st Century." This conversation takes place between three friends who are about to graduate from college. One of the friends, named Mike, is packing up to go home and discovers a paper he wrote for a course earlier in his college career.

Skill A—Learning Strategy: Critical Thinking

Skill B—Language Function: Speculating about the Future; Reminiscing about the Past

DID YOU KNOW?

Yogi Berra being interviewed

- Benjamin Franklin, the famous American inventor and statesman who helped establish the first public library and the first mail delivery service in Philadelphia, said of the future, "Nothing is certain but death and taxes."
- Yogi Berra, a baseball player and manager who is famous for his comic misuse of the English language said, "Prediction is very hard, especially when it's about the future."
- People everywhere are fascinated with the idea of burying time capsules containing evidence of what life is like today so that future generations can use them to discover more about how we lived. These capsules contain newspapers, photographs, and other documents and are sometimes placed in the hollow cornerstones of new public buildings. It is estimated that there are over 10,000 time capsules in the world.
- Historian Philip Toynbee said, "I have seen the future, and it does not work."

Getting Started
Sharing Your Experience

activity **1**

Imagine for the next few moments that it is now the year 2025. For you, it is an ideal world; all your hopes for yourself and humanity have been realized. Take a moment to let this image of an ideal world sink in. Then, as a class or in small groups, share your responses to the questions on the opposite page.

1. How old are you?
2. What kind of job do you have?
3. Where do you live?
4. What do you see when you look out the window at home? At work?
5. Is there romance in your life?
6. What do you do during your leisure time?
7. What do you do on vacations?
8. In what ways are you involved in community or government affairs?
9. What are your friends like?
10. What is a typical day like for you?

activity 2

Think about the following questions and then share your responses as a class or in small groups.

1. Do you think that the ideal world you described in Activity 1 is really a possibility? Why or why not?
2. Do you think that the future will basically be good, or do you fear a dark future?
3. What are some of your worst fears about the future?
4. How did these fears arise? For instance, is the source of one of your fears a program you saw on TV? A movie? An article in a newspaper? Is the source something a friend, acquaintance, or family member said?
5. Are your fears reasonable? Are they based on hard evidence such as statistics or scientific surveys or are they based on things such as feelings, opinions, or gossip?
6. Do you think you have enough hard evidence about any one of your fears to help persuade a government body to do something?

Vocabulary

exercise

The definitions of the words in this list reflect the ways in which they are used in the discussion in this chapter.

apathy	*indifference; lack of care, interest, or emotion*
to commission	*to authorize, command, empower*
to deplete	*to use up*
extinct	*no longer existing (refers to a group or class, not to an individual)*
to implement	*to put into action*
inflation	*the decrease in the worth of paper money as more and more of it is printed*
to replenish	*to replace or restore*
scarcity	*shortage*
to have strings attached	*to have obligations, often not formalized, beyond a basic agreement*

Each of the incomplete analogies below contains one blank. Read the items and fill in the blank with a word or group of words from the vocabulary list to complete the analogy. Compare your answers with your classmates'.

example: polar bear : living :: dinosaur : _extinct_
Polar bear is to living as dinosaur is to extinct.

1. add : subtract :: replenish : _____

2. present : absent :: excitement : _____

3. fish in the sea : plenty :: bald eagles : _____

4. rising prices : _____ :: hard economic times : depression

5. wild animal : free :: zoo animal : _____

6. make : recipe :: _____ : plan of action

7. black : white :: use up : _____

8. ask : request :: authorize : _____

SKILL A

Critical Thinking

Critical thinking involves evaluating facts, concepts, and opinions and then making your own decisions. Making accurate analyses is not always easy, however. Effective critical thinking involves careful deliberation, withholding judgment and stepping back to view things as objectively as possible.

Throughout this book you have been introduced to learning strategies that can help you develop your ability to think critically. For example:

1. As you consider a speaker's ideas you can compare and contrast your (or someone else's) ideas with the speaker's ideas (Chapter Six).

2. Seeing cause-and-effect relationships (Chapter Seven) may help you break down complicated ideas into a simpler sequence of causal events and their results.

Critical thinking (and listening) also requires you to distinguish facts and opinions (Chapter Nine). Here are some further suggestions to help you think critically.

Facts and Opinions

As you refine your critical thinking ability, you will find that the ideas you encounter generally fall into one of three categories:

1. *Facts* Facts can be proven either right or wrong by comparing them with data known to be accurate.
2. *Questionable concepts* Explanations of vague terms and abstract ideas can be evaluated by comparing them to other explanations.
3. *Opinions* Personal judgments—beliefs, values and tastes—can be evaluated in light of your own personal preferences and by asking yourself the following questions:
   - Is the speaker using emotions rather than logic to persuade me?
   - Is an issue being oversimplified or misinterpreted?
   - Is the information relevant to the main issue?
   - Is the speaker basing his or her ideas on valid theory?

Guide for Critical Thinking

1. Don't believe everything you hear. Be skeptical.
2. As you look for questionable concepts, question not only the controversial, but the plausible concepts as well.
3. Find out the speaker's attitude and purpose. Does the speaker have a bias? Is he or she being paid to support a specific concept? Are important points of an argument left out so as to "weight" the argument in favor of one side?
4. Look for inconsistencies so that you are not fooled by arguments based on poor reasoning.
5. Examine data to ensure that the speaker has presented it accurately and that you are interpreting it correctly.

Listen In

exercise 1

If you wish, you can read along as your instructor reads aloud this passage about what life might be like in a space colony. Answer the questions that follow. Then compare your responses with those of your classmates.

Gerard O'Neill, author and scientist, has seriously considered the idea of colonies in space. He believes that by the year 2010 it will be technically feasible to build a space city in the shape of a cylinder that would rotate through space. O'Neill is convinced that such colonies would provide an adequate

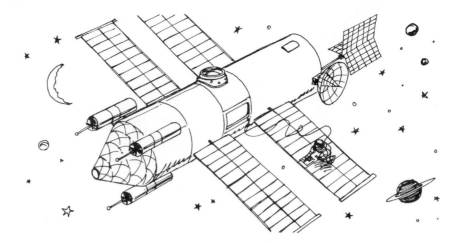

alternative to life on earth for our ever-expanding population. Fiber-optic light would duplicate the passing of the sun overhead, so people would continue to function in the daytime and nighttime they are used to. These space citizens would live in a cylinder, and their view up would be of other people and buildings standing upside down. I think this would be the most serious drawback: the sky would be missing.

1. What are the facts in the passage? _____

_____

_____

2. What are the questionable concepts? (Hint: How are the key terms defined

and who is defining them?) _____

_____

_____

_____

_____

_____

_____

3. What are the opinions of Mr. O'Neill? _____

_____

_____

_____

_____

_____

4. Do you agree with Mr. O'Neill? ___ _____ Why or why not? (Use the suggestions in the boxes on pages 130 and 131 to guide your evaluation) _____

_____

_____

_____

5. What is the opinion of the speaker? _____ _____

_____

Do you agree? _____ Why or why not? _____

_____

exercise 2 You will hear three friends, Mike, Jenny, and Ted, as they discuss an old paper that Mike wrote for one of his courses.

Step 1 Listen to the discussion once all the way through.

Step 2 Listen once or twice more and fill in facts, questionable concepts, and opinions in the appropriate sections here and on the next page.

FACTS

1. _____

_____

2. _____

_____

3. _____

_____

4. _____

_____

In the year 2025, will our planet be able to accommodate a population that seems to be increasing geometrically?

Drought-stricken area

Irrigated farmland

QUESTIONABLE CONCEPTS

1. _____

   _____

2. _____

   _____

OPINIONS

1. _____

   _____

2. _____

   _____

3. _____

   _____

4. _____

   _____

   _____

   _____

   _____

   _____

Family planning is a worldwide concern.

 **exercise 3** Analyze your responses in Exercise 2 according to the criteria in Skill A and answer the questions that follow.

1. Do you think the statements of fact hold up on closer examination? _____ Why or why not? _____

_____

_____

_____

_____

_____

2. Do you agree with the ways in which Mike uses terms in the statements of concepts? _____ Why or why not? _____

_____

_____

_____

_____

_____

3. Do you agree with Mike's opinions? _____ Why or why not?_____

_____

_____

_____

_____

_____

4. Do you think that Mike is trying to persuade his friends to accept a particular point of view? _____ If so, what are the techniques he uses to do this? _____

_____

_____

exercise 4

Step 1   Listen to the discussion again and make notes on Mike's proposals to remedy the world's problems.

_____

_____

_____

_____

_____

_____

Step 2   Share your list of proposals with your classmates.

Step 3   In pairs or small groups, evaluate the proposals using the criteria suggested in Skill A.

Speak Out

activity 1

Step 1   Break up into groups of three or four. Each person should choose one of the following methods of gathering information about the future.

Step 2   Group members complete their individual assignments, taking notes on what they find out.

Step 3   Each person shares with the others what they learned from their interviews, readings, and investigations of photographs and advertisements.

Method 1

1. Design a questionnaire that includes five to ten questions such as:

- What do you think life will be like in the year 2025?
- Do you think the future will be better than the present?

2. Administer the questionnaire (interview) to two or three people.

Method 2

Explore some new viewpoints by reading newspaper articles, magazine articles, and material in books that deal with life in the future. (*Hint:* The study of the future may be called "futurology" in your bookstore or library.)

Find an interesting photograph or advertisement intended to depict life in the future. Make notes on your ideas about what the item is trying to say about the future, whether or not you agree with this statement, and why you think the photo or ad was displayed where it was.

activity **2**

Step 1 To further practice critical thinking, read the following statements and decide if you agree with each one and why or why not?

Step 2 Discuss with your classmates as many of the statements as time permits.

Washoe the chimp knows sign language.

- Do you agree with your classmates about the validity of each statement?
- Do you agree on the definition of terms in each statement?
- In particular, do you agree on definitions of the more abstract terms?

STATEMENTS

1. All people are born equal.
2. The United States was a democracy before women were allowed to vote.
3. Animals have language.
4. Morality is not important to someone living alone on an island.
5. Virtue is its own reward.
6. Thirteen is an unlucky number.
7. Blondes have more fun.

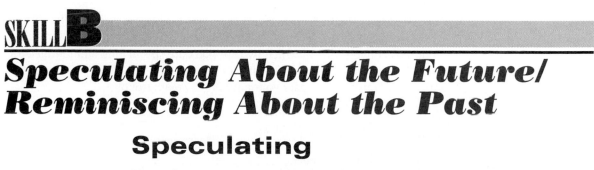

SKILL B

Speculating About the Future/ Reminiscing About the Past

Speculating

Most of us cannot see exactly what will happen in the future. In order to prepare ourselves for unknown future events, we often speculate about various possibilities. The following expressions are used to introduce all types of speculations, whether they are about globally significant issues such as life on earth in the 21st century, or about more local daily events such as the chance of rain.

Reminiscing

Inevitably, some possibilities of the future become events of the past. When someone asks you a question or says something that reminds you about a past event and you want to share your recollections, your reminiscences, the following expressions will be useful.

Conversations

Listen to this conversation in which two speakers are speculating and reminiscing. Answer the questions you hear after the conversation in the spaces provided. When you are finished, compare your answers in small groups.

1. Who are the two speakers? _____

2. What are they doing? _____

3. What is their relationship? _____

4. What topics do the speakers speculate about, and what expressions do they use to introduce their speculations?

	TOPICS	EXPRESSIONS
Speaker A	_____	_____
	_____	_____
	_____	_____
Speaker B	_____	_____
	_____	_____
	_____	_____

5. What topics do the speakers reminisce about, and what expressions do they use to introduce their reminiscences?

	TOPICS	EXPRESSIONS
Speaker A	_____	_____
	_____	_____
	_____	_____
Speaker B	_____	_____
	_____	_____
	_____	_____

6. Why does Speaker A want Speaker B to stop reminiscing?

_____

_____

_____

Listen In

exercise 1

In the discussion in this chapter there are many speculations about what the world will be like in the 21st century. Some of the speculations are from the study commissioned by President Carter in 1975. Some of the speculations are personal opinions of the speakers.

- Listen to the presentation.
- Each time a statement is (or could have been) introduced by one of the expressions used for speculating, write down the expression used (or a possible one).
- In response to the speculations, make a few speculations of your own.
- The following speculations have been paraphrased from the lecture to get you started. Add as many more as you can. Then compare your answers and speculations with those of your classmates.

EXPRESSIONS	SPECULATIONS	YOUR SPECULATIONS
1. ＿＿＿＿＿	The number of poor and hungry will rapidly increase.	Do you agree? ＿＿＿ Explain. ＿＿＿＿＿ ＿＿＿＿＿＿＿＿ ＿＿＿＿＿＿＿＿ ＿＿＿＿＿＿＿＿
2. ＿＿＿＿＿	Food and farmland will rapidly decrease.	Do you agree? ＿＿＿ Explain. ＿＿＿＿＿ ＿＿＿＿＿＿＿＿ ＿＿＿＿＿＿＿＿ ＿＿＿＿＿＿＿＿
3. ＿＿＿＿＿	100 million people will be born each year.	Is this certain? ＿＿＿ Why or why not? ＿＿＿＿＿＿＿＿ ＿＿＿＿＿＿＿＿ ＿＿＿＿＿＿＿＿
4. ＿＿＿＿＿	The gap between the wealthy industrialized countries and the developing countries will widen.	Do you agree? ＿＿＿ Explain. ＿＿＿＿＿ ＿＿＿＿＿＿＿＿ ＿＿＿＿＿＿＿＿ ＿＿＿＿＿＿＿＿
5. ＿＿＿＿＿	The industrialized countries will use too much of the world's resources.	Why might this be so? ＿＿＿＿＿ ＿＿＿＿＿＿＿＿ ＿＿＿＿＿＿＿＿ ＿＿＿＿＿＿＿＿
6. ＿＿＿＿＿	The loss of forests will lead to the loss of topsoil.	How will this change planet earth? ＿＿＿＿＿＿＿＿ ＿＿＿＿＿＿＿＿ ＿＿＿＿＿＿＿＿

EXPRESSIONS	SPECULATIONS	YOUR SPECULATIONS
7. _____	For many nations, starvation will become the greatest problem.	Do you believe this? _____ Explain. _____ _____ _____ _____
8. _____	The United States, with its relatively stable economy, might lead a global program of providing food.	Is this realistic? ____ Why or why not? _____ _____ _____
9. _____	Exports should be priced according to the incomes of the consumer nations.	Why won't this happen? _____ _____ _____ _____ _____
10. _____	The only thing that will make people change is disaster.	What does this mean? _____ _____ _____

Speak Out

activity 1

Are you wondering what the future will bring? Why not visit the local psychic or fortune teller?

- In groups of three to five, take turns playing the role of a psychic or fortune teller who "sees all, knows all, and tells all."
- Let your classmates ask you whatever questions come to mind about future global or personal events.
- As you answer each of their questions, use an expression listed in Skill B to introduce your speculation about the future.

A class of 1926 at its
fiftieth reunion

activity 2

Reunions are popular in many cultures. There are family reunions, class reunions, and team reunions, to name a few. In fact, any gathering of people who have not seen each other for a long time can be called a reunion.

- Imagine that you and your classmates have decided to come back together for a reunion.
- At a party, you are getting reacquainted in small groups by sharing what has happened in the last twenty-five years, reminiscing about the past, and speculating about the future.
- Throughout the activity, try to stay in character as you move from group to group as at a party. Play yourself as you might be twenty-five years from now.
- If possible, you might want to have some refreshments at your reunion party to get you into the mood.

activity 3

Role-play a family reunion in the 21st century.

- Divide the class into four groups to represent four generations of a family, which will include great-grandparents and great-grandchildren.
- Decide what your individual roles and relationships will be.
- Staying in character, imagine that you are all attending a family reunion. It's like most other family reunions, except for one thing—it is taking place in the year 2076.
- Circulate at the party and chat with various family members. Share your reminiscences and speculations about the future.

You will hear a short presentation. After the presentation, you will be asked some questions. After you hear a question, read the four possible answers and decide which one is the best answer. Circle the letter of the best answer.

QUESTION 1

A. Seers.
B. Forecasters.
C. Futurologists.
D. All of the above.

QUESTION 2

A. In 1950.
B. In 1915.
C. In 1903.
D. In 1900.

QUESTION 3

A. Because oil and gas stoves were developed.
B. Because unexpected things keep happening.
C. Because being popular doesn't make you right.
D. Because not everyone can write a best-seller.

QUESTION 4

A. The rise in the number of people who watch a lot of TV.
B. The rise in the number of people who work at home.
C. The rise in the number of women who work outside the home.
D. The rise in the number of marriages for each person.

QUESTION 5

A. Pessimistic.
B. Optimistic.
C. Backward.
D. Gentle.

QUESTION 6

A. Because Boston had a lot of crime.
B. Because high-tech inventions create slave societies.
C. Because they had dark and haunting visions in 1984.
D. Because scientists had produced better weapons.

Appendix

Scoring for risk-taker test, pages 28–29

QUESTION	STRONG YES	WEAK YES	MAYBE	WEAK NO	STRONG NO
1.	4	3	2	1	0
2.	6	5	3	2	1
3.	5	4	3	2	1
4.	6	5	3	2	1
5.	7	6	4	2	1
6.	2	1	5	0	0
7.	3	2	1	.5	0
8.	6	5	3	2	1
9.	7	6	4	2	1
10.	7	6	4	2	1
11.	9	8	6	4	2
12.	7	6	4	2	1
13.	10	9	8	4	2
14.	8	7	5	3	1
15.	10	9	8	4	2
16.	10	9	8	4	2
17.	5	4	2	1	0
18.	4	3	2	1	0
19.	5	4	2	1	0
20.	9	8	6	4	2
21.	8	7	5	3	1
22.	7	6	4	2	1
23.	3	2	1	.5	0
24.	2	1	.5	0	0
25.	7	6	4	2	1

Crossword Solution, from Page 129

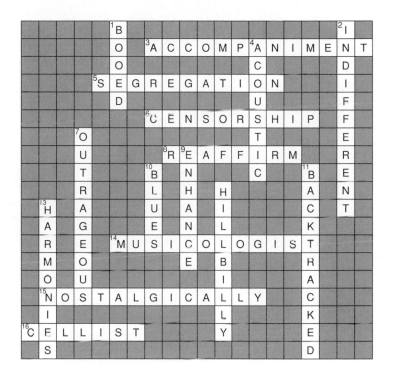

Tapescript

Language and Learning

To School or Not to School

LECTURER: Good afternoon. Before we jump into the practical substance of this course—the actual methods you will use as teachers—I would like to discuss a more general issue. Potentially great artists and scientists will appear in your classrooms. Will you recognize them or not? Will you encourage them or not? When someone asks the next Einstein or Marie Curie who was important in his or her schooling, will your name come up? Will the answer be, "It was my third grade teacher. That teacher really made a difference"? Do teachers, in general, help the gifted student along the path to greatness or don't they? What are the chances of you making a difference? How well do schools serve scientific or artistic geniuses? These are very important questions for you, so that's why I've made them the focus of our first class.

So, first of all, I think we have to separate the arts and the sciences. Why do you think I want to do this? Amy?

AMY: Well, artists are temperamental, moody, inconsiderate, and self-centered.

LECTURER: Is that different from the rest of us?

AMY: Well, yes. I think so. They seem different because they often must "get away from it all," go off to their lofts, workrooms, or studios to be creative. You know. And you read about those opera stars and actors that have to be handled with kid gloves, VERY CAREFULLY, so that they won't get angry and walk off the job.

LECTURER: Right, Amy. And because these people can be temperamental, moody, and self-centered, we might expect that it is unlikely that they would do well in school. School environments usually are quiet, calm, well organized, and students are expected to be disciplined, after all.

These are not, of course, the only—and perhaps not even the most important— reasons why artistic people may not do well in our schools. But just what are the important reasons? We would certainly not be surprised to hear that great writers, actors, painters, and dancers have been less than enthusiastic about their early education. In *Huckleberry Finn* and *Tom Sawyer,* two famous American novels, Mark Twain writes about boys who constantly play tricks in class or don't go to school because they find it so boring. This reflects the experience of the author. Twain was beaten again and again in school because he refused to obey the rules and complete his assignments.

Yes, Peter.

PETER: Didn't Charlie Chaplin (in my opinion a great comic genius) also hate school?

LECTURER: You're right on both counts, Peter. He *was* the comic genius of both silent films and "talkies" and he had little interest in school subjects, except for plays he could watch or act in.

Here's another one. Vincent van Gogh, the Dutch impressionist artist, could barely keep up with his studies. He spent five years at a boarding school. At the age of eleven he already acted like an artist. Yup! You guessed it! He was moody, so his classmates didn't like him. He only wanted to draw and paint. He loved being outside watching the colors of the countryside as the seasons passed, or as the light changed from early morning to night. Later he drew and painted this countryside, and his works made him famous.

Mark Twain, Charlie Chaplin, and Vincent van Gogh are examples of what we expect to find: that is, that the schools don't serve the artist. But there are exceptions to this rule. Martha Graham, the dancer and choreographer who revolutionized the art of dance in America, did her schoolwork so quickly and well that her teachers sent her to the library to read during her free time. And Maria Tallchief, another dancer, considered by some to be this country's greatest ballerina, was an obedient child who tried to please her parents and teachers and excelled in every subject she studied. The famous British poet William Wordsworth was also happy at school as a child. He did well in the classics and math and felt he had a free and happy life at school. Wordsworth was a curious child who was interested in the fresh and the new, and he found his teachers to be sympathetic and kind.

And now what about great scientists? How well did they do in school? Did their teachers see the greatness in them? Generally not. Let's take Thomas Edison as our first example. He was a truly great inventor. He patented 1,099 inventions in his lifetime, including the lightbulb, the phonograph, and the motion picture projector. His elementary school teachers, however, thought he was from another planet, or at the very least, mentally unbalanced. He always asked a lot of questions, and this made his teachers feel uncomfortable. So Edison's mother decided to teach him at home. By the time he was nine, he had read most of the English classics, including Gibbon's *Decline and Fall of the Roman Empire*, a monumental book that covers thirteen centuries of Roman history. He was a curious person who bought all the books he could afford and read his way through many libraries. But Edison's first love was doing experiments.

Yes, Susan.

SUSAN: Didn't Edison once set fire to his father's barn in order to "see what happened"?

LECTURER: He sure did. He also built himself a chemistry laboratory in the basement of his parents' house. Instead of going to school, he worked to earn money so he could conduct more experiments.

Now Charles Darwin, the scientist who first fully developed the theory of evolution, was another curious, creative thinker. He didn't do any better in school than Edison. In grammar school his grades ranged from average to poor. And Darwin, unlike Edison, did *not* read the classics, even though they were required reading in his British school. He preferred to follow his own interest in natural history. He continuously collected insects, plants, and rocks. And he did lots of experiments. In this way he was like Edison. He started his scientific career as an unpaid naturalist on the ship *The Beagle*.

Perhaps the most well-known scientist of modern times is Albert Einstein, and our discussion would not be complete without a look at his schooling. Although he generally did fairly well in school, he didn't like it at all. In fact, he once said "I hate school. It's like being a soldier . . . School is like a barracks, the teachers are like officers who tell the soldier what to do. If you don't learn your lessons by heart, they scold or beat you. Even if you don't understand what the books say. They are angry when you ask questions—and I like to ask questions."

Even though these scientific giants experienced great conflict between the demands of school and the development of their own minds, we should not jump to conclusions. There are other examples of scientists who performed well in school and found it to be a good place to prepare for their careers. Marie Curie, who discovered the element radium and invented radiation therapy, did well from her very first day in school. Curie was a star pupil in all subjects. While most children were having difficulty learning because of the excessive strictness of her Polish school, she *refused* to fail.

Another example of success in school is Lillian Moller Gilbreth, one of the founders of industrial engineering. Because of her shyness, Gilbreth did not attend school until the age of nine, when she entered the fourth grade and was an excellent student. And Alexander Fleming, who discovered penicillin. He loved the one-room schoolhouse he attended in Scotland. He passed his medical school entrance examinations with the highest marks that any student had ever received.

So what can we learn from these examples of famous people and their experiences at school? Yes, Sasha.

SASHA: Well, they were very curious.

LECTURER: Yes! They asked questions. And the bad teachers were unaccepting of their questions. Part of your job as future teachers in this country is to encourage your students to ask questions. You may have the next great artists or scientists in your classes. How can you tell which ones they are? They are the ones who will ask you more than you know.

STUDENTS: (laughter)

LECTURER: Well, that's it for today. See you next time.

SKILL **B**   *Requesting the Main Point*

Conversations

In the following conversations, you will hear the expressions used appropriately and inappropriately. Sometimes the intonation is what makes the difference. Listen to the speakers and answer the questions. When you are finished, compare your answers in small groups.

CONVERSATION 1

Randy tries to tell Sandy some interesting news.

RANDY: Did you see the seven o'clock news last night?

SANDY: No, what about it?

RANDY: Well, they showed the wilderness-preservation march that I participated in with my ecology class. You know, the one where we went to the state capitol building and we protested and there were some people dressed up as trees and plants and stuff, and, anyway, I was really surprised at the way the newscaster handled it. Remember I told you it was raining terribly hard that day and some people were even throwing things at us and I forgot my umbrella—most people did—and we all got drenched, absolutely soaking wet. Well, the march was picked up by the major news networks and, boy, did their reports surprise me! I didn't think the march was so controversial. It didn't feel like a very daring thing to do at the time.

SANDY: Get to the point, would you? How did the networks handle it?

Question 1: Was this conversation friendly or unfriendly?
Question 2: Was it formal or informal?

Professor Draper is talking about the midterm exam.

PROFESSOR DRAPER: Well, students, I want to reorganize our schedule and change the date of the midterm. You know, we had scheduled the readings of Jones and Tomkins for the sixteenth and the readings by Rockford and Pebble for the fourteenth and those by McVey and Gill for the twelfth. Well, I want to move McVey and Gill to the fourteenth, the midterm to the twelfth, Rockford and Pebble to the sixteenth, and Jones and Tomkins to the nineteenth.

STUDENT: So, what are you driving at? I don't get it. Are you trying to tell us that we only have two more days until the midterm?

Question 1: Was the student's request for the main point polite or impolite?
Question 2: What would you have said in the same situation?

CONVERSATION 3

Professor Werner and Richard discuss an upcoming field trip.

PROFESSOR WERNER: Okay, now students, let me explain how we'll organize this plant-hunting expedition. You'll want to have a buddy and to keep your buddy with you at all times. You are to search for the various plants of the genus Rhus, but remember many of them are quite poisonous, so make sure your arms and legs are well covered and wear plastic gloves when you pick the plants. Of course, you will be free to wander wherever you like, but the terrain changes quickly and is unmarked. We did have a problem with students getting lost two years ago, and one of them broke her leg.

STUDENT: Excuse me, Professor Werner, I don't quite understand what you're getting at.

PROFESSOR WERNER: Well, Richard, the point is: This trip could be dangerous if you don't follow all the rules carefully.

Question 1: Did Richard handle the situation well?
Question 2: Was he polite or impolite?

Listen In

exercise   Now listen to another version of the lecture "To School or Not to School." In this version, some of the main points have been omitted. During the lecture, your instructor will stop the tape so that you can ask for the main point. Each time your instructor stops the tape, several of you should practice requesting the main point by using an appropriate expression from Skill B. Note: The omitted material is indicated by the blank lines. Stop the tape at the first bracket.

LECTURER: Good afternoon. Before we jump into the practical substance of this course—the actual methods you will use as teachers—I would like to discuss a more general issue. Potentially great artists and scientists will appear in your classrooms. Will you recognize them or not? Will you encourage them or not? When someone asks the next Einstein or Marie Curie who was important in his or her schooling, will your name come up? Will the answer be, "It was my third grade teacher. That teacher really made a difference"? Do teachers, in general, help the gifted student along the path to greatness or don't they? What are the chances of you making a difference? How well do schools serve scientific or artistic geniuses? These are very important questions for you, so that's why I've made them the focus of our first class.

So, first of all, I think we have to separate the arts and the sciences. Why do you think I want to do this? Amy?

AMY: Well, artists are temperamental, moody, inconsiderate, and self-centered.

LECTURER: Is that different from the rest of us?

AMY: Well, yes. I think so. They seem different because they often must "get away from it all," go off to their lofts, workrooms, or studios to be creative. You know. And you read about those opera stars and actors that have to be handled with kid gloves, VERY CAREFULLY, so that they won't get angry and walk off the job.

LECTURER: Right, Amy. [_____

_____
                                    *
_____

_____]

These are not, of course, the only—and perhaps not even the most important— reasons why artistic people may not do well in our schools. But just what are the important reasons? [_____
                                    *
_____] In *Huckleberry Finn* and *Tom Sawyer,* two famous American novels, Mark Twain writes about boys who constantly play tricks in class or don't go to school because they find it so boring. [_____
                                    *
_____]

Yes, Peter.

PETER: Didn't Charlie Chaplin (in my opinion a great comic genius) also hate school?

LECTURER: You're right on both counts, Peter. He *was* the comic genius of both silent films and "talkies" and he had little interest in school subjects, except for plays he could watch or act in.

Here's another one. Vincent van Gogh, the Dutch impressionist artist, [_____
_____*_____] He spent five years at a boarding school. At the age of eleven he already acted like an artist. Yup! You guessed it! [_____
_____*_____] He only wanted to draw and paint. He loved being out- side watching the colors of the countryside as the seasons passed, or as the light changed from early morning to night. Later he drew and painted this countryside, and his works made him famous.

[_____
                                    *
_____

_____] Martha Graham, the dancer and choreographer who revolutionized the art of dance in America, did her schoolwork so quickly and well that her teachers sent her to the library to read during her free time. And Maria Tallchief, another dancer, considered by some to be this country's greatest ballerina, was an obedient child who tried to please her parents and teachers and excelled in every subject she studied. The famous British poet William Wordsworth was also happy at school as a child. He did well in the classics and math and felt he had a free and happy life at school. [_____
                              *   ]
[_____
                                    *
_____] Let's take Thomas Edison as our first example. He was a truly great inventor. He patented 1,099 inventions in his life- time, including the lightbulb, the phonograph, and the motion picture projector. His

elementary school teachers, however, thought he was from another planet, or at the very least, mentally unbalanced. [_____
_____
_____* _____]

By the time he was nine, he had read most of the English classics, [_____
_____
_____* _____
_____] But Edison's first love was doing experiments.

Yes, Susan.

SUSAN: Didn't Edison once set fire to his father's barn in order to "see what happened"?

LECTURER: He sure did. He also built himself a chemistry laboratory in the basement of his parents' house. Instead of going to school, he worked to earn money so he could conduct more experiments.

Now Charles Darwin, the scientist who first fully developed the theory of evolution, was another curious, creative thinker. [_____
_____
_____* _____
_____] He preferred to follow his own interest in natural history. He continuously collected insects, plants, and rocks. [_____* _____
_____] He started his scientific career as an unpaid naturalist on the ship *The Beagle*.

Perhaps the most well-known scientist of modern times is Albert Einstein, and our discussion would not be complete without a look at his schooling. Although he generally did fairly well in school, he didn't like it at all. In fact, he once said "I hate school. It's like being a soldier . . . School is like a barracks, the teachers are like officers who tell the soldier what to do. If you don't learn your lessons by heart, they scold or beat you. Even if you don't understand what the books say. They are angry when you ask questions—and I like to ask questions."

[_____ _____
_____
_____* _____
_____ _____] Marie Curie, who discovered the element radium and invented radiation therapy, did well from her very first day in school. [_____* _____] While most children were having difficulty learning because of the excessive strictness of her Polish school, she *refused* to fail.

Another example of success in school is Lillian Moller Gilbreth, one of the founders of industrial engineering. Because of her shyness, Gilbreth did not attend school until the age of nine, when she entered the fourth grade and was an excellent student. And Alexander Fleming, who discovered penicillin. He loved the one-room schoolhouse he attended in Scotland. [_____
_____* _____]

So what can we learn from these examples of famous people and their experiences at school? Yes, Sasha.

SASHA: Well, they were all very curious.

LECTURER: Yes! [_____ _____
_____
_____* _____
_____] You may have the next great artists or scientists in your classes. How can you tell which ones they are? [_____ _____* _____
_____]

STUDENTS: (laughter)

LECTURER: Well that's it for today. See you next time.

Focus on Testing

Understanding spoken English on standardized listening comprehension tests (such as the TOEFL) is more difficult than in other contexts. For example, during standardized tests you cannot interact with the speaker to get clarification or rewind the tape to listen again. You get only one chance to listen for important information. The Focus on Testing exercises in this book will help you practice this skill.

You will hear a short presentation. After the presentation, you will be asked some questions. After you hear a question, read the four possible answers and decide which one is the best answer. Circle the letter of the best answer.

Presentation

Artificial intelligence, or AI, is the ability of a machine to exhibit intelligent behavior. Artificial Intelligence systems are modeled after the human brain. Like the brain, an AI system receives information, processes it, and then produces an appropriate action or response. Since the 1940s, many specialists, including computer scientists, mathematicians, philosophers, and electrical engineers have tried to make a machine as intelligent as the human brain, but so far no computer even comes close.

AI, however, has proven to be better than the human brain for answering certain types of questions. For example, AI seems to be better, and certainly faster, than the human brain for problem solving when you must remember and process a large amount of information. However, AI is still not capable of any type of adaptable, or truly intelligent behavior. So far, AI programs are quite primitive when compared to the kinds of reasoning, language, and learning the human brain can do.

Although the fastest computers are able to perform about 10,000,000,000 calculations per second, AI systems still cannot recognize or produce natural language as well as the human brain. Also, all knowledge contained in AI systems is based on logical rules. Intuition does not come into it. Someday, when scientists completely understand the mysteries of human language and learning, they may be able to create an AI system as good or even better than the human brain.

Question 1: What is the main topic of the presentation?
Question 2: What is the model for Artificial Intelligence systems?
Question 3: When is an Artificial Intelligence system better than the human brain?
Question 4: What is all knowledge contained in Artificial Intelligence systems based on?

CHAPTER two

Danger and Daring

LECTURE   *Hooked on Thrills*

PROFESSOR: Good morning.

STUDENTS: Good morning.

PROFESSOR: Did you know that the towers of New York City's World Trade Center are exciting to other sorts of people besides international businesspeople and sightseers? Since they were built, these twin towers, which are two of the world's largest buildings, have been irresistible to a variety of daredevils. Does anyone know what a 27-year-old French high-wire artist named Philippe Petit did on August 17, 1974?

STUDENT A: Well, it's a little before my time, but I think I read about him somewhere. Didn't he disguise himself as a construction worker or something and manage to sneak by the building guards? And then didn't he string a cable between the two towers?

PROFESSOR: Yes! He did! Then he did something I'd never do in a million years!

STUDENT A: Me neither! I read that Petit balanced on that cable—around 1300 feet above the street—for 45 minutes!

PROFESSOR: Right. And did anyone read about an unemployed construction worker named Owen Quinn?

STUDENT B: Yes! I guess I must have read the same article. I think it was sometime in the summer of 1975 that he jumped off the roof of one of the towers.

PROFESSOR: Yes, that's true. But you left out a very important part. He was wearing a parachute.

STUDENTS: (laugh)

PROFESSOR: A few years later, another parachutist, whose name is unrecorded, pulled off an even more amazing stunt: He jumped from an airplane and landed on the roof of the South Tower.

STUDENTS: Scary. Amazing. Wow!

PROFESSOR: But the most famous of all the stunts performed on these towers of world trade and high finance was the one performed by George Willig. He was a twenty-seven-year-old toy maker from Queens, New York, who had already gotten the nickname "the human fly." Between 6:30 and 10:10 in the morning on May 26, 1977, using only ropes and clips that he designed himself, he climbed the smooth vertical face of the North Tower all the way to the top, 110 stories.

STUDENTS: Wow! Incredible! Awesome!

PROFESSOR: Along with the reporters waiting to question George on the roof, were several New York City policemen. They handcuffed him and charged him with the same criminal offenses that had been brought against previous daredevils: trespassing, disorderly conduct, and criminal endangerment.

STUDENTS: Really? That doesn't seem fair. What for?

PROFESSOR: Then they handed him a notice saying that he was being sued for damages totaling $250,000, because, as a spokesperson for the mayor said, "We've got to discourage this kind of antic performance in the future."

STUDENTS: Awwwww!

PROFESSOR: But to the thousands of spectators on the street, and the millions who watched his stunt on TV, George Willig was not a criminal. He was a hero. On his way to jail, women kissed him, reporters cheered wildly, and even the policemen who arrested him asked for his autograph. By the following morning, Willig had delighted and captured the affection of so many people that the mayor himself attended a ceremony honoring Willig, and he reduced Willig's fine from $250,000 to $1.10, just a penny for each floor of the tower.

STUDENTS: (cheer and laugh)

PROFESSOR: What motivates daredevils like Philippe Petit and George Willig to perform such dangerous stunts, risking criminal prosecution, injury, and even death? Is it the hope of gaining fame and fortune, the thirst for headlines and business deals? This may be true of some, but certainly not of Willig. Willig said he was "amazed at the hullabaloo" he created and insisted that his motives were pleasure, not profit, and increased self-esteem, not glory. Willig told a reporter that "far above the streets I was very much alone with myself and at peace with myself. . . . It was a personal challenge; I just wanted the prize of getting to the top."

Psychologists who study what motivates people to do this kind of thing agree with Willig. They have categorized stunts such as Willig's as "thrill and adventure seeking"—a subdivision of the larger class of activities labeled "sensation seeking." According to Marvin Zuckerman, a leading researcher in this field, sensation seeking is a fundamental human characteristic. That is, sensation seeking is built into the human nervous system, passed on from one generation to the next, and encouraged by the social community. He claims that sensation seeking is a major factor that can be used to determine and classify personality types. It was not ambition or greed that led George Willig to the top of the World Trade Center. Rather, it was a need for the intense stimulation of a risky activity. Zuckerman and his colleagues theorize that we all seek our own "optimal levels of stimulation." Some of us are most comfortable with a low level of sensation and feel overstimulated in risky situations. Others of us require higher levels of stimulation to be content, and without such stimulation we become anxious or bored. Still others of us require unusually high levels of stimulation to be happy. These are the thrill and adventure seekers, the ones who take up race-car driving, parachute jumping, and climbing buildings.

Researchers distinguish four types of high-level sensation seeking. Thrill and adventure seeking, which we've already mentioned, involves the desire to participate in activities that involve speed and danger. These physical conditions stimulate intense sensations in the tissues and nerves of the body.

In contrast, another type of sensation seeking, called experience seeking, involves the search for powerful and unusual mental rather than physical activities. Examples of experience seeking include the longing to travel, exhibitionistic behavior (such as dressing up in unusual clothing), and the use of mind-altering drugs such as LSD. Experience seekers may also choose to associate with bizarre people, involve themselves with avant-garde music and art, and rebel against established authority. Zuckerman has nicknamed this kind of sensation seeking the "hippie factor," because many of these behaviors were characteristic of the hippies of the 1960s and 1970s.

A third form of sensation seeking is known as disinhibition and is nicknamed "the swinger factor." Disinhibitors find their optimal stimulation level in activities such as heavy social drinking, frequent sexual encounters, wild parties, and gambling.

The fourth type of sensation seekers are boredom avoiders. They dislike repetition, routine work, and people who are predictable and unexciting. They frequently feel restless and generally prefer variety over sameness.

To determine whether people are higher-level or lower-level sensation seekers in each of the four categories, Zuckerman and his colleagues developed a questionnaire called the "Sensation Seeking Survey," or SSS. The survey requires yes or no responses to statements such as these:

1. I like to ride in open convertibles.
2. I sometimes like to do "crazy" things just to see the effects on others.
3. A person should have considerable sexual experience before marriage.
4. The worst social sin is to be a bore.

"Yes" responses to all of these items on the questionnaire indicate a person who tends toward higher levels of sensation-seeking, "No" responses indicate an individual who is content at a much lower stimulation level.

Using the SSS as a tool, researchers have discovered several patterns. First, who do you think are higher level sensation seekers—men or women?

STUDENTS: Men! No, no I think women are! No way. It's *got* to be men! Why should it *have* to be that way?

PROFESSOR: Okay, Okay. Let me tell you. Men tend to be higher-level sensation seekers than women, particularly in the subcategories of thrill and adventure seeking, and disinhibition. I suppose that's not too surprising considering when this research was done, but somehow I think we might get different results if we surveyed *this* class.

STUDENTS: (laugh)

PROFESSOR: And what do you all think the results might be according to age?

STUDENT B: I'd bet people our age tend to take the most risks.

STUDENT C: Well, could be. But it could also be the adolescent age group.

PROFESSOR: Well—you're *both* right! Among different age groups, adolescents and college students have the highest number of high-level sensation seekers. Sensation seeking tends to decrease steadily with age, and young children do not seem to be high-level sensation seekers. Researchers can also correlate levels of sensation seeking with different personality types. They do this by comparing individual scores on the SSS with the results of other psychological tests. Extraordinarily high sensation seekers have psychological profiles similar to those of sociopaths.

STUDENTS: Wow! Really?

PROFESSOR: Yes, we do tend to label the behavior of these high-level sensation seekers as crazy. In Willig's case, both the police and the spectators were sure that the man climbing the building was insane until a suicide rescue worker spoke to Willig when he was halfway up the tower. After three minutes of conversation, the rescuer determined that "the human fly" was okay. He decided this, he said, because of Willig's responses to questions, by the type of equipment he used, and simply by the look in his eye. Every response he gave was reasonable; the only unreasonable thing was that he was climbing up the outside of a building.

STUDENTS: (laugh along with professor.)

PROFESSOR: Another personality trait that is strongly correlated with high-level sensation seeking is creativity. Willig certainly provides a good example of this. Willig designed and built all of his equipment to carry out his stunt. But just thinking up some of these stunts takes a good deal of creativity, too, I think.

Other personality traits correlated with higher levels of sensation seeking include nonconformity, impulsiveness, dominance, and extroversion. Although high-level sensation seekers are somewhat concerned with other people because having an audience is nice, they are ruled more by their own needs and feelings than by the rules of society. Willig's statements certainly bear this out. On the other hand, high-level sensation seekers' scores on the SSS do not correlate with those of schizophrenics and victims of anxiety. In other words, high-level sensation seekers are *not* crazy, even if we think what they are *doing* is crazy.

Now you may wonder what use this information might be. Psychological research in the area of sensation seeking has had many practical applications, ranging from career counseling to psychotherapy. For example, the fact that women have lower optimal stimulus levels than men is one explanation for the past hesitation of women in taking the kinds of risks that lead to success in business. As a result, new techniques for breaking down the fear of risk and for encouraging women to develop "guts" or nerve are now being taught by counselors and popularized in magazines, in newspapers, and on talk shows.

On the flip side, excessive and dangerous sensation-seeking behavior in preadolescents and teenagers is a serious problem. For example, two teenage boys jumped off the Brooklyn Bridge. One of them was killed instantly, but the other boy survived. When authorities asked him if he and his friend had understood how foolish this stunt was, he replied that they realized the danger involved but they jumped anyway, "just to see what it felt like." By recognizing the creative functions of sensation seeking, doctors are helping children and parents find ways to decrease the self-destructive aspects of sensation-seeking behavior and to increase the self-expressive and creative ones.

Well, that's all we have time for today. Finish reading Chapter 17, and we'll go on with this discussion next time.

SKILL B   *Saying "Yes" and "No"*

Conversations

Listen to the following conversations and note the various ways in which the speakers say *yes* and *no*. Fill in the blanks in each conversation. When you are finished, compare your answers in small groups.

CONVERSATION 1

Ted and Paul are discussing their plans for the weekend.

TED: I'm going white-water rafting this weekend, Paul, and one of my buddies, Phil—you know Phil, don't you?

PAUL: Uh-huh.

TED: Well, Phil can't go because he sprained his back playing soccer, so there's room for one more. You wanna go with us?

PAUL: Are you kidding? I've never gone white-water rafting.

TED: Aw, come on. There's a minicourse being given by the Explorers' Club Wednesday night this week. Take it and you'll be ready to go with us.

PAUL: No way! I'll never learn enough in two nights to go on a trip for a whole weekend.

TED: Sure you can! The instructor is great. I know of lots of people who've done it.

PAUL: Well, it's probably not such a good idea, but how much does it cost?

TED: Well, the trip'll cost you about $150 with everything—food, equipment, everything. The course is only twenty bucks.

PAUL: That's not too bad. I'll think about it.

TED: Don't just think about it; do it! You've got the money, don't you?

PAUL: I think so.

TED: Well, then, it's settled. Let's go over to the student union, have something to drink, and then sign you up.

Terry and Lynn are discussing vacation possibilities.

TERRY: Hey Lynn, I saw the greatest trip advertised in this travel magazine I get. It's a mountain-climbing trip in Nepal—you know, in the Himalayas. We'd go all the way to the base camp on Annapurna. That means we'd follow in the footsteps of the women's expedition that climbed Annapurna in 1978! Wouldn't that be great? Let's go!

LYNN: Not on your life! You won't get me up there! I don't even like riding in those glass elevators that go up and down the outside of fancy hotels.

TERRY: Come on! Think about it a bit. There's a month-long training program and then the trip is three weeks. Think how strong and brave you'll feel at the end.

LYNN: You may feel strong and brave after a month. But not me! Never in a million years!

TERRY: Oh, don't be like that. It's important to overcome these fears. You'll be a better person for it!

LYNN: I won't climb a mountain! Not for all the tea in China, and that's that! Find someone else to go with you.

TERRY: But I want you to go. You're my best friend. Besides, there won't be any technical climbing with ropes and all that—just some high-altitude hiking—really! Come on! It'll be fun. We'll have a good time!

LYNN: I like having a good time, but my idea of a good time is seeing a movie, going out to dinner, or watching a baseball game on TV. Wanna go out to dinner?

TERRY: Definitely! Maybe I'll even convince you by the time we order dessert.

Focus on Testing

You will hear a short news program feature. After the news feature, you will be asked some questions. After you hear a question, read the four possible answers and decide which one is the best answer. Circle the letter of the best answer.

News Feature

Bungee jumping is a popular daredevil sport among the young, particularly in California, New Zealand, and France. Bungee jumping was once done by only a handful of sky divers, mountain climbers, and other daredevils. Recently however, dozens of bungee adventure clubs have opened. One club, Bungee Adventures in California, has already sent more than 10,000 thrill seekers over the edge. There have been no fatal accidents so far in the United States, but two French jumpers fell to their deaths when their bungee cords severed. The cords just snapped apart as they were stretched to the limit. A third jumper died when he bounced off of the jump tower.

Bungee jumpers claim that the thrills are greater than the risks. Jumpers leap headfirst from bridges, towers, cranes, and even hot-air balloons. They leap from 90 to 300 feet above the ground, with only the long nylon and rubber bungee cord to break their fall. The bungee cord is a lot like a giant rubber band. Tied around the ankles or the body, the cord is only long enough to allow a few seconds of free fall before it stretches to the limit, stopping the jumper just a few feet short of the land or water below. The jumper is then thrown skyward as the cord snaps back to its original length. Bungee jumping does not require any special physical training or ability. The strength required is only psychological.

Bungee jumping is based on a ritual practiced by the villagers of Pentecost Island in the South Pacific. Every spring the villagers collect vines and wind them into long cords or ropes. Then young men climb high wooden towers, tie the vines around their ankles and jump. A successful jump is considered to be a demonstration of courage—and a sign that there will be a plentiful yam harvest.

Question 1: What kind of a sport is bungee jumping?
Question 2: What do bungee jumpers do?
Question 3: What equipment must bungee jumpers use?
Question 4: Why do the Pentecost Islanders leap from the towers?

CHAPTER three

Man and Woman

<u>LECTURE</u>   *Becoming a Man, Becoming a Woman*

STUDENTS:	Hi. Nice haircut. Can I borrow a pen? When's the midterm?
LECTURER:	Good morning. Today's lecture is about rites of passage. What are rites of passage? Randy?
RANDY:	Aren't they the ceremonies that take place when people go from one stage in life to another?
LECTURER:	That's right. Rites of passage are the ceremonies and rituals that take place in every society in the world as people go from one stage in life to another. They mark the transition from infancy to childhood, from childhood to adolescence, adolescence to adulthood, adulthood to maturity and maturity to old age, and, finally, old age to death. What rites and rituals mark these transitions in the United States and Canada? Get into groups of three and quickly write down what ceremonies mark these stages.

> Note: Stop the tape at this point and discuss the answers to the lecturer's questions in small groups.

LECTURER:	O.K. group 1. What did you get for the transition from infancy to childhood?
STUDENT FROM GROUP 1:	Graduation from kindergarten or entrance into first grade in elementary school.
LECTURER:	Good. Group 2, the change from childhood to adolescence?
STUDENT FROM GROUP 2:	Confirmations at church; graduation from elementary school; and starting middle school or junior high school.
LECTURER:	Good. What about adolescence to adulthood, Group 3?
STUDENT FROM GROUP 3:	Graduation from high school or college, or maybe even a marriage.
STUDENTS:	(laugh)
LECTURER:	Yes, that's right. What about old age, Group 4?
STUDENT FROM GROUP 4:	How about a retirement party, you know, like people have when they retire at 65?
MARTI, FROM GROUP 4:	Or 70. And at that age they get the title "senior citizen."
LECTURER:	That's right, Marti. And funerals, of course, mark death. All of these transitions from one stage of life to another involve changes that might be difficult. For example, children starting school no longer have the freedom to play all day long. Newly retired people no longer have the routine of work to occupy their lives. Instead they have the freedom, sometimes the

frightening freedom, of unscheduled days. Such changes may be extremely stressful. Anthropologists believe that ceremonies and rituals help relieve some of the anxiety and stress that come with the changes. Rites of passage are celebrations of the "passage," or transformation, of people from one social identity or role in society to another as they grow older. The rites may also signify a transformation of the mind of an individual; that is, a deepening of the understanding of the meaning of life.

Today we will focus on tribal rites that mark the change of girls into women and boys into men in the eyes of their society. These rites of passage, rites of becoming a man or a woman, are called puberty rites.

Puberty rites are the most dramatic of the rites of passage. This passage to womanhood or manhood is based on two things: (1) physical maturation and (2) the emergence of secondary sexual characteristics. Puberty is regarded as the most radical change in a person's life. For girls, it is obvious when the ceremony should take place. It depends on when a girl gets her first menstrual period. With boys, it's more subtle, but usually their voices change and body hair begins to grow.

Although the first menstruation is the obvious occasion for a girl's initiation, in some societies—for instance, the Bimin-Kuskusmin of New Guinea, who we will discuss later—the change from child to adult takes place over a period of years. This is also true of the Carrier Indians of British Columbia, who have the adolescent girls live for three or four years in complete isolation after their first menstruation.

STUDENTS: Wow! No kidding?

LECTURER: In other societies, as I already mentioned, the transition from child to adult is considered to be completed on a single occasion.

All tribal rites of passage are similar in some basic ways. The first stage is the rite of separation. In this stage, the person going through the transformation—the initiate, as he or she is called—is removed from his or her previous surroundings. For example, among the Bimin Kuskusmin of New Guinea and the Kurnai of Australia, this involves abruptly taking the boy from his mother's house and the company of the women who raised him and never letting him return there.

RANDY: Imagine that! No more home cooked meals.

STUDENTS: (laugh)

LECTURER: Furthermore, all sports and games of boyhood are forbidden from that time on.

Now, the second stage is the rite of transition. This involves either a physical or symbolic journey to a place outside normal time and space. The journey usually begins with an ordeal involving one or more of the following: fasting, being kept in isolation, or suffering sleep deprivation, humiliation, or intense physical pain of some sort. Among the Omaha and Ojibway Indians of the Great Plains, the child and all his relatives are taken to a sacred hut. The child is attached to a board and acts lifeless during the entire ceremony. The other participants arc then symbolically murdered by medicine men. This ceremony represents the death of the childlike person and the emergence of the man. In his mind, the child can now identify with the adult males. He has been made one of them. He will now be thought of as a productive adult member of the society. All those who participate with him in the ceremony develop a feeling of solidarity. Perhaps you have had this feeling?

MARTI: Yes, I really felt that when my friends and I climbed Mount Shasta. Boy did that feel great!

RENÉ: I know it's not the same as climbing a mountain, but a group of us really had a feeling of solidarity after we stayed up all night together to study for your last exam.

STUDENTS: (laugh)

LECTURER: That's great René. It's just this sort of solidarity that holds any society together. After an experience like this, the members of the group have a renewed feeling of closeness to each other.

Here's another example: During the puberty rites of certain tribes in the lower Congo, the young man must speak a special language and wear no clothes. In this way, all his previous self-concepts, all his ideas about himself and images of himself, are removed. The idea is that he must face his own true nature and, by doing this, come to understand the nature of God.

Okay, now, the third stage is the rite of incorporation. The initiate is healed, welcomed back to the ordinary world, and given a new social status. For example, the Omaha and Ojibway Indians end the ritual with a great feast. They exchange gifts and the initiate's grandfather makes a welcoming speech and the initiate receives his new adult name. In both North American Indian and Australian aboriginal societies, these rites of incorporation include the revealing of sacred objects, such as masks that the child has never before been permitted to see. In the lower Congo, the initiates pretend to relearn all the forgotten gestures of ordinary life, such as walking and eating. In all cases, though, after the rites of incorporation, the initiates look back upon their previous identities as foreign and definitely no longer worthy of respect.

So far, the examples of puberty rites that I've mentioned involve young men. Now I'd like to present a couple of examples of female puberty rites. In Nigeria, a girl who is a member of the Tiv tribe lies quietly on the ground next to her mother while an old man cuts the skin of her stomach with a razor. He inscribes three circles around her navel and a vertical line to her chest. Other lines branch outward to either side and downward. These lines signify the structure of time, and they symbolically place the girl at the point where past and future generations meet. The old man rubs ground charcoal into the cuts. In three days, the cuts will become infected. Then the girl will bathe and cover the cuts with palm oil. When the cuts have healed, a suitor will kill a chicken and present it to her as a gift. Then she can make fun of all the younger, unmarked girls of her society, who do not have suitors.

In New Mexico, in the United States, there's a very different kind of ceremony. A Navajo Indian girl is dressed in many layers of colorful clothing. Then she spends four days and nights in isolation in her family house. After the four days and nights, she places a corn husk in a pattern drawn in the sand, and her relatives sing and dance to celebrate the arrival of her first menstrual period. By chanting a series of traditional verses, she identifies herself as the daughter of the mythical goddess, Changing Woman. Then the older women of the tribe give her a vigorous massage, symbolically rubbing away the old identity. Now she is considered to be a re-formed person, one who is capable of bearing children and enabling the human race to continue.

Although all of the ceremonies I've mentioned are somewhat different, they do have one important similarity. The person who goes through the puberty ritual changes from a receiver of the culture to a giver of the culture. The lengthy preparation periods, the chanting of myths, and the singing of ritual songs during the rites provide formal education both in the social customs and in the sacred traditions of the society. In fact, as I said before, many puberty rites are dramatizations of the death of the old self and the birth of the new.

RENÉ: Excuse me, but some of these rites seem really painful and difficult. I don't see why this is necessary.

LECTURER: Well, you're certainly not the only one who feels that way! Researchers who observe the tribal rites of passage often hold conflicting moral views about them. On the one hand, many of the ordeals are seen as unnecessarily painful and oppressive. On the other hand, anthropologists admit that for outsiders to change or threaten these rites also threatens the life and equilibrium of the society as a whole, and in that way threatens all of its individual members. But whatever judgment we make about these rites, the fact remains that rites of passage are one of the primary ways in which human beings give meaning to the changes that occur in life.

Okay, that's enough for today. See you next week. And don't forget there will be a test the following week.

SKILL B *Extending Congratulations and Condolences*

Conversations

Step 1 Listen to the following short conversations. In each conversation, the second speaker offers congratulations to the first. In some conversations, the second speaker is sincere (his or her tone of voice is enthusiastic) and in others he or she is indifferent (not enthusiastic). Listen to each conversation and circle the word that best describes the *second* speaker. When you are finished, compare your answers in small groups.

CONVERSATION 1

A: Guess what! I'm getting married next month!
B: Oh! Terrific! I'm so happy for you.

CONVERSATION 2

C: Guess what! Louise and I are engaged!
D: Congratulations. I'm so happy for you.

CONVERSATION 3

A: Hey! I've got some news! I got a promotion at work.
B: Congratulations! I'm so pleased for you.

CONVERSATION 4

C: Hey, listen to this! I got a raise this week.
D: No kidding! Congratulations! I'm thrilled.

CONVERSATION 5

A: It's my 90th birthday today!
B: Congratulations! May you have many more!

CONVERSATION 6

C: Guess what! I'm 25 years old today!
D: Congratulations! Many happy returns!

Step 2 Listen to the following conversations in which congratulations and condolences are made as part of longer on-going conversations. In the spaces provided, write down all the expressions of congratulation you hear in the first conversation. For the second conversation, write down all of the expressions of condolence you hear.

CONVERSATION 1

A: Boy! The traffic downtown sure was terrible today.
B: Yeah—sure was. Are you still having trouble with your car overheating in heavy traffic?
A: Oh, no! I finally got a new car.
B: Congratulations! What kind of car did you get?
A: A blue Toyota with all the extras.
B: Great! Does it get good mileage?
A: Sure does! It's so much better than my old car!
B: Well, I'm really glad to hear that! Use it in the best of health!
A: Thanks! I will!

CONVERSATION 2

A: What have you been up to lately?
B: Not much—just work, work, and then a little more work. But things will look brighter when we get this project finished in December.
A: Are you still driving to Los Angeles every week to take care of your mother?
B: No, I'm not doing that anymore. She died in September.
A: Oh! I'm so sorry. Is there anything I can do?
B: No, I don't think so. Everything's under control now. My father had a rough time for a while, but he's doing much better now.

Focus on Testing

You will hear a short conversation. After the conversation you will be asked some questions. After you hear a question, read the four possible answers and decide which one is the best answer. Circle the letter of the best answer.

Conversation

PATTY: Jacobson's class is pretty interesting, don't you think? I especially enjoyed the lecture yesterday on puberty rites. How 'bout you, Alphonso?

ALPHONSO: Yeah, really! Some of that stuff was pretty strange though, right? I mean, going on a vision quest, climbing a mountain and meditating for a while sounds kinda neat, but some of that other stuff was too much.

PATTY: What do you mean?

ALPHONSO: Well, I can't exactly see myself sacrificing an animal or anything, can you?

PATTY: No way!

ALPHONSO: Right! And how about scarification? Could you sit there while they carved sacred designs into your body?

PATTY: Oooh. I don't think so. I see what you mean now. But it's all based on your cultural perspective, isn't it?

ALPHONSO: Huh?

PATTY: I mean, what seems okay, what seems normal in terms of these kinds of rituals is all a matter of what you're used to. You know, what the cultural norms are. In fact, I wonder what people in tribal cultures think of some of our rites of passage. Or for that matter, I wonder what people in the year 3000 will think of the things we do to mark becoming a man or a woman in our society.

ALPHONSO: You're right! I hadn't quite thought of it like that. I wonder if getting your driver's license will be as big a deal then as it is now?

PATTY: I swear, all you ever think about is cars! How about when we went out on our first date? Wasn't that a big moment for you?

ALPHONSO: Of course it was, Patty. But are you saying that our first date was a rite of passage? You know, my first date with *you* wasn't exactly my first date.

PATTY: Is that so? Well, you could have fooled me.

PATTY AND ALPHONSO: (both laugh)

Question 1: Who is Jacobson?
Question 2: What does Alphonso think about vision quests?
Question 3: Which statement about cultural norms is *not* true?
Question 4: What does Patty say Alphonso thinks about most?

CHAPTER four

Mysteries Past and Present

The Origins of Our Solar System

STUDENT 1: This stuff is just like what I'm learning in my philosophy class!

STUDENT 2: Yeah, and there was a history unit in my physics class and the prof, you know, she talked about similar stuff in there, too!

PROFESSOR: Good evening, class. I'm happy to inform you that the astronomy texts for this class have finally arrived at the bookstore . . .

STUDENTS: (cheers and applause)

PROFESSOR: So . . . no more excuses for not getting the reading done, right?

STUDENTS: (groans and laughter)

PROFESSOR: Okay. Now . . . tonight we're going to trace some of the most influential ideas about the origin of the solar system. As we said last time, we will really be talking about our ignorance. When you get right down to it, the bottom line is: We just don't know how the solar system originated. Last time we had just started to talk about Descartes. Do you remember what century we were talking about? Larry?

LARRY: I'm sorry, but I can't remember.

SEVERAL STUDENTS: Thirteenth century. Fifteenth! No, I think it was the 1400s. That's the same thing, silly. Okay, then seventeenth century. How about the eighteenth?

PROFESSOR: Well, it was in the seventeenth century, 1644 to be exact, that the French philosopher and mathematician, René Descartes, proposed a theory that is still accepted by some scientists. According to this theory, at the very beginning there was only a cloud of dust and hot gases. Descartes speculated that currents of movement within this hot cloud took the shape of vortices, or whirlpools, just like the whirling winds in tornados. As the cloud cooled, these vortices came together somehow to form a large central body and other smaller bodies revolving around it.

Yes . . . Toni?

TONI: Did Descartes work on that theory for many years or did it come to him all of a sudden in 1644?

PROFESSOR: That's a good question, but I'm afraid I don't know the answer. Sorry. Let's see, now where was I? Oh, yes. During the late eighteenth century, the German philosopher Immanuel Kant and the French astronomer Pierre-Simon Laplace worked on Descartes's hypothesis. They further developed this hypothesis about the formation of our solar system. They combined Descartes's ideas with Sir Issac Newton's new theory of gravitation.

Kant and Laplace developed a theory known as the "nebular hypothesis." According to this theory, after the sun was formed, a disk-shaped cloud of dust and gas was attracted by the sun's gravitational pull. As this dust cloud revolved around the sun, lumps within the cloud became smaller

Tapescript

	centers of gravitational attraction. Do you know what this process led to? Jonathan, do you know?
JONATHAN:	I'm very sorry, I have no idea.
PROFESSOR:	That's okay. I just wanted to see if anyone had any background in this. Well, this process of gravitational attraction led first to the formation of a series of concentric rings. Eventually this led to the formation of dense, round planets. So you see, according to the nebular hypothesis, the formation of planets is a natural result of the existence of stars. Therefore, solar systems like our own could very possibly be found throughout the universe.

At the turn of the twentieth century, however, the British astronomers James Jeans and Harold Jeffries proposed another hypothesis. They suggested that our solar system was special, was unique in the universe, and that the creation of our solar system was the result of a highly unlikely accident. They argued that millions and millions of years ago another star passed very close to the sun. The gravitational attraction between the two stars caused lines of dense matter to break off from the surface of the sun. But this matter was still affected by the sun's gravity, and so it remained trapped in orbit around the sun. The matter then cooled and condensed, shrinking inward upon itself to form the planets.

By 1920—less than twenty years later—new discoveries led to even newer theories. James Clerk Maxwell and some other scientists demonstrated that a newly discovered principle, the law of conservation of angular momentum, makes both Descartes's model and the nebular hypothesis impossible. Does anyone know what the law of conservation of angular momentum states? Margaret, how about you this time?

MARGARET:	Oh gosh. I'm afraid I couldn't tell you right now.
PROFESSOR:	Anyone else? No? Well, don't worry about this; you'll have a chance to go over this again in discussion session after you get your textbooks. Just bear in mind that the law of conservation of angular momentum states that the amount of circular movement within a closed system must remain constant. That is, the amount of movement cannot change.

So if the sun and the planets had been produced by the contraction of larger clouds of matter, each of these bodies would have picked up speed just as a whirling skater who pulls in his or her arms picks up speed. Furthermore, the sun and the planets would now have to be spinning faster than the speed of light, and we know that they don't spin that fast.

Astronomers were confused by this paradox until the late 1950s. That's when discoveries were made about the nature of plasmas. Plasmas are the gases that make up the clouds between the stars. Astronomers discovered some interesting interactions between these plasmas and electromagnetic fields. These discoveries led a Swedish physicist, Hannes Alfvén, to revise the nebular hypothesis of the eighteenth century. Does anyone know what Alfvén's hypothesis is called? Frank, do you know?

FRANK:	I'm not certain, but I'll guess. Is it the plasma-nebular hypothesis?
PROFESSOR:	Yes, Alfvén's hypothesis is quite naturally called the plasma-nebular hypothesis. According to this hypothesis, our solar system appeared between $4\frac{1}{2}$ and 5 billion years ago, and our sun began as a protostar. A protostar is a highly dense cloud of hydrogen and helium, with some smaller quantities of heavier elements such as mercury. The protostar measured about a light year in diameter. Our sun was formed as the cloud condensed—shrank inward upon itself. As it turned faster and faster, it built up enough electromagnetic energy, heat, and light to set off a permanent ther-

monuclear reaction—the kind of reaction that powers true stars and hydrogen bombs. While the center of the cloud came together into a dense, explosive sphere, the outer sections of the cloud shrank into a disk-shaped mass of gas. This gaseous mass was held rigid by spokes of magnetic force radiating from the dense center—much like the spokes of a wheel—as you can see in the picture on your handout. At first, the disk turned much more slowly than the sphere. Later the disk gained speed until it was turning much faster than the sphere. This aspect of the plasma-nebular hypothesis accounts for the fact that, in general, younger stars appear to spin faster than older ones.

Now, as the central sphere cooled, the cloud around it began to condense in a way similar to the way rain and snow condense from a storm cloud. But instead of drops of rain or snowflakes, spherical grains of matter were formed. Then these spherical grains of matter bumped into each other and stuck together, accumulating into lumps. Evidence of these lumps has been found in meteors and—anyone know where else? Eloise?

ELOISE: I'm afraid I don't remember for sure, but I think it might be in rocks from the moon and maybe from Venus.

PROFESSOR: Well, good, you're half right. Evidence of these lumps has been found in rock samples from the moon and from Mars. Then as a result of gravitational attraction, the lumps accumulated into larger and larger bodies, with the larger bodies swallowing the smaller ones. In this way, the planets and their moons were formed, at least according to this theory.

Also according to this hypothesis, the chemical composition of the lumps varied according to the temperature. Close to the sun, where the heat was greater, only the heavier, denser chemical compounds like metals and silicates condensed. And since there wasn't very much of these compounds, the planets close to the sun remained small. Farther out, away from the sun, where temperatures dropped sharply, the lighter substances like hydrogen, helium, and methane condensed. Since there were a lot of these compounds, the larger planets like Jupiter and Saturn were formed.

The plasma-nebular hypothesis accounts for the chemical composition and sizes of Mercury, Venus, Earth, Jupiter, and Saturn. This hypothesis does not, however, explain why Mars is smaller than the earth, nor does it in any way account for the sizes and compositions of the outer planets: Uranus, Neptune, and Pluto. It has been further hypothesized that in the process of decreasing in size and increasing the rate at which they turn, two bodies the size of Jupiter and Saturn split into unequal parts, producing Mercury and Venus from one body and Earth and Mars from the other.

As you can see, it is evident from our look at some scientific hypotheses about the origin of the solar system that we really don't know exactly how the solar system originated. The data scientists are collecting has not yet been organized into a clear and coherent theory. Physicists and astronomers hope that all of the information that comes from developing technology will soon reveal a comprehensive and comprehensible explanation. But it is also possible, as has happened before, that more data will only complicate rather than clarify this issue.

ROBERTO: Excuse me professor, do you have any ideas about what the next theories might be?

LECTURER: I'm afraid as of now Roberto, I couldn't even begin to guess.

Admitting a Lack of Knowledge

Conversations

Listen to the following conversations in which one person admits a lack of knowledge. In some conversations, the second speaker is polite and in others he or she is rude. Listen to each conversation and circle the word that best describes the *second* speaker. When you are finished, compare your answers in small groups.

CONVERSATION 1

WOMAN: Excuse me, sir, could you give me directions to the Statue of Liberty?

MAN: I'm sorry, I don't know. I'm not from around here myself.

CONVERSATION 2

SAMANTHA: Professor Hill, what did the Druids believe about the origin of the universe?

PROFESSOR HILL: I'm afraid I don't remember the answer to that anymore, Samantha, but almost any text on Druid history should tell you.

CONVERSATION 3

PHIL: When is the next space shuttle supposed to take off?

BOB: Beats me. I haven't a clue.

CONVERSATION 4

CARMINE: How long does it take to get to Machu Picchu?

DOROTHY: Don't ask me. I haven't any idea.

CONVERSATION 5

GARY: When were the statues on Easter Island carved?

SARAH: I'm sure I don't know!

Focus on Testing

You will hear a short tale. After the tale, you will be asked some questions. After you hear a question, read the four possible answers and decide which one is the best answer. Circle the letter of the best answer.

Tale

Once upon a time, Silver Fox was the only one living. There was no earth. There was no water. Only fog.

Silver Fox walked along through the fog feeling lonely. So she began to sing:

I want to meet someone.
I wish I would meet someone.
I want to meet someone.
I really want to know someone else.

She sang this song over and over as she walked along. Soon she met Coyote.

"I just knew I was going to meet someone," Silver Fox said. "Why are *you* traveling?"

"I don't know," Coyote said. "Why are *you* traveling?"

"I am traveling because I am lonely," Silver Fox said.

"Me, too," Coyote said. "So, why don't we travel together?"

Then, as they traveled, Silver Fox spoke. "I know what we should do. Let's make the world!"

"How will we do that?" Coyote said.

And Silver Fox answered, "We will sing the world."

So the two of them began to sing and to dance. They danced around and around in a circle and sang and sang. Soon a small lump formed in the fog below their feet.

"Look down, Coyote. Do you see something?" Silver Fox said.

"I see something, but it is very small," Coyote said.

"Oh, then let's close our eyes and keep dancing and singing," Silver Fox said.

And that's what they did. They sang and danced and danced and sang until the earth took shape beneath them.

"Look down now," Silver Fox said.

"I see it! It's big enough now!" coyote said.

Then the two of them jumped down onto the earth. They sang and danced until they made everything on earth with their footsteps and their song. They jumped up and down and made the valleys and the mountains. They skipped up and down and made the lakes and the rivers. They sang all the songs of the trees, the birds, the fish, and the animals.

And then they danced the dance and sang the song of the people.

Question 1: Who was traveling?
Question 2: What did Coyote and Silver Fox decide to do?
Question 3: How did they do it?
Question 4: What is the best title for this tale?

Transitions

RADIO PROGRAM — The Stages of Life—A View from Shakespeare

GRACE WIDMARK: In some ways life is like a giant puzzle. To construct a puzzle you have to gather and put together the parts. Similarly, we gather and piece together our life experiences as we learn and grow and change.

Hello. This is Grace Widmark and welcome to "Transformations," the show that addresses dynamic changes in the self, the society, and the universe. Tonight we present the sixth program in our series on "Transformations Described in Literature." We are pleased to air a tape of a lecture presented at the University of Wisconsin by the distinguished professor of English Literature, Francis Salinger. The topic is "The Stages of Life—A View from Shakespeare."

We're sure you'll enjoy the program, and we'll have a call-in discussion afterwards as usual. Those of you who receive our newsletter will find Jacques' speech from "As You Like It" in the latest issue. Parts of this speech are quoted in today's presentation.

And now, Professor Salinger.

PROFESSOR SALINGER: Many of us seem obsessed with time and change. We hope the future holds great promise for us and will bring us good fortune, yet we also know from looking at the past that not all changes are good. These conflicting views of time and change trouble us. We want to see time and change as positive, but let's face it—we also know them to be negative because inevitably they will bring our decline and eventual death.

If we try to count them, the ways in which people react to change in their lives seem infinite. Frankly, some people waste their time worrying about what they weren't able to do or what they didn't become. Others learn to accept and take pleasure in what is—in what they were able to do and in what they did become. For example, if they've managed to live an ethical life and provide some comfort to others, they don't worry about the fact that they've never sailed around the world, earned a million dollars, or won a Nobel prize.

And there are those people whose professions demand that they think hard about life: scientists, philosophers, doctors, artists, monks, and naturalists, for instance. Some of these thinkers have positive feelings toward humanity. They believe that a lifetime is a period in which to develop and perfect ourselves and that we must work hard to accomplish this task. On the other hand, some of these thinkers aren't as hopeful about the potential of people's minds or the goodness of their natures. Those who believe that humankind is not worthy of trust, and therefore not worth caring about at all, are known as misanthropes.

Clearly, there are many ways to view people and the stages that they go through in life. A Buddhist would probably see transformation or change as an opportunity for spiritual growth. A business executive may see change only in terms of financial growth or decline. And there are, of course, as many ways to deal with the transformations within our lives as there are points of view. In Western civilization, we seem to be afraid that perhaps all the planning, working, and struggling for success are simply meaningless moves in a game that can't be won. We fear that our efforts will produce, as Shakespeare wrote, merely "sound and fury, signifying nothing." One of the most disturbing visions is the idea that we are just actors playing out roles created for us by circumstance, genetics, the choices our families made, or any number of other things. Even worse, what if we are just puppets whose strings are pulled by forces beyond our control? I'm sorry to tell you that if this is the case, we do not even have the freedom to interpret the role, to move as we would like to within our circumstances. And each and every moment, every gesture, every thought is decided for us.

Of course, we don't like the idea of being puppets, because this limits our freedom. As we grow older, though, we are often willing to settle for less freedom. We settle into our roles, which are determined by our own characters and society's expectations of us. These roles sometimes make us feel that we're in a rut, but we often seem content to live our lives confined and restrained in this way. As we grow older, we seem to grow more sympathetic toward cynics—people who sneer at the idea of freedom of choice and who distrust human nature and people's motives. Cynics believe that most people basically are selfish. And when the cynics describe our cowardice and failures, we listen eagerly. Why do we do this? Well, perhaps the cynics' view of humanity reassures those people who are weak. You see, if that's the way humanity is, then the weak just can't help themselves. They have the best possible excuse for their behavior: That's simply the way all people are. The cynics' view also provides support for those who want to criticize whoever represents authority in society, because all people, especially those in power, always make a mess of everything. The cynics, however, offer nothing constructive, no suggestions or solutions. They merely moan, whine, and complain about the inevitable state of affairs of the world and humanity's poor part in it.

Because we are so painfully aware of the human condition and the fact that eventually we will die, the dark visions of the cynics and even darker visions of the misanthropes can be fascinating to us. One of the most famous speeches in literature about the stages in life that we all pass through is the one given by Jacques in Shakespeare's play *As You Like It*.

Let me tell you a little about Jacques. Jacques is one of the lords serving the duke in the play, but he also presents himself as a philosopher who has separated himself from the rest of humanity. He wanders from place to place, has no connections with other people, no attachments to speak of, and no desire for them. At the drop of a hat, though, he will comment freely to anyone about the corrupt nature of humanity.

As I read the speech, you can decide for yourselves whether you think Jacques is a cynic or a realist, a misanthrope or someone who sees things as they really are. Keep in mind that in deciding this, you are probably deciding which of these *you* are, as well. Now please follow along on your handout:

All the world's a stage,
And all the men and women merely players.
They have their exits and their entrances,
And one man in his time plays many parts,
His acts being seven ages.

So, Jacques says that we are all simply actors going through our lives as if they were real, when actually we are only playing roles already determined for us. He says the seven stages of life are like acts in a play. In the next few lines, he describes the first two stages:

At first the infant,
Mewling and puking in the nurse's arms,
Then the whining schoolboy, with his satchel
And shining morning face, creeping like a snail
Unwillingly to school.

Now, all Jacques has to say about the sweet, innocent babe in the first act of life's drama is that he whimpers (that's the "mewling") and he spits up his milk, or "pukes." And the next twelve years, according to Jacques, don't get any better. The child is sent off to school with his face washed and his books in his "satchel"—in his bag. He does nothing of importance, but continues to whine and complain as he goes unwillingly to school. The only choice he makes is to go to school slowly, "creeping like a snail." Soon he reaches adolescence—his teenage years—and his interest in the opposite sex quickens:

And then the lover,
Sighing like a furnace, with a woeful ballad
Made to his mistress' eyebrow. Then a soldier,
Full of strange oaths, and bearded like a pard,
Jealous in honor, sudden and quick in quarrel,
Seeking the bubble reputation
Even in the cannon's mouth.

So, now, in this third stage of life, our hero burns with desire ("sighing like a furnace") and not much else. He becomes possessed by the passion he feels for his sweetheart. Jacques makes the youth seem foolish by having him write a poem about the beauty of his girlfriend's eyebrow. That is certainly silly stuff, and it is all the lover has to say.

The next stage of his life, however, is not as amusing, nor perhaps as understandable. The youth soon grows beyond love and sexual desire into anger, jealousy, and the most forceful emotion: ambition. And to him, fulfilling the ambition of becoming a man means becoming a soldier. His language changes. It becomes more coarse; to put it bluntly, he swears a lot. He begins to hate his enemies more than he loved his sweetheart—his "mistress." He grows a beard, hoping to look as fierce as a "pard"—that is, leopard. He does this to intimidate his enemies. He fights—"quarrels"—in order to make a name for himself, to gain a little bit of glory. He is so driven by his ambition for recognition that he pursues this path to glory even if it endangers his life. That is, he pursues the "bubble of reputation" even into "the cannon's mouth," even if someone is about to shoot him. He ignores the fact that he is mortal and puts glory and reputation before reason and thought. He makes a wonderfully fierce but thoughtless soldier.

If the youth manages to survive these years, he will achieve the fifth stage, making a career and accumulating things and ideas. He will shift from liberal to conservative, from adventurous to cautious, from passionate to self-controlled. Listen:

> And then the justice,
> In fair round belly with good capon lined,
> With eyes severe and beard of formal cut,
> Full of wise saws and modern instances,
> And so he plays his part.

So, you see, now our young man has managed to become a justice—a court judge. His belly has grown to match his inflated self-satisfaction. He has become fat from eating chicken (that is, lining his belly with "capon") and other tasty foods. His beard is no longer bushy and fierce-looking, but is now well trimmed. Furthermore, he is full of sayings and examples. Not to beat around the bush, he's boring. If this were the last stage, he might be quite content, but there are two stages yet to come. And the next stage brings the trouble of aging:

> The sixth age shifts
> Into the lean and slippered Pantaloon,
> With spectacles on nose and pouch on side,
> His youthful hose, well saved, a world too wide
> For his shrunk shank and his big manly voice,
> Turning again toward childish treble, pipes
> And whistles in his sound.

And here our man puts on the clothes of old age: loose comfortable pants and warm slippers. His eyes are weak, and glasses pinch his nose. He carries his tobacco, and perhaps his money too, in a pouch or purse at his side. There it will be easier to reach and easier to guard. The colorful stockings that he once wore on his strong, youthful legs are too large to fit his tired, shrunken legs now. He no longer has the clear voice of lover, soldier, and judge, but speaks in a high, childlike voice, often whining in sharp tones like those of Scottish bagpipes. To add insult to injury, his missing teeth give a whistling sound to his words. His life has almost come full circle, and the next stage concludes life's play:

> Last scene of all,
> That ends this strange eventful history,
> Is second childishness and mere oblivion,
> Sans teeth, sans eyes, sans taste, sans everything.

And so he returns, without teeth, without sight, without taste, without any of the senses, to the emptiness from which he first came into the world.

We all travel the same path. Sometimes the circumstances of our life are disappointing, even tragic; sometimes they are delightful; sometimes they are merely routine. We might be glad to be alive, worried about it, or uncertain of life's value. In any case, only when we die is our role in the play completed. And the kind of life that we have lived, the roles we were forced to accept by our parents, our culture, and our time in history are only part of the story. Let's face it, what is equally important is how we have handled ourselves, how we have behaved along the way. What it all means—the significance of life—for better or for worse—is left for each of us to decide for ourselves.

Whether we are simply actors in a play that we have not written or are in fact the controllers of our own fates is a fascinating question. If you found the answer, would it make a difference in the way you lead your life? I'll leave you with that question.

GRACE WIDMARK: Hello again, listeners. Professor Salinger's question seems like a good place to start the call-in segment of our program. Our phone lines are now open for your thoughts. If you knew for certain whether or not you could control your own fate, would it make a difference in the way you live your life? Go ahead, Salim in Milwaukee, you're on the air.

SKILL B *Making Negative Statements or Comments Politely*

Conversations

You will hear three pairs of conversations. Each pair of exchanges uses exactly the same words, but each version conveys a different meaning because of the tone of voice used by one of the speakers. Listen to each conversation and answer the questions. When you are finished, compare your answers in small groups.

CONVERSATION 1A

MICKEY: Gloria, have you seen my Uncle Ted lately?
GLORIA: Yeah, I saw him last week at the club meeting.
MICKEY: Oh, really? How was he?
GLORIA: Well, to be honest with you, I don't think he looked very good. He seemed so thin and pale and . . . well, just old.
MICKEY: Well, he's been working very hard and, let's face it, he's no youngster anymore. I've been trying to persuade him to retire, but he just won't do it.

QUESTION 1: Is Gloria really concerned about Ted? Is Mickey?
QUESTION 2: How do you know?
QUESTION 3: How would Ted feel if he overheard this conversation?

CONVERSATION 1B

MICKEY: Gloria, have you seen my Uncle Ted lately?
GLORIA: Yeah, I saw him last week at the club meeting.
MICKEY: Oh, really? How was he?
GLORIA: Well, to be honest with you, I don't think he looked very good. He seemed so thin and pale and . . . well, just old.
MICKEY: Well, he's been working very hard and, let's face it, he's no youngster anymore. I've been trying to persuade him to retire, but he just won't do it.

QUESTION 1: Is Gloria really concerned about Ted now? Is Mickey?
QUESTION 2: How do you know?
QUESTION 3: How would Ted feel if he overheard this conversation?

CONVERSATION 2A

MIRANDA: Dad, I've something to tell you.

MARK: What is it, sweetheart?

MIRANDA: Jeremy asked me to marry him.

MARK: And?

MIRANDA: And I said yes. We'd like to be married right away. What date this month would be best for you?

MARK: To tell the truth, if you go ahead with this plan, you'll have to get married without me.

QUESTION 1: How does the father feel about not going to his daughter's wedding?

QUESTION 2: How do you know?

QUESTION 3: What reason might he have for not going?

CONVERSATION 2B

MIRANDA: Dad, I've something to tell you.

MARK: What is it, sweetheart?

MIRANDA: Jeremy asked me to marry him.

MARK: And?

MIRANDA: And I said yes. We'd like to be married right away. What date this month would be best for you?

MARK: To tell the truth, if you go ahead with this plan, you'll have to get married without me.

QUESTION 1: How does the father feel about not going to his daughter's wedding?

QUESTION 2: How do you know?

QUESTION 3: What reason might he have for not going?

CONVERSATION 3A

PAUL: Well, how do you like it? I know it's not professional quality yet. I've only taken one course. But what do you think? Should I quit my job and become a photographer?

JANE: To tell the truth, I can't make out what it is.

PAUL: It's a bird soaring over a rainbow. See the little point here? That's the beak. Well, what do you think?

JANE: Well, not to beat around the bush—don't quit your job just yet.

QUESTION 1: Does Jane like Paul's artwork?

QUESTION 2: How can you tell?

QUESTION 3: Does Jane like Paul?

QUESTION 4: How can you tell?

CONVERSATION 3B

PAUL: Well, how do you like it? I know it's not professional quality yet. I've only taken one course. But what do you think? Should I quit my job and become a photographer?

JANE: To tell the truth, I can't make out what it is.

PAUL: It's a bird soaring over a rainbow. See the little point here? That's the beak. Well, what do you think?

JANE: Well, not to beat around the bush—don't quit your job just yet.

QUESTION 1: Does Jane like Paul's artwork?
QUESTION 2: How can you tell?
QUESTION 3: Does Jane like Paul?
QUESTION 4: How can you tell?

Focus on Testing

You will hear a short presentation. After the presentation you will be asked some questions. After you hear a question, read the four possible answers and decide which one is the best answer. Circle the letter of the best answer.

Presentation

Nearly 85 percent of the population of India is classified as Hindu. Unlike most other religions, Hinduism, which began to develop about 4000 years ago, has no single founder or creed. It consists of a vast variety of beliefs and practices and has no centralized organization or leadership. Hinduism does, however, suggest a commitment to or respect for an ideal way of life, known as DHARMA.

Hinduism divides DHARMA, or the ideal way of life, into four stages. In each stage there are different duties. The first stage is studentship, or BRAHMACARYA, which lasts from initiation into the Hindu community at 5 to 8 years of age until marriage. During the second stage of the ideal life, GRIHASTHYA, one marries, raises a family, and takes part in society. Forest dwelling, or VANAPRASTHYA, is the third stage. It is during this stage, after one's children have grown up, that the Hindu leaves the household and prepares for the spiritual search or quest. The fourth and final stage is SAMNYASA, renunciation. This is when one gives up attachment to all worldly things and seeks spiritual liberation.

The ideal stages of life and their duties encompass males only. The position of women in Hinduism has always been highly ambiguous. They are, on the one hand, venerated as a symbol of the divine. On the other hand, women are often treated as inferior beings. Women are traditionally expected to serve their husbands and to have no independent interests.

Question 1: What percentage of the population of India is Hindu?
Question 2: During which of the four stages of Dharma is the ideal time for a Hindu to marry
         and raise a family?
Question 3: Which of the statements is *not* true?
Question 4: What is the Hindu ideal way of life called?

CHAPTER **SIX**

The Mind

SKILL **A** *Listening for Comparisons and Contrasts*

Conversations

You will hear some conversations that illustrate the informal use of comparison and contrast. Listen to the conversations once and discuss them with a partner. Then listen a second time and list which indicators of comparison and contrast were used by the speakers. When you are finished, compare your answers in small groups.

CONVERSATION 1

Otto and Henry

OTTO: I really like that German restaurant on Second Street, Henry. You know, the one with the giant beer stein on the roof?

HENRY: I don't think I've ever been there, Otto. Why do you like it?

OTTO: They cook the food the same way my mother did when she was alive. It makes me dream about my childhood.

CONVERSATION 2

Judy and Paula

JUDY: Paula, do you think we should drive or take the train to the concert in Chicago? I can't decide. There are advantages and disadvantages to both.

PAULA: Well, let's see. Driving means that we can leave whenever we want. On the other hand, Judy, taking the train means we don't have to worry about parking and we can both sleep on the way home.

CONVERSATION 3

A teaching assistant and students

T.A.: I've talked with Professor Thornton and there's gonna be some changes this week. What do you want first—the good news or the bad news?

STUDENTS: Oh no—What?

T.A.: Well—the good news is we're not going to have a quiz today.

STUDENTS: Really? That's great! No kidding?

T.A.: And the bad news is that this means that next week we'll have *two* quizzes—one on the mind on Wednesday, and one on dreams and the dream state on Friday.

STUDENTS: Oh, no. Great!

LECTURE *Dreams and Reality*

PROFESSOR: Hello, everyone. Well . . . how did you do with the reading for this week? Any problems?

STUDENT 1: Oh, yes. I thought that the textbook was really hard to understand.

STUDENT 2: Yeah, me too. I thought I knew something about the topic for this week, you know, *Dreams and Reality,* until I started doing the reading.

STUDENT 3: I agree. I finally went to the library and got another book on the subject.

PROFESSOR: Okay. How many others had problems? Yes, well, it looks like about half of you had some difficulty. This is about what I expected, so I thought we would put the textbook aside today. Instead, I'm going to share with you some ideas that occurred to me last summer when I was sitting under my favorite tree, relaxing and reading a great science fiction book.

STUDENT 2: Really? You mean like *Dune*? You know, that really great book about the giant worms? I loved that one.

STUDENTS: (laugh)

PROFESSOR: Yes, I liked that one, too. But last summer I read another science fiction book called *The Lathe of Heaven*. Today's lecture is based on some of the ideas in this book. And I'm very interested to hear your reactions. So let me just share a few thoughts with you, then we'll open it up for discussion. Okay?

STUDENTS: Sure. Yeah. Great. Sounds good.

PROFESSOR: Most of us have had extremely vivid and intense dreams. While we are sleeping, these dreams seem real, but once we wake up, the dream images become more subtle, like the scent of flowers through an open window. Even though the dream images have become more subtle—not so intense, so strong—they still stay with us and drift into our daily routines; they find their way back into our lives as we go about our daily activities. We may be only partially aware of these images and only partially aware of the changes in perception that they may cause. But our dreams can even affect the course of a day without our conscious awareness. During the day, they may influence our seemingly rational, thought-out decisions and choices.

Sometimes scientists or artists will see an everyday object and become inspired. Likewise, many breakthroughs in science and inspirations in the arts come during dreams. In the sciences, for example, a German chemist, F. A. Kebule von Stradonitz, dreamed about a snake with its tail in its mouth. He said that this dream led him to his visualization of the benzene molecule. The dream helped him with the conceptualization he needed in order to build a model of this molecule.

Similar stories can be found in the arts. There is a famous English poem entitled "Kubla Khan" written by Samuel Taylor Coleridge. Coleridge said that he created the poem during a dream and that the minute he woke up, he began to write it down. While he was doing this, a visitor came to see him and interrupted his writing. When he returned to his desk to finish the poem, he found he could not. He had forgotten it. But, on the bright side, critics still consider it one of his best poems, even though it is unfinished.

Often, however, our dreams seem trivial and useless. For example, the other night I dreamed about buying a suit, something I had actually done during the day. And one night last week I dreamed about hot dogs piled up on a bridge—no useful images for scientific discoveries or artistic creations there that I can figure out. But at least I do dream. And research has shown that dreaming, any kind of dreaming, is essential to maintaining good physical and mental health.

It would seem, then, that the mind can create two basic types of dreams: on the one hand, the powerful and intense images that can change our lives, and, on the other hand, the fleeting, chaotic, meaningless images that contain no important messages.

Ursula Le Guin, a popular and respected science fiction writer, explores the world of dreams in a novel entitled *The Lathe of Heaven*. In this book, she considers the relationship between dreams and reality in a fascinating way. Let me briefly summarize the story for you. Then I'll discuss some of her ideas in detail.

George Orr, the main character in the story, has a peculiar problem. When he has certain kinds of dreams, the world changes according to his dream. So he frequently awakens to a different world from the one that existed when he fell asleep.

STUDENT 2: Wow! That would be neat.

STUDENT 3: Yeah! Far out!

PROFESSOR: Yes, that's quite an extraordinary power. But as you can imagine, it frightens him because he doesn't believe that it is right to change reality in this way. His fear grows bigger when he realizes that no one else knows that he is changing the entire world night after night. Everyone else changes completely to become a part of the new reality—the new world—that George creates in his dream. Every time George dreams a new reality, each person acquires a new set of memories to fit this new reality. They remember nothing of the former reality that existed only the night before.

STUDENT 1: That sounds awful!

PROFESSOR: Yes, this may sound awful, but I can think of some days when I'd like to awaken to a new reality.

STUDENTS: (laugh)

PROFESSOR: So George is extremely upset and seeks help from a psychiatrist named Haber. Fortunately, Dr. Haber eventually comes to believe George's story and does not think he is insane. However, Dr. Haber wants to use George's power for his own purposes, so at first he does not tell George that he knows that the dreams really change things. But someone else finds out that George can actually change reality through his dreams, and Dr. Haber is forced to admit that he has not been trying to cure George of his fear of dreaming. Instead, Dr. Haber has been trying to use George's dreams to change the world.

The positive side of this is that the doctor wants to change the world for the good, into his own vision of a "better" place.

STUDENT 4: That sounds okay, but I bet there's a catch, right?

PROFESSOR: Right. Dr. Haber has built a special machine that records George's dreams, so that even without his patient's cooperation, he can transfer George's brainwave patterns during dreams to his own dreams.

This technique works, up to a point. Dr. Haber does, in fact, gain some power to change reality through his own dreams. But he fails to understand what is real and what is unreal. Because he sees only the concrete, material world as real, his dreams produce nightmarish realities with no flexibility, no poetry. For example, Dr. Haber decides that he would like there to be absolute equality in the world—for all people to be absolutely equal in all ways. So he dreams, and when he wakes up, everything is gray. People's skin, their clothes, the houses, the trees, the animals— everything!

STUDENTS: Oh, no! How awful!

PROFESSOR: Everything is indeed equal, but only in a material sense. But things could be worse. Just imagine if Dr. Haber were an evil person rather than a basically good man with a limited view. Eventually Dr. Haber goes mad from the stress of never getting it quite right.

STUDENTS: (laugh)

PROFESSOR: Well, now. What might be the point of such a bizarre story? One clue lies in the title, *The Lathe of Heaven*. A lathe is a machine on which objects are turned and shaped into new forms. If the wood or the metal is not flexible, it will crack when it is put on the machine to be shaped. The same thing happens with the lathe of heaven. If a person is inflexible and clings to only one aspect of the mind—the rational, logical aspect—he will be destroyed by the lathe.

In this novel, Dr. Haber represents the rigid, rational, materialistic person who thinks that he can control nature, that he can bend nature to serve himself. He is never still, never quiet. His mind is always active, seeking new ways to manipulate what he sees as reality. George, on the other hand, is mentally quiet. He never thinks of manipulating reality. His dreams are powerful, not because he wants power, but because he is in tune with nature.

This book suggested to me that reality cannot be fixed or held still in order to be controlled. Reality is vast and mysterious and cannot be defined by the rational, logical mind. Also, anyone who tries to manipulate the world will only suffer like poor Dr. Haber.

But Le Guin does not suggest that George, even though he is in harmony with reality, will not suffer. Imagine what it would be like to wake up to a new world with a new history every few days and to be the only one who can recall the old world.

Likewise, the lathe of heaven forms and re-forms the world and plays with time like a child playing with a tape recorder. Time is moved forward or backward in response to George's dreams. There's a real advantage to this. Because he is in tune with reality in all its aspects, he can change the course of history.

This idea is difficult for most of us to grasp, but certainly it is an intriguing one to think about. To help us, Le Guin asks us to let go of our concept of time, which is the idea that time continuously moves forward, inch by inch, as on an infinite ruler. Instead, she wants us to see time as relative to a central point. George represents that point around which time flows. Perhaps Le Guin wants us to see that change cannot be pushed from behind along a straight course, but only exists in relation to a stable central point.

Now, if we stretch this idea a little, we can see that the lathe of heaven might be the main tool, the most important mechanism we have, for forming and re-forming the world we live in. Although this might be a frightening idea to some, the lathe of heaven and our notion of time are what we use to create our daily world. But not only that. The lathe of heaven—its nature and rhythms—is what can lead us to the mysterious power of the dream.

Uh-oh. I can see there are mixed reactions to this idea. So . . . let's take a short break and then open it up for discussion. I'm really anxious to hear what *you* think.

SKILL A *Expressing the Positive View*

Conversations

You will hear several conversations. Answer the questions you hear after each one. Then discuss your responses as a class or in small groups.

CONVERSATION 1

Gary and Julius

GARY: Hi, Julius. How's it going?

JULIUS: Hi, Gary. I'm really tired. I didn't sleep much last night because I had this terrible dream. I dreamed that I got the second-to-lowest grade on the history final.

GARY: Oh, yeah? And who got the *lowest* grade?

JULIUS: Henry Mitchell. Gee—what a horrible dream!

GARY: Oh, yeah! But it could have been worse!

JULIUS: Yeah? How?

GARY: Well, you could have woken up and discovered *you* were Henry Mitchell.

Question 1: What expression does Gary use to help Julius "look at the bright side"?
Question 2: Is Gary's suggestion amusing? Why or why not?

Tapescript

CONVERSATION 2

Christine and Eric

CHRISTINE: Oh, shoot, Eric! It's raining again, and I was looking forward to going to the soccer team picnic.

ERIC: Yeah—too bad—but look at it this way. Now we'll have time to go see that hypnotherapist I was telling you about.

CHRISTINE: Oh, well—maybe . . .

ERIC: Now come on, Christine. You said you wanted to stop smoking, didn't you?

Question 1: What does Eric suggest doing instead of going to the picnic?
Question 2: What expression does he use to introduce this suggestion?
Question 3: Do you think Eric was glad the picnic was rained out? Why or why not?

CONVERSATION 3

Clara and Joyce

CLARA: Hi, Joyce. What's up?

JOYCE: Hi, Clara. I'm on my way over to my study skills class. We're starting a unit on speed-reading, and I'm not looking forward to it.

CLARA: Really? Why not?

JOYCE: Well, I'm afraid that those speed-reading techniques might interfere with my reading comprehension. And I already have so much trouble understanding a lot of the material in my classes.

CLARA: Oh, but just think. You'll learn to read everything so quickly that you'll at least read everything once. You *were* having trouble completing all of the reading assignments on time, weren't you?

JOYCE: Yes, but remember what the comedian Woody Allen said a speed-reading course did for him?

CLARA: No—what?

JOYCE: He said: "Well, after the speed-reading course I really improved. I was able to read Tolstoy's *War and Peace* in five minutes . . . Yes, uh, huh—it's about war."

Question 1: What is Joyce's complaint?
Question 2: What does Clara suggest?
Question 3: What expression does Clara use to introduce her suggestion?
Question 4: Was Clara able to convince Joyce to see the bright side? How do you know this?

Focus on Testing

You will hear a short conversation. After the conversation you will be asked some questions. After you hear a question, read the four possible answers and decide which one is the best answer. Circle the letter of the best answer.

Conversation

KELLY: Hi, Brian. What's up?

BRIAN: Uh? What, what?

KELLY: Oh, sorry. I didn't mean to startle you. Am I interrupting anything?

BRIAN: Oh, Kelly. It's you. No, no, you're not interrupting anything. I was just dreaming. Or at least I *think* I was dreaming.

KELLY: What do you mean *think*?

BRIAN: Well, I'm so tired, I may be losing touch with reality. You know, I've been studying for final exams and it's really important that I get all A's and B's this semester. Anyway, I've been up about three nights in a row now. And just before you came in I was reading this psychology book and I guess I sort of drifted off. Only I didn't realize it until you came in.

KELLY: What do you mean? What happened?

BRIAN: Well, I thought I was awake and then this girl came in and she said that I needed to rest and that I should go with her to the garden and sit there and she would bring me some refreshments.

KELLY: Refreshments? Nobody uses that word any more. Sounds to me like you just fell asleep for a few minutes and you were dreaming.

BRIAN: But it seemed so real. She took my hand in hers and it was so soft. I followed her and sat at the table in the garden. She left for a minute. I leaned over to smell the roses and I picked a really beautiful pink one. Then she came back and gave me a cup of tea and the most delicious cookies I've ever tasted. I was eating the cookies and just about to ask her her name when . . . well, I guess that's when you came in.

KELLY: I don't know who she was, Brian, but these cookies are really good. Where did you get them?

BRIAN: What? What cookies? I didn't have any cookies here a few minutes ago!

KELLY: Relax, Brian. I'm just teasing. I brought you the cookies. You're not losing touch with reality. You were just dreaming.

BRIAN: Yeah, I guess you're right. It sure was a great dream, though.

KELLY: Sounds like wishful thinking. You know, that's what Freud said about dreams—that they can represent what we hope for or what we need.

BRIAN: Well, after this dream, I'm sure Freud was right. A lovely lady to share some tea and cookies with me is exactly what I need right now.

KELLY: Well, here I am.

Question 1: What was Brian doing when Kelly arrived?
Question 2: Why is Brian so tired?
Question 3: What did the girl in the dream do?
Question 4: Why was Brian surprised and a little anxious about the cookies?
Question 5: What does Brian think he needs right now?

CHAPTER Seven

Working

DOWNLINK DISCUSSION

Japanese and American Business Management

TECHNICIAN:	Phil, you're on in 10 seconds.
PHIL:	Okay, thanks. Are we ready, everybody? Here we go.
TECHNICIAN:	Five, four, three, two, one. You're on the air.
PHIL:	Good evening. I'm Philip Grant and I will be your moderator for tonight's Downlink Discussion. As usual we have a live audience here in our broadcast studio and I'm very proud to announce that we have a record-breaking 2,072 Downlink sites that are watching us via satellite and will be able to interact with tonight's speakers.
AUDIENCE:	(applauds)
PHIL:	Yes, it's really great, isn't it? Well—tonight's discussion is "Japanese and American Business Management." And we are fortunate to have with us here two very knowledgeable people on this topic—Laura Gordon and Brian Mani. Laura and Brian are independent management consultants and have worked for over fifteen years with corporations in Japan and America.
	First, Ms. Gordon and Mr. Mani will give us some background information and then we will open up the discussion to participants from our studio audience and all of the Downlink sites. So, without further delay—Laura Gordon and Brian Mani.
LAURA:	Good evening. Let me begin by saying a few familiar, well-loved words: Nikon, Honda, Mitsubishi, Sony, Nagoya, Matsushita. . . .
AUDIENCE:	(laughs)
LAURA:	Yes, we laugh because a few years ago these names would have sounded remote and exotic. But today they are household words to Americans. They demonstrate the success of Japanese goods in the American marketplace.
	From cars to cameras, from videorecorders to violins, from stereos to steel, we are surrounding ourselves with more and more products "Made in Japan." We choose them because they are easy to get, they are well made, and what's more, they are not too expensive. As a consequence, the increased demand for Japanese goods has cut deeply into the sales of American companies, and American industries are losing a great deal of business.
	In response to this situation, some leaders in business, labor, and government have called for protective taxes and import quotas to help the American industries by keeping Japanese products out of the United States. Other leaders, however, have suggested a different approach. They say that instead of keeping the Japanese out, we should learn from them. Furthermore, they say, we should learn from this economic challenge by studying and using Japanese methods for producing better goods at lower cost.
	What are these methods? What are the differences between Japanese business management techniques and our own? Before I answer these questions, let me ask you a few. Take a look at the blue handout in your study packet. It says Audience Survey at the top. And the title is "How Would *You* Run a Doorbell Company?"

Tapescript

Okay. Everybody got it? Good. Look at the handout. As you read through it, imagine that you are the personnel manager of a large corporation that is setting up a new electronic doorbell assembly factory. For each item, decide which of the choices, *a* or *b*, you would use to increase productivity at your company. On your handout, mark *a* or *b,* depending on which choice you think is better.

We'll give you a few minutes to complete this, and then Brian will go over the handout with you.

Note: Stop the tape while students complete the survey.

BRIAN: Okay. It looks like everybody is just about finished here in the studio. How's everybody doing at the Downlink sites, Phil?

PHIL: Fine, Brian. The studio engineer is telling me that every site is indicating that they're ready to continue.

BRIAN: Great. So, if you haven't figured it out already, let me explain what we've got here.

The *a*'s and *b*'s describe the two systems of management, Japanese and American. All the *a*'s describe one system, and all the *b*'s describe the other system. Which is which? Do you know? If you think that the *a*'s describe the American system of management, you are right. If you chose mostly *a*'s you were choosing the American management system. And, of course, if you chose mostly *b*'s, you were choosing the Japanese management system.

Let's look at the *a*'s first, the statements that describe typical American management. As the American manager, you try to encourage and reward individual initiative. Therefore, you separate the people who are moving up in a company from those left behind. Not only that, but you keep a clear division between management and labor.

On the other hand, as the typical Japanese manager illustrated in the *b* statements, what you try to do is encourage the group to work together. You reward the group for working together. You don't focus on individual initiative. So, what you believe is that long-term security for everyone in the company is important. In addition, you feel that it is imperative to keep the organization as stable as possible. Therefore, you don't try to make rapid changes. Furthermore, you believe it is unnecessary to keep a clear division between management and labor. In fact, you work to promote a stronger identification between management and labor.

Now just why is it that the Japanese and American business management styles are so different? Over the last twenty years or so many researchers and management specialists have studied the contrasting styles of Japanese and American managers. What they have found is that the different styles of management reflect a contrast between the traditions and national character of the two countries. While the Americans have treasured the values of individualism, self-reliance, and freedom from rules, the Japanese have preferred group identity and interdependence of the workers themselves as well as the interdependence of workers and management and a complex system of rules.

The researchers believe that the contrast has its roots in the geography, history, and the traditions of the two countries. Japan, as you know, is small, isolated, and poor in natural resources. As a result, it is necessary for Japan to pool the available wealth and labor in a cooperative effort to succeed economically. The United States, in contrast, is large and has been a nation of open frontiers—with many areas that are still unpopulated. In the past, the United States had unlimited natural resources and populations that moved from place to place, not to mention the fact that the people in the United States seem to love unconventionality. They like breaking rules. They also love competition.

So researchers are now noting that the American tradition may not be as well suited to modern industrial production as the Japanese system. Modern industrial production demands cooperation and supportive behavior among workers and between workers and management, rather than competition within the company itself. Did you know that the very word *corporation* stems from the root meaning "a single body"? Both scholars and businesspeople have come to the conclusion that a shift in the direction of the Japanese cooperative system is just what American industry needs to improve its performance.

Laura, why don't we change things a little bit here and have you talk about Ouchi's work now rather than later? What do you think?

LAURA: Yes, great idea. I was just thinking the same thing. It makes more sense to do it now, I think.

Okay, now, as Brian mentioned, one scholar who has done much to teach the principles of Japanese business management to American managers is Professor William Ouchi. He asserts, in his widely read book, *Theory Z: How American Business Can Meet the Japanese Challenge,* that if U.S. managers take steps to strengthen the bond between workers and their firms, U.S. productivity will increase dramatically and eventually surpass the Japanese. Among the steps that he mentions are: lifetime employment contracts, promotions in small but regular steps, nonspecialization of executives, and consensus decision-making at all levels—that is, with input from all employees. Although these measures suggest a certain slowing down of the highly valued corporate processes of innovation and advancement as well as decision-making, Ouchi claims that in the long run such reforms will lead to higher levels of agreement, morale, corporate strength, *and* profits.

PHIL: Excuse me, Laura. I've heard that a great many American companies have already adopted the Japanese corporate model. Could you name a few of the well-known ones for our audience, please?

LAURA: Of course. There's IBM, Intel, Proctor and Gamble, Hewlett-Packard, the Cadillac and Saturn divisions of General Motors, to name a few. Oh, and lots of power companies such as Wisconsin Power and Light and Florida Power and Light. For some reason the basic principles of the Japanese management style work particularly well at power companies.

These firms have divided employees into project teams that govern their own jobs and they have reduced firing during economic slumps by cutting back everyone's working hours and not laying off anyone. I might add, too, that they have allowed workers themselves to manage quality control procedures. These changes have produced encouraging results. There has been a decrease in worker discontent and in labor-management disputes along with gains in workmanship and productivity. If this trend continues, it may turn out that Japan's most valuable export to the United States is a philosophy of business organization that will make citizens prefer their own cars, cameras, and TV's to those produced elsewhere.

PHIL: But didn't some of the Japanese management practices originate in America?

LAURA: Yes, in a way. W. Edwards Deming, an American, brought many innovative management concepts to Japan after World War II. The Japanese quickly put them to use, but American companies just weren't ready until recently.

PHIL: Laura—Brian—I think this would be a good place to take a short break. Okay?

LAURA AND BRIAN: Sure. That's fine.

PHIL: Okay. We'll take a fifteen-minute break, audience. And when we come back we'll open up the discussion to everyone in the audience here and at the Downlink sites. And thanks so much to Laura Gordon and Brian Mani for doing the background presentation tonight.

AUDIENCE: (applauds)

SKILL B *Persuading and Giving In*

Conversations

Step 1 Listen to the conversation which involves persuading and giving in. Then answer the questions you hear following the conversation.

EXECUTIVE: Our company is one of the most successful of its kind in Japan. We are sure to be successful here as well.

CITY OFFICIAL: That will be good for your company, but exactly how will it help our town?

EXECUTIVE: Well, first of all, we will hire only local people to work in the factory.

CITY OFFICIAL: Does that include all the employees? Even those in management positions?

EXECUTIVE: Yes, for the most part. We will, of course, have some of our personnel from Japan in management positions to get things started and to teach our management system.

CITY OFFICIAL: That sounds good. Now what about your waste products? What will you do about them? We don't want any industrial waste problems here!

EXECUTIVE: There really isn't any waste to speak of. Not only that, the industry is very quiet as well. So you will have no noise pollution from us.

CITY OFFICIAL: I'm sold. It sounds like an ideal situation. How about you, Mayor? What do you think?

MAYOR: Well, I'd like to know more about your management system. I'm not so sure the people in our town will be happy with that system, not to mention the fact that I have my doubts about how well your product will sell over here.

EXECUTIVE: You may have a point there. But our company is willing to take that chance. What's more, if the management system does prove to be unsatisfactory, we're willing to modify it as necessary to keep the employees satisfied and to keep our production rate up. And I might add that our company is willing to pay top dollar to the city for the use of that land by the railroad tracks where we want to build our factory.

MAYOR: I see. In that case, you've talked me into it!

Question 1: Where is the company executive from?
Question 2: What does he want to do?
Question 3: Who is he trying to persuade?
Question 4: Who will work for the company?
Question 5: Who will manage the company?

Question 6: What does the company executive say about pollution problems?
Question 7: What is the mayor concerned about?

Question 8: What enticing offer does the executive make?

Question 9: Is the mayor persuaded?

Step 2   Listen to the conversation a second time and write down all the expressions you hear for persuading and giving in. When you are finished, compare your answers in small groups.

Focus on Testing

You will hear a short segment from a radio interview. After the interview, you will be asked some questions. After you hear a question, read the four possible answers and decide which one is the best answer. Circle the letter of the best answer.

Interview

HOST: Good evening, listeners, I'm Frank Taylor, your host for "Business Day," the program that knows America's business and keeps you informed. Our guest today is June Randolph from the University School of Business. June is an expert on the work of W. Edwards Deming, and she has agreed to explain Deming's seven-step quality improvement process.

June, thank you so much for joining us today.

GUEST: My pleasure, Frank.

HOST: First, I'd like to ask a simple, but very basic question. Is the seven-step quality improvement process useful for all businesses or only very large corporations?

GUEST: Oh, it's definitely useful for all businesses—of all types and all sizes. In fact, it's useful for any organization or group that needs to get a job done well or to provide a service. I've even found it useful at home with my family.

HOST: Really? In what way?

GUEST: Well, the seven-step process helps us to look at a problem or project in a very systematic way. We analyze the issue, take steps to deal with it, or improve the situation, and then check our results. If we like the results we can then take steps to make sure we keep improving in the future.

HOST: Can you give us an example of what you mean?

GUEST: Sure. At our house, we had a problem with training our dog, Gracie, to stay out of the garbage. Now the first step in the improvement process is to understand the reasons for improvement. In this case, with our dog, they were pretty obvious: (1) She was making a big mess in the kitchen every day that none of us enjoyed cleaning up, and (2) she was eating things that were not good for her.

HOST: And the second step is to collect data on the current situation, right?

GUEST: Right. So we counted exactly how many times in a month Gracie got into the garbage. We even tried to note the exact times of the day, but sometimes this was difficult because she tended to do this only when no one was home.

HOST: Of course!

GUEST: The third step is to analyze the data. We found out that she only did it about three days a week. That was really a surprise to us. It had seemed as if she was doing it all the time, but it turned out that she was doing it only when we ate meat.

The fourth step is to plan and implement a solution to the problem. With our dog, that was easy. Every time we ate meat, we gave her a little of it in her bowl and also took out the garbage right away after dinner, so we didn't tempt her too much.

HOST: And how were your results? The fifth step is to check your results, right?

GUEST: Right. The results were great. And then the sixth step is standardization. This means that you take steps to make sure your results continue into the future. So all of us in the family agreed to take turns taking out the garbage on time! And to take turns giving Gracie some meat in her bowl if she left the garbage alone. The seventh step, of course, is to make plans for the future, for further improvement.

HOST: Well, this is very interesting. It sounds like you got great results, but I wonder whose behavior actually improved as a result of using the seven-step process—the dog's or your family's?!

Question 1: What groups can profit from the seven-step quality improvement process?
Question 2: Who got into the garbage?
Question 3: What did steps two and three of the seven-step process reveal?
Question 4: What is the fourth step in the quality improvement process?
Question 5: What was part of the solution the Randolph family found for their problem?
Question 6: What did the family members agree to take turns doing?

CHAPTER eight

Breakthroughs

LECTURE *Discovering the Laws of Nature*

STUDENT 1: Boy! I don't usually have trouble in science class, but I'm having a really hard time understanding this stuff. How about you?

STUDENT 2: Yeah! Me, too. Say, let's get together at my place and compare notes later, okay?

STUDENT 3: Hey! Did I hear you guys say something about comparing notes later? Count me in! This class is impossible. I just don't get this stuff.

STUDENT 1: Yeah, I know. But I think the three of us together can probably figure it out.

STUDENT 2: Right. Come over about 6:00. I'll order a pizza.

STUDENTS 1 & 3: Great! You're on!

STUDENT 2: Shhhh. Here he comes.

PROFESSOR: Good morning. We're going to do a little history of physics today. I know you're taking this course to learn more about Einstein's unified field theory, but I thought it would be a good idea to put his search for a unified field into a historical perspective.

You know, physics has not always been considered to be a separate science. In fact, long ago the study of physics was combined with an exploration of religious and metaphysical ideas about the nature of the cosmos. So is our current view of the science of physics the one true and final view? Or is it like other views of the past—a series of temporary beliefs about nature that may be overturned at some future time?

If we look at history, we find many examples of common beliefs about nature that turned out to be false or that seem foolish today. For instance, for many centuries millions of people believed that the earth was the center of the universe. Others believed that lead could be turned into gold . . . or that doctors could cure sick people by bleeding them.

Now, in the field of physics, it wasn't until the seventeenth century that someone "discovered" the law of gravity. Of course, this doesn't mean that people in the past who didn't understand about the laws of gravity were completely wrong about their world. They were just organizing their view of the world according to a different set of principles. Physics is, in some sense, the attempt to describe an infinite number of events in nature in terms of general principles or models, sometimes called paradigms.

These principles of physics, however they have been expressed at various times in the past, reveal the harmony of the physical world and the intelligence that seems to operate within it. The Greeks called this intelligence *logos,* meaning the invisible cosmic power that shaped the world and set in motion all the laws and forces of nature. Paradigms of past ages should be regarded as contributions to the sum total of human knowledge, rather than merely as mistakes or superstitions.

The first great age of physics began with the ancient Greeks. They developed many theories about the beginnings of the universe. These theories were based on the interactions of the four basic elements of nature: earth, air, fire, and water. The Greek philosopher Plato caused a revolution in physics by showing the connection between nature and humanity. He claimed that physics and philosophy were one science because knowledge of one led to knowledge of the other. He also did not regard the earth as the center of everything. In contrast, another Greek, named Aristotle, also saw the universe as a highly ordered, tightly governed system but with the earth at the center and the sun and the planets traveling around it in neverending circles. Ptolemy, an Egyptian astrologer, confirmed this view.

As ridiculous as it might seem to us now, this view was the accepted one for the next 1800 years, until the work of Sir Isaac Newton. But even before Newton's time there were serious doubts about Aristotle's paradigm. For example, Copernicus, Kepler, and Galileo all had attempted to prove that the sun and not the earth was the center of the solar system.

However, it was Newton who finally demonstrated that the sun is the center of our solar system by using mathematics. He also showed that mathematics was the key to understanding the unity of nature. He showed that the stars in the distant skies as well as the earth under our feet obey the same mathematical laws. What's more, for Newton the mathematical principles of gravitation were *the* logos, *the* law, *the* paradigm that explained all events in the physical world. Gravitation was *the* unifying principle—or unified field theory—of its time, the principle that provided the model for all other forms of knowledge.

Are you surprised? That's nothing. Listen to this. . . . While Aristotle's paradigm lasted 1800 years, Newton's lasted only about 200 years before it began to look a little shaky and was seriously questioned. The problem with Newton's theories was not that they were wrong, but that they just didn't cover everything. When scientists began to look at atomic and subatomic particles, they found that Newton's mathematical equations simply did not explain what they were observing. So again there was a need for someone to fit the new observations and knowledge in with the old—to reformulate this knowledge into a single set of laws—to come up with another unifying theory to explain how the objective world works.

The person who came along to do just this was Albert Einstein. In the early twentieth century, Einstein gave us a new way of describing natural events. He gave us a new way of perceiving the world. His Special Theory of Relativity proposed that time and space were not constant and separate. He said that time and space were not discrete principles of nature. Rather, they were relative to each other and even interchangeable. The unifying principle that Einstein proposed was light. Light—whose speed remains constant—remains the same no matter where it travels.

Einstein went on to develop a General Theory of Relativity that joined elements of gravity, space/time, and matter into a cohesive or unified system. This theory was later used as a basis for theories of the origin of the universe. But Einstein was not content with this. He did not believe that his theories explained the events in the world of subatomic particles, such as electrons. You see, an observer cannot say that an electron is in a certain place at a certain time, traveling at a certain speed. An observer can say only that there is a *probability* of finding an electron in such and such a place at such and such a time when it is traveling at such and such a speed.

Einstein was puzzled by this problem most of his adult life. He tried and tried to find a unified field theory that could explain all electric, magnetic, optical, and gravitational events and locate them in space and time. He died, as we know, without succeeding. Nevertheless, he tried until the end of his life to prove his belief that "God does not play dice with the universe"—that everything is not just left to chance.

So how long will Einstein's paradigm last? You think it will last a long time, don't you? It certainly does explain some aspects of our world very well. Ah, yes, but so does the mathematics of Newton.

So where do we stand now in terms of a unified field theory? Is it a myth—or perhaps a religious notion—that we inherited from our ancestors? Or is all of nature truly unified in ways we can't see yet, but may one day discover. Is the unified field theory within reach, or is the search for it just a wild-goose chase? Neils Bohr, one of the fathers of quantum theory, has suggested that we simply may not be looking in the right places. He believes that we have reached the limits of mathematical models to describe events in nature. Perhaps now we must use symbols and metaphors from other areas of human interest to explain the world. Yes, you guessed it. Back to where we started: combining physics, the study of nature, with religion and myth. In fact, several physicists have written books showing the similarities between certain ideas from the field of *meta*physics and the current theories in the field of physics.

Well, I think this is a good spot to break. Next time we'll continue our look at the search for a unified field theory. So be sure to review the chapters on Einstein's Special and General Theories of Relativity and begin the next chapter on quantum mechanics.

SKILL B   *Giving and Receiving Compliments*

Conversations

You will hear four conversations; the first two involve an instructor and some students, and the last two include several senior citizens. These conversations contain examples of both appropriate and inappropriate ways of giving compliments. After listening to each conversation, answer the questions you hear in the spaces provided. When you are finished, compare your answers in small groups.

CONVERSATION 1

Ron and Mr. McGovern are in the hall after class.

    RON: Mr. McGovern, you are such a very good teacher. I like your class so much. I'm learning so much. I like you so-o-o much.

MR. MCGOVERN: Oh, uh . . . thank you, Ron. Well, I'm on my way to an appointment right now. I'll talk to you later.

Question 1: Ron's compliments to Mr. McGovern are inappropriate. What's wrong with Ron's timing?
Question 2: What's wrong with the number of compliments?
Question 3: What's wrong with the phrasing?

CONVERSATION 2

Sandra and Mr. McGovern are in his office, during office hours.

    SANDRA: Oh, Mr. McGovern, that was a great class. I never understood the second law of thermodynamics before, and now I feel like I could explain it to anyone else who doesn't understand it.

MR. MCGOVERN: Thank you, Sandra. I appreciate your saying that.

Are Sandra's compliments to Mr. McGovern appropriate?
Why or why not?

CONVERSATION 3

Helen, Larry, and Martin are chatting at a retirement home.

MARTIN: Larry! Helen! Hello! Who's winning?
HELEN: Oh, hello, Martin.
LARRY: Hi, Martin. Not me! I can never seem to beat Helen at checkers. Just between you and me, she's definitely the checkers champion around here.
HELEN: Oh, I wouldn't say that. I just win a few games now and then.
MARTIN: Oh, no, Helen, Larry's right. You're definitely the best player here.
HELEN: Well, thank you both very much.
LARRY: Hey, Martin, you were looking pretty good last night at the party. I couldn't believe how well you danced! I didn't know you knew how to do all that.
MARTIN: I don't! It was my first time—my daughter pulled me out onto the dance floor and I had to do it. But I wasn't really any good. In fact, I was terrible. You know that law of nature that says, "You just can't teach an old dog new tricks"!
HELEN: Come on, Marty. That's not a law of nature! This is the generation dedicated to the principle of lifelong learning! And I don't mind telling you that you looked just fine out on the dance floor. And what's more, your daughter looked simply beautiful!
MARTIN: Well, thanks. Coming from you, that means a lot. You're quite a dancer yourself.
HELEN: Oh, I can't take all the credit. My partner helped some.
LARRY: Oh, no—I hardly did anything. Helen really is a wonderful dancer. She's so graceful and light on her feet. She should give lessons. Better yet, she should go on stage in New York or be in the movies. She's as good as any of the dancers you see there.
HELEN: Now Larry, flattery will get you nowhere today. You're losing this game of checkers, and I'm not going to let you win no matter how many compliments you give me.
MARTIN: That's telling him, Helen!

Question 1: How does Larry first compliment Helen?
Question 2: What is Helen's response?
Question 3: Why do you think she says this?
Question 4: How does Martin compliment Helen?
Question 5: How does Helen respond this time?
Question 6: What do Helen and Larry tell Martin about his dancing?
Question 7: Who looked beautiful on the dance floor?
Question 8: How does Martin feel about the compliments from Helen?

CONVERSATION 4

Later in the day at the retirement home Helen, Larry, and Martin continue chatting.

LARRY: Martin, what's wrong? You look a bit worried.
MARTIN: Well, I'm not worried exactly, but I am confused and feeling very old. I wish I had Helen's attitude about the principle of lifelong learning. You always seem so in touch with current ideas, Helen.
HELEN: I appreciate your saying that, but what brought all this on?

MARTIN: Well, I was trying to help my grandson with his physics homework, and I'm afraid I wasn't much help at all. I don't really understand some of the new theories.

LARRY: Well, if you ask me, Martin, you were wonderful to even try to help him. A lot of grandfathers wouldn't take the time.

MARTIN: Thanks, I needed that. But I still wish I knew more about what's happening in the field of physics these days.

LARRY: Why is that so important to you?

MARTIN: It seems to me that young people today have a different view of the world than we did when we were young, and I'd like to understand it.

HELEN: Well, that's admirable, Martin. Sounds to me like you *are* interested in lifelong learning after all. In fact, I've been meaning to tell you that you're one of the brightest, most stimulating, most adventuresome and forward-thinking men I know.

MARTIN: Why, thanks, Helen! That kind of flattery will get you everywhere!

Question 1: What's wrong with Martin?
Question 2: Is the compliment Martin gives Helen appropriate?
Question 3: How does Helen accept this compliment?
Question 4: How does Larry try to cheer Martin up?
Question 5: What does Helen say to encourage Martin?
Question 6: Does it work?
Question 7: How does Martin respond?
Question 8: What does he mean by this?

Focus on Testing

You will hear a short presentation. After the presentation, you will be asked some questions. After you hear a question, read the four possible answers and decide which one is the best answer. Circle the letter of the best answer.

Presentation

The German-American physicist Albert Einstein, was born on March 14, 1879 and died on April 18, 1955. He contributed more than any other scientist to the breakthroughs in our perception of physical reality. No other scientist has received so much public attention for his or her work.

Einstein was not always so successful, however. He lived in Munich until he was about 15 years old. At that time, the family business failed and he and his family moved to Milan, Italy. After a year, Einstein still had not completed secondary school, and he failed an examination that would have allowed him to study to become an electrical engineer at the Swiss Federal Institute of Technology. In 1896, at the age of 17, Einstein returned to Switzerland to attend the Zurich Polytechnic. He graduated in 1900 as a secondary school teacher of mathematics and physics.

After two difficult years on a teacher's salary, he obtained a position at the Swiss patent office in Bern. The patent-office work required Einstein's careful attention, but during the two years he was employed there, he also completed an astounding amount of work in theoretical physics. For the most part, these papers were written in his spare time and without the benefit of books to read or colleagues to talk to.

Einstein submitted one of his scientific papers to the University of Zurich to obtain a Ph.D. degree in 1905. In 1908 he sent a second paper to the University of Bern and was offered a position as a lecturer there. The next year Einstein received a regular appointment as associate professor of physics at the University of Zurich.

By 1909, Einstein was recognized throughout German-speaking Europe as a leading scientific thinker. He worked for a brief time as a professor at the German University of Prague and at Zurich Polytechnic. In 1914, at the age of 35, he advanced to the most prestigious and best-paying post that a theoretical physicist could hold in central Europe: professor at the Kaiser-Wilhelm Gesellschaft in Berlin. Einstein remained on the staff in Berlin until 1933. At that time he came to the United States and held a research position at the Institute for Advanced Study in Princeton, N.J., until his death in 1955.

Question 1: When did Einstein die?
Question 2: Why did Einstein's family move to Milan?
Question 3: What was Einstein's first job?
Question 4: What did Einstein do in his spare time when he worked at the patent office?
Question 5: Which institution gave Einstein his Ph.D. degree?
Question 6: Where did Einstein die?

CHAPTER nine

Art and Entertainment

The Rise of Rock 'n' Roll

ANNOUNCER: "Music in America." This series is a production of Wisconsin Radio. Program 6: "The Rise of Rock 'n' Roll."

LECTURER: So far in this series on "Music in America," we've talked about music and its importance to all people. Musicologists agree that music is a universal phenomenon.

Stop tape: Example A

LECTURER: Music may be a universal phenomenon and every society may have music, but it is very different from culture to culture. Music reflects the social order. I think musicians and their audiences use music to reaffirm their feelings about themselves and their society. So it seems to me the music of a particular culture reflects that culture's values. Therefore, I also think that music has the most meaning for the people from the culture in which it was created.

Stop tape: Example B

LECTURER: Now, from that perspective, let's look at the rise of rock 'n' roll in America. The term *rock 'n' roll* comes from Alan Freed, who was a popular disc jockey in the 1950s. He got the phrase from a line in an old blues song that goes, "My baby rocks me with a steady roll."

Stop tape: Item 1

LECTURER: This reflects an important element in rock 'n' roll—its origins in the blues. As you know, the blues are part of the black musical tradition in America. But I think that the actual beginning of rock 'n' roll music occurred on April 12, 1954, in New York City when Bill Haley and the Comets recorded "Rock Around the Clock." Let's hear a few bars of this famous song. Notice the blues harmonies as we listen.

ROCK AROUND THE CLOCK

One, two, three o'clock, four o'clock, rock—
Five, six, seven o'clock, eight o'clock, rock—
Nine, ten, eleven o'clock, twelve o'clock, rock—
We're gonna rock around the clock tonight.
Put your glad rags on and join me hon',
We'll have some fun when the clock strikes one.
We're gonna rock around the clock tonight.
We're gonna rock, rock, rock 'til broad daylight.
We're gonna rock, gonna rock around the clock tonight.

Stop tape: Item 2

LECTURER: What you just heard is an example of how the blues harmonies of black music mixed with the hillbilly sounds of white music to become the earliest form of rock 'n' roll. This early form of rock 'n' roll was called rockabilly at first. But this name didn't stick, even though there were a few rock 'n' roll groups in the '80s that nostalgically called their music rockabilly. You can easily pick out the blues harmonies and hillbilly sounds in Elvis Presley's music. Let's listen to a few bars of his hit from the 1950s "Heartbreak Hotel."

HEARTBREAK HOTEL

Since my baby left me found a new place to dwell
Down at the end of Lonely Street at Heartbreak Hotel.
I get so lonely baby.
I get so lonely.
I get so lonely I could die.

Stop tape: Item 3

LECTURER: Another famous artist of the '50s was Paul Anka, who was raised in Ottawa, Canada. When he was fourteen, he was already writing and performing hit songs. His song, "Diana," is the sad story of a young boy in love with an older girl. This generation, the '50s generation, was probably eager to grow up, and the song, "Diana," spoke about these feelings. Only a few instruments and voices were used. Let's listen. See if you can pick out the instruments.

DIANA

I'm so young and you're so old;
This, my darling, I've been told.
I don't care just what they say
'Cause forever I will pray
You and I will be as free
As the birds up in the trees.
Oh, please, stay by me, Diana.

LECTURER: Rock 'n' roll music of the '50s was, for the most part, youth music, music of young people. And not all people enjoyed it—not even those people with youthful spirits. Pablo Casals, the famous classical cellist, said that rock 'n' roll is "poison put to sound." Mitch Miller, the famous bandleader, said, "The reason kids like rock 'n' roll is because their parents don't." Most likely teenagers in every society have rebelled against or resisted their parents in some way. In the '50s in the United States, rock 'n' roll was a focus for this adolescent rebellion.

LECTURER: The songs of the '50s, however, did not speak out strongly against the values of the adults in the society. But the songs of the '60s certainly did. Teenagers who listened to rockabilly in the '50s became college students in the '60s. In the '60s, there was a mood of confusion and instability. The Vietnam War was beginning; the civil rights movement in the early '60s pointed out that there were many racial injustices in America. College students looked to folk values of the past for strength and peace of mind. The music that supported these values was called folk-rock.

LECTURER: In the early '60s, the star of the folk scene was Bob Dylan. His song, "The Times They Are a'Changing," was a protest against tradition and indifference. In the song "Blowin' in the Wind" he asked that people stop being indifferent, that they become involved with important issues in the world. Listen to the folk-rock sound of this song.

BLOWIN' IN THE WIND

[Consult a record album for the lyrics when you have time.]

Many people thought that Bob Dylan was more of a poet than a songwriter. A lot of his poetry dealt with the dishonesty of people in authority, and frequently his songs became songs of protest.

LECTURER: In the middle '60s, with Dylan's music, protest-rock was born. Dylan generally provided his own accompaniment at folk-rock concerts using only acoustic guitar and mouth organ, a simplicity of style that was connected to a return to simple, basic folk values. At the Newport Folk Festival in 1965, he appeared on-stage with an electric guitar and was booed off the stage. Although his concert audiences obviously didn't care for the electronic sound, record buyers apparently did, and protest-rock became a major movement of the electronic age.

Some other participants in this movement were P. F. Sloan, who wrote "Eve of Destruction," about the fear of nuclear war, and Tom Paxton and Phil Ochs, whose songs protested segregation, the Vietnam War, and racism, as well as the evils of atomic warfare.

Stop tape: Item 8

LECTURER: Right along with folk-rock and protest-rock came the British sound. In 1960, a group called The Silver Beatles was playing in the Indra Club in Hamburg, Germany. They had made a record that showed the influence of Elvis Presley and the rockabilly of the '50s on their music. After several name changes and a change of drummers, they became the Beatles.

By 1963, the Beatles had a gold record, "She Loves You," and in 1964 they had four singles on the best-seller charts. Then they came to America. When they appeared on the Ed Sullivan show, three out of every four TV sets in New York were tuned in to watch them. Because of the way they looked, wearing stiff white collars under collarless jackets—almost like choirboy outfits—and having well-groomed if somewhat long hair, they appeared respectable to adults. This was a far cry from the black leather jackets and greasy hair of the '50s rock 'n' rollers, and it seemed to parents even further from the bare feet, stringy hair, and vacant eyes they associated with folk and protest-rock.

Stop tape: Item 9

LECTURER: The Beatles also had a good sense of humor. When they played for the Queen Mother and Princess Margaret in 1963 at a royal command performance, John said, "The people in the cheap seats can clap. The rest of you just rattle your jewelry." Unlike Dylan, the Beatles did not start out writing protest songs per se, but wrote humorous put-downs of values and conditions, not just of people in power. Take "A Hard Day's Night," for example. It's not anti-authority. Here's a bit of this song.

A HARD DAY'S NIGHT

Consult a record album for the lyrics when you have time.

Stop tape: Item 10

LECTURER: Well, that's all I remember. Anyway, in 1966, their music got mixed reviews. The American composer Aaron Copland said that their music had an unanalyzable charm, while Richard Rodgers, who wrote Broadway musicals, said it was monotonous and boring. Some music critics said it wouldn't last. By 1967, it was clear that it would. Richard Goldstein, the Rock critic, said the Beatles were creating the most original, expressive, and musically interesting sounds in popular music. A good example of their original sound is "Sgt. Pepper's Lonely Heart's Club Band." Probably most of you have heard this one.

A major British invasion came with the Beatles. For example, there were the Rolling Stones, who were outrageous compared to the Beatles. Their statements were not gentle or humorous, and they challenged social rules with the suggestive words in their songs. "Satisfaction" and "Let's Spend the Night Together," now famous worldwide, are good examples. When they were on the Ed Sullivan show, the words *the night* were changed to *some time* because of censorship regulations.

Stop tape: Item 11

LECTURER: Although the British did bring their own unique sounds, the blues, as I said before, is a major factor in all rock 'n' roll music. Eric Clapton, the famous British guitarist, said, "Rock is like a battery that must always go back to the blues to get recharged." An interesting combination of blues melody and soft-rock can be heard in Procol Harum's "A Whiter Shade of Pale." This is an interesting piece for another reason as well. Do you hear a familiar melody in the background?

WHITER SHADE OF PALE

One of sixteen vestal virgins
Who were leaving for the coast,
And although my eyes were open
They might just as well been closed.
And so it was that later
As the miller told his tale
That her face (at first) turned ghostly
Turned a whiter shade of pale.

LECTURER: Soul music also emerged in the '60s. Soul music emerged with the civil rights movement as an expression of Black pride. African-Americans were now a people who no longer would accept second-class citizenship. They were proud of their identity and proud of their music. And the rest of the country loved it, too. The most important soul music comes out of Motown—Motortown—the city of Detroit. Rather than trying to explain the essence of soul music, let's listen to "Natural Woman," a song made famous by Aretha Franklin, soul singer extraordinaire.

NATURAL WOMAN

When my soul was in the lost and found
You came along to claim it.
I didn't know just what was wrong with it [me]
'Til your kiss helped me name it.

Now I'm no longer doubtful
Of what I'm aiming [living] for,
And if I make you happy
I don't need to do more
'Cause you make me feel
You make me feel
You make me feel like a natural woman.
Oh, baby, what you done to me
You make me feel so good inside
And I just want to be
Close to you—you make me feel so alive
You make me feel
You make me feel
You make me feel like a natural woman.

Stop tape: Item 12

LECTURER: Today's popular music has come a long way from the rock 'n' roll of the '60s. On our next program we'll finish talking about the '60s and continue with "The Rise of Rock 'n' Roll" through the present day. Yes, rock 'n' roll is definitely here to stay.

SKILL **B** *Expressing Doubt or Disbelief*

Conversations

You will hear four conversations in which people's responses range from very formal to very informal. After listening to each one, answer the questions you hear in the spaces provided. When you are finished, compare your answers in small groups.

CONVERSATION 1

Carl discusses a project with Professor Johnson.

CARL: Professor Johnson, I'd like to talk to you about my art project for my senior thesis.
PROFESSOR JOHNSON: No time like the present, Carl. Have a seat. What would you like to do?
CARL: Are you sure it's okay? I know how busy you are.
PROFESSOR JOHNSON: It's fine.
CARL: Well, I'd like to do something really imaginative and creative, something like my friend Howard did for his Master's thesis.
PROFESSOR JOHNSON: What was that?
CARL: He filled the administration building entrance hall with white paper cups and that was his project.
PROFESSOR JOHNSON: And he got his Master's for that?
CARL: Yes, he did.
PROFESSOR JOHNSON: I find that hard to believe. You'll have to think of something else, Carl— another type of project.

Question 1: What expression does Carl use to express doubt?

Question 2: Why do you think he uses that expression?

Question 3: Professor Johnson expresses disbelief twice in this conversation. Is he polite to Carl?

Question 4: The first time he expresses disbelief through intonation alone. What words does he use?

Question 5: What expression does he use the second time?

CONVERSATION 2

Mr. Jones chats with Mr. Smith about his son's band.

MR. JONES: My twelve-year-old son is in a rock band, and the band is going to make $30 million in the next three months.

MR. SMITH: Get outta here. The Rolling Stones only make $58 million in a whole year!

MR. JONES: Yes, they really will. And the most amazing thing is that they have a twelve-year-old manager. She does all the negotiating for the concerts.

MR. SMITH: Oh, sure!

MR. JONES: Yes—and she's really first-rate. These twelve-year-olds are booked for concerts in New York, Chicago, Denver, Los Angeles, Atlanta, Detroit, and Philadelphia in the next four weeks alone.

MR. SMITH: Yeah, right   and I'm Mick Jagger.

Question 1: Is this conversation formal or informal?

Question 2: When the second speaker says "Get outta here," does he sound amused or angry?

Question 3: How does the second speaker sound when he says, "Oh, sure!"?

Question 4: When the second speaker says "Yeah, right—and I'm Mick Jagger," does he sound rude?

Question 5: Why do you think the second speaker expresses disbelief this way?

CONVERSATION 3

Jenny and Al talk about dancing.

JENNY: I'd really love to be a prima ballerina.

AL: Well then, you'll have to do more than take lessons once a week. Nureyev danced until his feet bled, and he kept on dancing.

JENNY: I find that hard to believe. How do you know that?

AL: I saw it in a movie. He was so dedicated you wouldn't believe it! With bleeding feet he just danced and danced and danced some more. I saw it all in the movie.

JENNY: Could he really do that?

AL: Yes, it was the most incredible thing I've ever seen.

Question 1: Are Jenny's expressions of disbelief formal or informal?

Question 2: Is she polite or rude?

Question 3: What are some expressions Jenny uses?

CONVERSATION 4

Rachael attends Professor Starr's music appreciation class.

PROFESSOR STARR: Today I'm going to talk about Mozart, the musical genius who performed concerts on the pianoforte for the royalty of Europe at the age of eight.

RACHEL: Oh, come on!

PROFESSOR STARR: It's true. Not only that, he was already composing music at the age of five.

RACHEL: I doubt it.

PROFESSOR STARR: Well, why don't you see me after class for my list of references if you'd like to look into the matter further. But for now we'll concentrate on a discussion of Mozart's music.

Question 1: Are Rachel's expressions of disbelief formal or informal?
Question 2: Is she polite or rude?
Question 3: Does the professor seem impatient with Rachel?
Question 4: What are some expressions Rachel uses?

Focus on Testing

You will hear a short review of a music festival. After the review, you will be asked some questions. After you hear a question, read the four possible answers and decide which one is the best answer. Circle the letter of the best answer.

Music Festival Review

Bethel, New York—August 29, 1969. The Woodstock Music and Art Fair in Bethel, New York was advertised by its youthful New York promoters as "An Aquarian Exposition" of music and peace. It was that and more—much more. The festival, quickly nicknamed "Woodstock" for short, may have turned out to be history's largest "happening." As the moment when the U.S. youth of the '60s openly displayed its strength, appeal, and power, Woodstock may rank as one of the most significant political and sociological events of the age.

By a conservative estimate, more than 400,000 people—the vast majority of them between the ages of 16 and 30—showed up for the Woodstock Festival. Thousands more would have come if police had not blocked off some of the access roads. Other roads turned into long, ribbon-like parking lots as spectators simply left their cars, rather than wait for hours in a traffic jam. If the festival had lasted much longer, as many as one million youths might have made the pilgrimage to Bethel to participate in the Woodstock Festival.

What lured our country's youth to Woodstock? An all-star cast of top rock artists, including Janis Joplin, Jimi Hendrix, and the Jefferson Airplane. But the good vibrations of good groups turned out to be the least of it. What the youth of America—and their worried elders—saw at Bethel was the potential power of an entire generation—a generation that in countless disturbing ways had rejected the traditional values and goals of the U.S. Over 400,000 young people, who had previously thought of themselves as part of an isolated minority, experienced the thrill of discovering that they were, as the saying goes, "what's happening." They were the current voice of America.

To many adults, the festival seemed like a monstrous Dionysian orgy, a wild party where a mob of crazy kids gathered to take drugs and groove and move to hours and hours of amplified noise that could hardly be called music. The significance of Woodstock, however, cannot be overestimated. Despite the piles of litter and garbage, the hopelessly inadequate sanitation, the lack of food, and the two nights of rain that turned Yasgur's farm in Bethel, New York into a sea of mud, the young people found it all "beautiful." One long-haired teen-ager summed up the significance of Woodstock quite simply: "The people," he said "are finally getting together."

Question 1: Which item describes the festival?
Question 2: What was the nickname for the festival?
Question 3: How many people went to the festival?
Question 4: How old were most of the people who came to the festival?
Question 5: Why did the young people go to the festival?
Question 6: According to the reviewer, which of the items was *not* a problem at the festival?

Ethical Questions

Organ Transplants

In this chapter you will hear about some ethical questions about organ transplants. Richard and his sister Susan are home from college for a few days. It is Sunday morning and they are sitting in the kitchen after breakfast reading the Sunday paper.

RICHARD: Hey, listen to this. Remember that kid, David, the five-year-old who was dying of an incurable liver disease? You know. His condition was irreversible and his parents were frantically searching for some sort of a solution?

SUSAN: Oh, yeah. I remember. They had been told that David's only hope was a liver transplant.

RICHARD: Right. David needed to get a healthy liver from another child who had just died and he was put on the waiting list for a compatible donor.

SUSAN: So what happened?

RICHARD: Well, the waiting list was just so long that David's parents took matters into their own hands. They made nationwide appeals on TV and radio looking for a donor. It was in the papers, too.

SUSAN: Yeah, I remember that, but were they successful?

RICHARD: Yeah, but it got pretty tense. Finally, just a few days before David was expected to die, a call came through. Another five-year-old child, two thousand miles away was hit by a car. The child was declared legally dead.

SUSAN: That means that the boy's brain is dead, but his body organs were still functioning, right?

RICHARD: Right. So anyway, this boy's parents hoped that their son's liver could help. They had heard about David's case on the news. So, within a few hours, their boy's liver was removed and flown—in a picnic cooler!—to David's doctors, who replaced David's diseased liver with the new one.

SUSAN: Gosh, that's fantastic.

RICHARD: Yup. And a week later David is playing with his toys in his hospital room, and his prognosis is very good. Pretty great, huh?

SUSAN: Yeah, pretty terrific for David. But, you know, there is a downside to this organ transplant thing.

RICHARD: Really? What's that?

SUSAN: Well, last term at school, you know, I took a medical ethics class. I thought it would be a great elective for my premed major, and it was! We talked a lot about the ethical questions involved in using organ transplants to help people who are dying of degenerative organ diseases. It's wonderful that there have been such great advances in immunosuppression and surgical techniques that people such as David can be given a second chance at life. But there *are* a few big ethical questions.

RICHARD: Like what?

SUSAN: Like who should be allowed to live.

RICHARD: Allowed?

SUSAN: Yup, allowed. The patients needing organs vastly outnumber donors— those who can give organs. It's been estimated that only 10 percent of the people who can donate organs actually do donate them, due to a variety of social, medical or legal complications. Because of this, each year, thousands of people who could be saved by a routine transplant die. And they die knowing that their lives might have been spared if only a suitable organ had been donated in time.

RICHARD: With such a small number of donated organs, I think that selecting recipients should be a question of national concern. What if there's only one organ available and many needy patients? Who should receive it? The nuclear scientist who can offer the country his future research? Or the retarded child who seems to have little to offer society? And what about the alcoholic or smoker who has voluntarily contributed to the degeneration of his or her own body? You're right. This is a big ethical question!

SUSAN: Yeah, and besides, who should make this decision and by what criteria? There was this one example the teacher gave. I'd heard it before. You probably have, too. It's the old lifeboat example. You know it?

RICHARD: I heard it once, but I've forgotten it. How does it go again?

SUSAN: Okay. Well, imagine that you are one of sixteen people in a lifeboat designed to hold only thirteen people. As the sea becomes rougher, it is clear to all of you in the boat that the boat will sink unless at least three people get out—jump overboard. Chances are that the people who go overboard will die—from drowning, shark attack, or the cold. So how would you determine who stays in the boat and who must go? Who should be given a chance to live and who must take their chances in the sea? What criteria should be used to make these decisions and who should make them? Should the person with the highest rank—such as the ship's captain—make the decision? If so, do you trust his fairness in making the decision? Should women, children, and married men always be saved first? Or perhaps the old and the sick should go overboard, because they have only a brief time left to live anyway? Maybe you think that each person should be regarded as equal to every other person? In that case, the only fair method of decision would be some sort of a lottery.

RICHARD: The lifeboat story is a good analogy, Susan. I don't know what the answer is, but I know that I wouldn't want organs just to go to the highest bidder—you know—the person with the most money.

SUSAN: You got it! The ethical dilemma is obvious. What if individuals or even companies start to make a business of buying and selling organs? Can we let private interests in this country control organ transplants? In other situations like this where the public welfare is affected so dramatically the government here has always intervened. You know, like with railroad or trucking strikes or with toxic waste disposal.

RICHARD: Uh-huh, the idea of buying and selling organs is definitely ugly. I thought that recently, laws have been proposed that would make this a crime. And that these laws would place the allocation of this precious commodity entirely in the hands of the federal government. Even in a capitalist country there is something appalling about the idea that life or death might depend only on the checkbook—only on the amount of money in your bank account. Not only that but . . .

SUSAN: Hold on a minute. Even if we decide that organs ought to be distributed fairly, with no discrimination for any reason, we still have another major problem. We still have too many needy people and not enough donors.

RICHARD: Oh yeah, right. I forgot about that for a minute. That was David's problem. I don't know how the government can help with that.

SUSAN: Well, in my class we talked about this dilemma from a number of points of view. First look at the donor side of the problem. The class came up with some interesting suggestions, I think. How about increasing the number of available organs by simplifying the donation process and the definition of brain death? Or how about writing laws that require everybody to donate organs if doctors say the brain is dead? And listen to this. This is really good. Why not establish a national organ bank and put all brain dead people in the same hospital?

RICHARD: What for?

SUSAN: Well, that way doctors in that hospital would keep their organs alive artificially until they are needed. I suppose this would be something like harvesting the dead, though.

RICHARD: Yeah, it would be like people were fruit trees grown only for the purpose of giving us their fruit. Ugh! I don't like the sound of that.

SUSAN: Yeah, I know what you mean. Our class also discussed the fact that some psychologists believe that this might present a greater psychological threat to humanity than we could justify by the number of lives saved.

RICHARD: Yeah, I agree. So much for increasing the number of donors. What about the recipients? Any good suggestions?

SUSAN: Maybe. We discussed the usefulness of the recipient to society.

RICHARD: Like the lifeboat example.

SUSAN: Exactly. Why not give those who might benefit society the most the best chance to live? The response to that argument has often been that few people, if any, have the wisdom to see what the social good is now. Nor can they see what it will be in the future. What if the convicted criminal we choose to push overboard today changes, and ten years from now helps hundreds of young people with drug problems.

RICHARD: Right. And the nuclear scientist could end up selling atomic secrets to terrorist organizations. Who can know the future for sure?

SUSAN: I don't know. But we came up with a couple of other solutions which have to do with basic health and humaneness. For instance, there could be an agreed-upon standard of health that every person is entitled to. People who are furthest from this state of health—but not yet irreversibly damaged—would be treated first. This means that the people who are the worst off would get the organs first.

RICHARD: Hey! Now you're talking. That sounds great.

SUSAN: Maybe. The problem with this position is still the shortage of organs and the large number of needy people. What if three people are in immediate danger of dying from kidney failure, but there is only one kidney? Then this solution doesn't help.

RICHARD: Of course. Boy! This is really a complex issue!

SUSAN: Uh-huh. And what about those people who have destroyed their organs with alcohol or drugs? Should we discriminate against them and put them last on the list? And first help the people who suffer from genetic or infectious diseases?

RICHARD: Good point. I don't know. Maybe the fairest thing would be a lottery. At least then the decision would not be made by any one person or group. And the people who do not receive organs in time might die more peacefully, knowing that their chance to live had been as good as anyone else's. What do you think?

SUSAN: Well, I don't know. At least they would know that no one discriminated against them for any reason. But special exceptions would probably have to be made. Like for the President, for example. If the President needed a transplant, should he or she be allowed to have it before the person who won the lottery?

RICHARD: Well, it looks like we aren't going to come up with the perfect solution—agreeable to everyone—this morning. It's really overwhelming to realize that certain ethical choices can mean that one person will live and others will probably die.

SUSAN: Right. So what else is happening in the news? Or better yet, why don't we look at the comics for a while?

SUSAN AND RICHARD: (laugh)

SKILL **B** *Taking the Floor and Keeping the Floor*

Conversations

You will hear two conversations in which people take and keep the floor. After listening to each one, answer the questions you hear in the spaces provided. When you are finished, compare your answers in small groups.

CONVERSATION 1

Erik and Sylvia are talking in the cafeteria after class.

ERIK: Sylvia, I hear they're doing great things now in the field of genetic engineering.

SYLVIA: Well, Erik, our biology professor spoke to us today about how experimenting with genes can be dangerous. He said . . .

ERIK: That's true, but . . .

SYLVIA: Wait, Erik. Let me just tell you the main point he made. He said that newly created genes could accidentally enter the gene pool and cause unimaginable . . .

ERIK: Yes, but Sylvia . . .

SYLVIA: Let me just finish what I was saying. These new genes could cause unimaginable genetic changes in the world. And what if these changes were worse than the problems the new genes were developed to correct?

ERIK: Yeah, I see what you mean. I hadn't thought of that.

Question 1: What nonverbal cue might Erik have used when he said, "That's true, but . . ."?
Question 2: What nonverbal cue might Erik have used when he said, "Yes, but . . ."?
Question 3: What nonverbal cue might Sylvia have used when she said, "Let me just tell you the main point he made."?
Question 4: What nonverbal cue might Sylvia have used when she said, "Let me finish what I was saying."?

CONVERSATION 2

A teaching assistant and some students are in class.

TEACHING ASSISTANT: Well, to continue with some examples of issues that fall into the area of ethics, I'd like to talk about some of the problems with euthanasia.

SALLY: (giggling) Oh, are the youth in Asia having problems these days?

TEACHING ASSISTANT: That's very clever, Sally—now where was I? Oh, yes, the issue of choosing to die instead of living in pain and suffering because of serious disease or aging. The first problem seems to be whether we ever have the right to take another life or not. The law, in fact, says that we certainly do not.

GINA: If I could interrupt, I believe some states allow for extenuating circumstances, and it may not always be such a black-and-white issue.

TEACHING ASSISTANT: Oh, I wasn't aware of that, Gina. Perhaps you could find out for us exactly what the laws in those states say regarding extenuating circumstances. It would be quite interesting to see how various governmental bodies deal with an ethical issue such as this.

FRED: Excuse me for interrupting, but I already have that information because of the research I did for a term paper I wrote on a similar topic for another class. I could bring it in next time, if you like.

TEACHING ASSISTANT: Sure Fred, that would save us quite a bit of time. Thank you.

Question 1.: Was Sally's interruption about youth in Asia polite or impolite? Why?

Question 2.: Was Gina's interruption about states allowing for extenuating circumstances polite or impolite? Why?

Question 3.: Was Fred's interruption about research for a term paper polite or impolite? Why?

Focus on Testing

You will hear a short human interest story. After the story, you will be asked some questions. After you hear a question, read the four possible answers and decide which one is the best answer. Circle the letter of the best answer.

Human Interest Story

This week a 14-month-old girl named Marissa Ayala donated a cupful of her bone marrow to her 19-year-old sister, Anissa. As Marissa lay anesthetized upon an operating table, a surgeon inserted a 1-inch-long needle into the baby's hip and slowly withdrew the bone marrow. The medical team then rushed the marrow to a hospital room where older sister, Anissa lay waiting. If all goes well, if rejection does not occur, and a major infection does not set in, the marrow will give life to the older sister, who otherwise could die of chronic myelogenous leukemia. Doctors rate the chance of success at 70%.

This dramatic story becomes even more poignant when we realize that Marissa's parents decided to make a baby—to conceive Marissa—in order to create a compatible bone marrow donor for their dying daughter Anissa. To many people, the fact that the Ayalas were able to accomplish this seemed like a miracle. To others, it seemed more like a profound horror. It called up brutal images—baby farming, harvesting living bodies for spare parts. Many saw in the story of the Ayala family the near edge of a dangerous slippery slope into a dark abyss.

A bone marrow transplant represents very little risk to the donor. And the Ayalas, of course, say they never considered aborting the fetus if its marrow did not match Anissa's. Still, what disturbed many people was that the baby was brought into the world to be used—and used without her consent. And the question remains: Would the baby have agreed to her own conception for such a purpose? And what if amniocentesis showed that the bone marrow of the fetus was not compatible for transplant? Should the Ayalas have been allowed to abort the fetus and then try again?

Just what sort of harvesting of living bodies is all right? Most organs come from cadavers, but the number of living donors is rising. There were 1,788 last year, up 15% from 1989. Of these, 1,773 provided kidneys, nine provided portions of livers. Six of the living donors gave their hearts away. How? They were patients who needed heart-lung transplant packages. To make way for the new heart, they gave up the old one; doctors call it the "domino practice."

There will never be enough cadaver organs to fill the growing needs of people dying from organ or tissue failure. Federal law now prohibits any compensation for organs in the United States. In China and India, however, there is a brisk trade in such organs as kidneys. Will the day come when Americans have a similar marketplace for organs? Turning the body into a commodity might, in fact, make families less willing to donate organs. A family would be willing to say, "We gave Joey's kidneys away." But would they want to have to say, "We sold Joey's kidneys?" I don't think so.

Question 1: Where did the bone marrow for the transplant come from?
Question 2: What are the chances that this procedure will save Anissa?
Question 3: What disturbed many people about this story?
Question 4: Why do living patients sometimes donate their hearts for transplants?
Question 5: Which country mentioned in the story prohibits people from selling organs?

CHAPTER eleven

Medicine

Laser Technology and Medicine

PROFESSOR: Hello, everyone.

STUDENTS: Hi. Good morning. Hello, Professor.

PROFESSOR: Well, as I promised you last time, today we're going to talk about practical applications of laser technology. Specifically, we're going to discuss how lasers are used by doctors to do surgery.

For centuries doctors have been operating on patients with a razor-edged instrument called a scalpel. While the scalpel has performed wonderfully in surgery and has helped many people, it is really no more than an extremely sharp knife. Therefore, it must first do damage to the body in order to begin to heal it.

Now, the laser, on the other hand, does not cut the body the way a scalpel does. It can also reach small, sensitive areas that a scalpel can't reach. I'm certain that lasers will entirely replace scalpels eventually—probably in the very near future.

The term *laser* is actually an acronym. L-A-S-E-R stands for light amplification by stimulated emission of radiation. That's Item 1, I believe, on your handout. Lasers work by producing a highly concentrated beam of pure light, usually of one color or wavelength. The light produced may be visible or invisible to the human eye. The wavelength of the beam of light produced by the laser depends on the material being used to emit the laser light.

Most lasers available today use gases, such as carbon dioxide, argon, or a mixture of helium and neon to stimulate the laser light. Look at your handout for the symbols for these gases. Other lasers use solids, such as semiconductor crystals, special glass rods, or various liquid dyes.

A particularly popular laser for surgery today is an yttrium-aluminum garnet laser—usually called YAG. That's Y-A-G, yag, not nag.

STUDENTS: (laugh)

PROFESSOR: But if it helps you to remember, you can think of me nagging you to get your papers on lasers in on time.

STUDENTS: (laugh)

PROFESSOR: Anyway, look again at the handout for the spelling of the full name of this laser.

Now here's something that may surprise you. Despite the fact that lasers are ideally suited to many types of surgery, they are not commonly seen in hospital operating rooms. This is because they cost from $20,000 to $100,000. Lasers are sometimes referred to as "the $50,000 scalpel." Also, their use requires a great deal of technical knowledge, which many doctors do not have. This means that doctors must go to school and take special classes before they can use lasers. The expense of the laser itself and the time it takes to learn how to do laser surgery is probably why laser surgery is not done everywhere yet.

Laser surgery is relatively new, having been performed for only about twenty-five years, and new applications are constantly being developed. Lasers are most commonly used to cut, burn, or fuse together living tissue during surgery. But a technique has also been developed that combines the use of the laser with a light-sensitive dye in order to kill cancerous tissue. I will explain a little more about each of these uses.

The first use I mentioned, involving cutting, burning, or fusing, is called photo-coagulation necrosis. This process destroys tissue. The heat or energy produced by the laser is shot into a group or cluster of diseased or unwanted cells. These cells absorb the energy of the laser beam and are vaporized, which means they are simply turned into moisture. The solid material that remains after the moisture in the cells has been removed is reduced to ash, which may be removed by suction, by sponging, or simply by being brushed away.

STUDENTS: No kidding. Wow. That's great.

PROFESSOR: Yes, it is quite something. Tumors, even cancerous ones, can be destroyed—can be simply turned into ash—if they are detected early enough.

Most large medical centers are considering the use of lasers to clear bockages in arteries now, too. For example, a patient might have a buildup of plaque, or cholesterol deposits, along the walls of an artery that threaten to close it completely. A physician can put a tube containing a laser lens into the blocked artery. Then, guided by an x-ray machine, the surgeon can locate the blockage and blast it with the laser beam. The plaque will simply melt away, and soon the blood will flow normally and easily through the artery.

The only real danger in this type of procedure is that the laser may not be aimed accurately and may burn away part of the arterial wall, which would cause severe bleeding. To prevent this, the surgeon can attach to the laser a small balloon that could be inflated to close the artery in case of damage.

The most exciting aspect of this use of laser technology is that it could lead to immense improvements in heart surgery. It could be used to clear blockages around the heart with less cost and less trauma for the patient. Today a patient with such blockages in the arteries generally has heart bypass surgery, in which arteries are taken from the leg to replace the blocked ones in the heart. Such a procedure can be painful and there are often postoperative complications.

The second way I mentioned that lasers are used in surgery involves the use of laser radiation in combination with a special dye to destroy cancerous tumors. This technique, called photoradiation therapy, uses a drug called HpD that is derived from blood and remains inactive until exposed to certain wavelengths, or colors, of light. The drug is injected into the tumors. When the pure light from the laser strikes those cells that have been injected with HpD, the drug becomes active and poisons only the cells it occupies, without damaging healthy tissue. No one knows why this drug only settles in cancerous cells, but its preference for diseased tissue makes it an ideal therapeutic tool.

I want to stress that the healing power of photoradiation does not involve cutting or burning with intense heat, but instead involves destruction of the cell by changing its internal chemistry. Photoradiation has been found to be most useful in treating isolated tumors in organs, but it can also provide some relief for more widespread disease. The only known side effect of photoradiation that can cause a problem is that patients become extremely sensitive to sunlight for thirty days after the procedure.

STUDENT A: That seems like a small price to pay, don't you think?

STUDENT B: Except if you're a surfer from California.

STUDENTS: (laugh)

PROFESSOR: Yes, right. Okay, where were we? Oh, Yes. I was about to explain that surgery performed with lasers is quite simple and straightforward. The patient lies on an ordinary examining table. Two pairs of bright blue plastic goggles to protect the eyes of both surgeon and patient are the only safety precautions necessary. A slender thread, actually a fiber-optic tube, relays the light to the tumor. The treatment takes only a few minutes, and in many cases only one treatment is necessary. The tumor often dies within one or two weeks. The most difficult part of the procedure is introducing the fiber-optic tube into the body and then guiding the laser beam to the target area. The patient may experience some pain in this phase of the operation, so a local anesthetic is generally used. But because lasers operate by vaporizing tissues instead of by cutting, the patient usually heals quickly and there is very little scarring or swelling.

STUDENT C: Excuse me for interrupting, but aren't there all different kinds of lasers? Can they all be used for any of these jobs?

PROFESSOR: Good question. No, the type of operation determines the type of laser to be used. For example, argon laser energy is easily absorbed by hemoglobin, the oxygen-bearing element in blood, and is therefore excellent as a tool to stop bleeding from ruptured small blood vessels. It is also highly successful in reattaching a detached retina by fusing it to the back of the eyeball. The argon laser is also used for removing tattoos and certain dark red birthmarks called port-wine birthmarks.

The YAG laser also has a particular use. It is not selectively absorbed by tissue, and so it is marvelous for penetrating blood clots, stopping the bleeding of large blood vessels, and reducing the size of large, abnormal tissue growths such as tumors.

Both argon and YAG lasers can be passed through fiber-optic tubes. The carbon dioxide or CO_2 laser, however, cannot be passed through the flexible fiber-optic tubes without loss of effectiveness. In surgery, the beam of the CO_2 laser must be applied directly or through a series of mirrors. So it's definitely more difficult to use. But it's still preferred for most cutting and burning procedures. The CO_2 laser is considered the workhorse of laser surgery and is favored for most surgical procedures in the ears, nose, mouth, and throat, as well as for delicate neurological, gynecological, and burn surgery. And overall, the CO_2 laser is considered best for treating cancerous growth because it causes only slight disturbance of tissue and practically no bleeding.

Lasers represent a considerable advance over the crude and traumatic cuts of the scalpel. But their overall effectiveness has been prevented by a lack of widespread knowledge of their use. As doctors come to accept and rely on lasers more often, we can expect to see the success of certain types of surgery increase and postoperative complications from those surgeries decrease. Lasers are no longer the stuff of science fiction—you know, speculation about death rays and all that. Lasers are now the focus of fruitful experimentation into the healing properties of light.

Well, that's all we have time for today. We'll continue with this topic next time.

SKILL **B** *Acquiescing and Expressing Reservations*

Conversations

Listen to these conversations between a doctor and two of his patients, in which the patients acquiesce or express reservations. Answer the questions you hear after each conversation. When you are finished, compare your answers in small groups.

CONVERSATION 1

DOCTOR: The hospital has just purchased a new laser machine. I think it would be the perfect treatment for your condition.

PATIENT: Those new-fangled things kinda' scare me. Are you sure they're safe?

DOCTOR: We have some of the finest technicians in the world here. No one can do it better than we can.

PATIENT: Yes, I know everyone here has a very good reputation and everyone has been so nice to me, but this is a big step. What happens if something goes wrong?

DOCTOR: Let me assure you that you are receiving the best medical care available anywhere in the world. The chances of something going wrong are almost nonexistent. This same treatment has saved hundreds of lives.

PATIENT: Well, I suppose you must know best.

Question 1: The patient asks two questions to express reservations. What are they?

Question 2: At the end of the conversation, does the patient acquiesce? What does the patient say?

CONVERSATION 2

DOCTOR: The hospital just purchased a new laser machine, and I think it would be the perfect treatment for your condition.

PATIENT: Perhaps, but I really don't know anything about it.

DOCTOR: Most people don't; it's so new. Now I suggest . . .

PATIENT: Excuse me, Dr. Jones, but I really do feel I should know what I'm getting into before doing this. Do you have any literature on laser-assisted operations?

DOCTOR: Well, not on hand, but why don't you leave it up to me to decide what's best?

PATIENT: I'm really not questioning your judgment, but I need to be certain for myself what the risks are.

DOCTOR: You certainly have that right, but I think you are wasting your time. The medical literature available is difficult for a layman to read, and besides, your condition could become very serious soon.

PATIENT: How long do I have to think it over?

DOCTOR: Two to three weeks at most.

PATIENT: That seems enough time to do some research, and I'd like to get a second opinion. I want to be 100 percent sure before I go ahead.

Question 1: The patient in this conversation also expresses reservations. What are this patient's concerns?

Question 2: At the end of the conversation, does this patient acquiesce? What does the patient say?

Focus on Testing

You will hear a short human interest story. After the story you will be asked some questions. After you hear a question, read the four possible answers and decide which one is the best answer. Circle the letter of the best answer.

Human Interest Story

Nicholas Green's family decided to take a month-long vacation in Italy in the fall of 1994. For about 3 months before the trip Nicholas, a 7-year-old second-grader read about Roman history. His mother Maggie, 35, and his father Reginald, 65, also took his sister Eleanor, 4, with them.

On Thursday, September 29, the family, who had already seen the Colosseum and the Forum in Rome and the ruins in Pompeii, started their trip from Naples to Palermo, Sicily. Reginald drove and Maggie, Nicholas, and Eleanor slept in the car. The road is notoriously dangerous, and robberies occur along the highway very frequently. At almost 11 p.m., highway robbers pulled up alongside the Greens' car. Rather than argue with the men, or turn around, Mr. Green drove faster. The robbers shot at the Greens' car. Before he could get away, two bullets smashed the windows and a third hit the hood. Nicholas was fatally wounded.

When the Greens saw the police and an ambulance several miles up the road, they stopped and the ambulance rushed Nicholas to the hospital. On Saturday, when the Greens heard that Nicholas had no brain activity, they decided to donate his vital organs. Seven people were helped by Nicholas. Maria Pia Pedala, 19, would have died within two days without Nicholas's liver. Tino Motta, 11, got one kidney and Anna Maria Di Ceglie 14, got the other. Andrea Mongiardo, 15, got Nicholas's heart. A 30-year-old woman from Rome got islet cells from Nicholas's pancreas to help her produce insulin.

Because of the Greens' act, organ donations went up in Italy 400%. The Italians honored the Greens. At a ceremony in Rome, they received the medal of honor from the President of Italy. The Greens still love Italy. At the funeral Mr. Green told grieving family and friends, "The main lesson of all this is the goodness that we've seen, rather than the badness. He has already saved the lives of other children: He could have lived to 100 and done less."

Question 1: How old was Nicholas?
Question 2: Where was the Green family driving to on September 29?
Question 3: How did Mr. Green react when he saw the robbers?
Question 4: Why did organ donations in Italy go up 400%?
Question 5: What was the "goodness" that Mr. Green saw in this experience?

CHAPTER twelve

The Future

The World in the 21st Century

MIKE: Wow! Far out! Here's the first paper I wrote when I started college. It's about the report President Carter commissioned on what the world will be like in the year 2000. Wanna hear it?

JENNY AND TED: Yeah, like I wanna knock my head against the wall. Yeah, if you'll pay me.

MIKE: Oh, come on. This is really great stuff. Honest. Listen. "What will the world be like in the 21st century?" How's that for an opening line?

TED: I like "Call me Ishmael" better.

JENNY, TED, MIKE: (laugh)

MIKE: Come on, guys. Gimme a break. Just listen to this. Then I'll give you the paper. You can sell it to the museum when I'm old and famous and you can reminisce and say you knew me back when.

JENNY: Yeah, right.

JENNY, TED, MIKE: (laugh)

JENNY: But, okay. I'm into it.

TED: Yeah. Me, too. Go ahead. Read it, Mike.

MIKE: Okay. Here goes.

"What will the world be like in the year 2000? The 21st century may bring many serious problems. According to a study commissioned by President Carter in 1975, the number of poor and hungry people will rapidly increase between now and the year 2000. At the same time, there will be a decrease in the available food to eat and land on which to plant food crops. The four billion people living on earth today will balloon to over six billion by the year 2000 and to over ten billion by the year 2030. This means that the population of the world will more than double in less than forty years. The report estimates that 100 million people will be born each year.

Because of the population increase, it is likely that the gap between the wealthy industrialized countries and the developing countries will continue to widen."

TED: Yeah? Why is that?

MIKE: Well, I didn't write about it in my paper, but my guess is that the industrialized countries will use up more and more of the world's resources, while the developing countries will produce more and more people.

JENNY: Right. But I'm not sure industrialization is the answer for everyone. You know, I just read in *Newsweek* recently that a lot of the people in China are moving from the country to the cities and that by the turn of the century there won't be enough work for everyone in the cities. The article said that there will be at least 30 million workers in the cities without jobs.

TED: That doesn't surprise me. Unemployment in urban areas seems to be a problem everywhere.

MIKE: Yeah. And there are other problems that I included in my paper. Listen to this.

"The Carter Commission said that oil reserves, water reserves, and forests will all be seriously depleted because of the increase in population. Furthermore, the loss of forests will lead to the loss of topsoil. Without trees to hold the soil in place, there will be more deserts. Also there will be greater amounts of carbon dioxide in the air. So, in less than twenty years, up to 20 percent of all plants and animals will be extinct."

JENNY: Gosh! I knew it was getting bad, but I didn't know it was that bad. But here's some good news. I read somewhere that the African black rhino will definitely make it into the 21st century. And there are only about 500 of them left.

TED: That's because they implemented those restrictions on poaching, right?

MIKE: Right. Listen to this.

"The Commission also predicted that the cost of everything will increase at alarming rates, primarily because of scarcity. Food costs alone will increase over 100 percent. The cost of energy—gas and electricity—will rise 150 percent. Inflation will also contribute to rising costs. Our incomes, however, will not increase. Therefore, our actual buying power will be considerably less."

TED: I think that's true already. I definitely feel like I have less money to spend than I had four years ago. My scholarship is still the same amount of money it was four years ago. They haven't increased it to keep up with inflation.

JENNY: Yeah, I know what you mean. Hey, Mike. I remember studying that Carter Commission report, too. Didn't it also say that renewable resources such as wood and land will not be replenished after they are used up, so there will be less and less land, wood, and water to feed and protect people as the population increases? And that for many countries, starvation will become the most serious problem in the 21st century?

MIKE: You got it. You know, this is a *good* paper. And I go on to make some really good suggestions. Listen and tell me what you think.

"Given these predictions about the future that were made by President Carter's Commission, let's think now about what steps can be taken to create a better future. The basic problem for humanity, especially the poorer peoples, is that there is no minimum standard of living. That is, there is no bottom limit where we say, 'No. People just can't live like that. We must provide for them.'

"The United States, which is economically and socially one of the most influential countries in the world, is a good candidate for making a commitment to solving this problem. The United States might, for example, lead a global program of distributing food and resources equitably throughout the world. Ideally, this should be done without political 'strings' attached. In order to provide such a global program, an international consensus must be reached, possibly through the United Nations, to lessen the sufferings of human beings, to take care of basic human needs, and possibly to prevent all of the bleak predictions in the Commission's report from coming true."

TED: Wait a minute, Mike. I hate to be a pessimist, but I'm beginning to doubt if the United States has that much influence anymore. I used to think so, but I'm not sure anymore.

JENNY: I know what you mean, Ted. And there are just so many terrible needs in the world. I don't know how the United States could take care of them all.

MIKE: Wait, wait. That's not exactly what I meant. I meant that the United States could be a leader in working toward a global consensus on how to solve this problem. I didn't mean that we could do it alone. Let's see. Maybe it will get clearer as the paper goes on. Now where was I? Oh, yes.

"Although this sort of cooperative global program may relieve the immediate needs for food and shelter for some people, more long-term economic planning is needed to reverse dangerous losses of natural and human resources. One long-range plan that has been proposed is a cooperative solar energy project. Some say that a full commitment of international resources—of scientists, technology, facilities, and money—could help replace the world's dependency on oil, which is a finite resource, with an infinite resource—the sun. The sun could be used as a source of inexhaustible energy, and the technology for tapping this resource could be made available to all peoples of the world.

"Another proposal aimed at altering the bleak future predicted by the Carter Commission is that exports of grain and other food products, as well as oil exports, should be priced according to the incomes of the consumer nations. That is, prices should be based on ability to pay."

JENNY: Wait a minute. Isn't that a little like welfare? I thought you were opposed to welfare.

MIKE: No, no. It's not like welfare. It's more like workfare, I think. Listen.

"This plan would assure that lower-income nations could build themselves up without depleting all of their own natural resources. Also, technical and economic help should be given as payment to lower-income nations for nonrenewable resources such as oil, coal, or certain rare minerals. This would give developing countries the needed technology and monies to develop farmland, build irrigation systems, and complete other practical projects.

"Now, the big question is: Can any of this really be implemented? Can the bleak future forecast by the Carter Commission Report be averted? Most people would say 'probably not,' but it is this negative response that is at the heart of the problems we face. We feel intuitively that the economics and politics of international relations have become too massive, too complex for anyone to comprehend or change them. We sense that somewhere, somehow, things have gotten out of control and that we have lost the power to determine our own future. It's as if we have become victims or prey to the systems we spent hundreds of years creating.

"There is also another reason why people may be pessimistic about the possibilities of averting a bleak future. It is because we are presented daily with almost certain proof by the media that the entire planet faces catastrophe—if not from political and economic strife, then from nuclear weapons in the hands of terrorists. And yet, it seems that nothing is being done about it, that things are only getting worse and worse.

"In the face of these things, a feeling of helplessness easily turns into apathy or indifference. When we no longer have the power to make meaningful changes, we lose interest in even trying."

JENNY: Well, I remember reading that Paul Schmid, one of the directors at the Institute for the Future in California somewhere, believes that it is very hard to get people to change. And that the only thing that makes people change is disaster. He gave examples like Hitler, the civil rights movement, and the Vietnam War.

MIKE: Yup. That's what I was coming to. I concluded my paper like this.

"If we can begin to think through some of our beliefs, we may realize that much of what we have come to believe about human nature may not be true. For example, some say that it is not natural for human beings to cooperate in this way. I think that this is not the problem—whether human beings are basically cooperative or not is not the issue. I think that the main obstacle is a basic ignorance of global economics. If people could come to understand that what is best economically for the whole world, will also be best for each individual, then we might avert the future that is described in the Carter Commission Report. If people would take courses in economics and would try to understand other cultures, this would help lay the groundwork for a cooperative global economy—one that is based on mutual aid rather than mutual destruction."

TED: Hey, not bad, Mike. The paper still holds up, I think. Thanks for sharing it. The Carter Commission left some things out, though. What about crime, and drugs? And what about how fast the technology is changing? Or did you just leave them out of your paper?

MIKE: No, not exactly. I dealt with those things in Part Two. Hmm. It's around here somewhere.

TED AND JENNY: Oh, no. That's okay, Mike. Oh, never mind. Maybe some other time.

JENNY: Hey, what do you say we get outta here for a while? Anyone up for Chinese food?

MIKE AND TED: I am. Let's get going. Sounds good to me. Chinese chicken salad here we come.

<hr>

SKILL **B** *Speculating About the Future; Reminiscing about the Past*

Conversations

Listen to this conversation in which two speakers are speculating and reminiscing. Answer the questions you hear after the conversation in the spaces provided. When you are finished, compare your answers in small groups.

SPEAKER A: Good morning.

SPEAKER B: Good morning. And how are you today?

SPEAKER A: I didn't sleep too well and I feel a bit tired, but I'm really eager to get home. . . . Well, let's get back to work. Where were we? As I recall, before I went to sleep, you were working on the calculations for our time of arrival.

SPEAKER B: That's right. You've been asleep exactly three years, twenty-one days, five hours, and ten minutes.

SPEAKER A: Now, now—no need to be sarcastic. Just tell me when we'll arrive home on Earth, will you?

SPEAKER B: Well, my guess is that we'll arrive at the spaceport in Dallas on February 23, 2047.

SPEAKER A: Your guess? You're supposed to know these things. And where did you learn that expression, anyway?

SPEAKER B: Same place you did, of course. Back on Earth. And you know as well as I do that some of our instruments were not functioning for a while. I can only speculate how long they were off. So based on this speculation, I can only guess our time of arrival. But don't worry, there's a good chance we'll arrive in February, as I said.

SPEAKER A: Swell— this reminds me of the time you broke down and miscalculated all of the readings from the instruments. I'm surprised we got home at all that time.

SPEAKER B: Well, that's not the case this time! I assure you I'm perfectly fine.

SPEAKER A: Okay, okay—well, anyway, it will be good to get home.

SPEAKER B: But don't be surprised if things are a lot different now. There's a good chance that Dallas will seem almost foreign to you.

SPEAKER A: Yeah—I'll never forget the time we took our first trip. What a jolt that was, arriving home and everyone was ten years older. The clothing styles, the music—everything was different.

SPEAKER B: Mmm. That takes me back to when you first decided to become a space pilot.

SPEAKER A: What? How do you know about that?

SPEAKER B: I know everything you know. Remember the time you and Salina Gravitz went to that party in Chicago and then . . .

SPEAKER A: Enough reminiscing! If you don't quit doing that I have a hunch that a computer I know quite well is going to have its circuits rearranged!

SPEAKER B: Oh, all right! But don't forget, it's bound to be lonely out here without me to talk to.

Question 1: Who are the two speakers?
Question 2: What are they doing?
Question 3: What is their relationship?
Question 4: What topics do the speakers speculate about, and what expressions do they use to introduce their speculations?
Question 5: What topics do the speakers reminisce about, and what expressions do they use to introduce their reminiscences?
Question 6: Why does Speaker A want Speaker B to stop reminiscing?

Focus on Testing

You will hear a short presentation. After the presentation, you will be asked some questions. After you hear a question, read the four possible answers and decide which one is the best answer. Circle the letter of the best answer.

Presentation

The future, which can seem so close—just days, hours, or even seconds away—is somehow always too distant to be seen clearly. But that has not stopped generations of seers and forecasters from squinting in that direction. Even Henry Adams, the respected historian, made predictions about the future. In 1903, he declared: "My figures coincide in setting 1950 as the year that the world must go smash." Sorry, Henry. The end of the world may indeed be coming, but your prediction for 1950 is definitely off the mark.

In this century, an entire futurology industry has been developed to meet the planning needs of corporations, governments, and military establishments. At the same time, the average person has become more and more interested in social trends and future talk. Numerous books on future trends, such as *Megatrends 2000* and *The Popcorn Report* have made it to the best-seller book list.

Being popular, however, does not make you right. The first rule of future forecasting should be that the unforeseen keeps making the future unforseeable. For example, in the 1890s it was widely predicted that the United States would have no trees left by the 1920s. It was assumed that all of the trees would have been chopped down for firewood. But something unforeseen happened. Oil and gas stoves were developed. Now the major threat to the trees is acid rain.

Futurologists in recent decades correctly predicted the rise of the number of "couch potatoes" addicted to television, the increase in the number of home offices, and the prevalence of multiple marriages in one lifetime. They missed out, however, on many other important developments, such as the economic power of OPEC and the mass arrival of women in the workplace.

Sometimes futurologists base their predictions only on what science is capable of producing, without taking into account what people actually need or want. Two-way picture phones, for example, have been available since the 1960s, but the prediction that they would soon be in every household never came true.

Many future forecasters become either excessively optimistic or excessively pessimistic about the future. Edward Bellamy, in his popular 1898 novel *Looking Backward,* described Boston in the year 2000 as a gentle, ideal city, where everyone enjoys equal pay and crime has all but disappeared. But the discovery in World War I that scientific advances could also produce better machines of death and destruction, turned speculation about the future to the darker side. Bellamy's radiant utopian city became the high-tech slave societies of Yevgeny Samyatin's novel, *We,* and the dark and haunting visions depicted in both Aldous Huxley's *Brave New World* and George Orwell's classic novel, *1984.*

Question 1: Who tries to see into the future?
Question 2: When did Henry Adams make his prediction about the end of the world?
Question 3: Why is it difficult for futurologists to make accurate predictions?
Question 4: What did futurologists *not* predict correctly?
Question 5: How did Edward Bellamy feel about the future?
Question 6: Why did some writers become pessimistic about the future?